HITLER'S IRISH VOICES

The Story of German Radio's Wartime Irish Service

DAVID O'DONOGHUE

D1428672

First published in 1998
by
Beyond the Pale Publications
PO Box 337
Belfast BT9 7BT
Tel: +44 (0)1232 431170
Fax: +44 (0)1232 301299
E-mail: btpale@unite.co.uk
Internet site: http://www.unite.net/customers/btp/

British Library Cataloguing-in-Publication Data.
A catalogue record for this book is available from the British Library.

ISBN 1-900960-04-4

Cover: Emty Design.

Printed by
Colour Books Ltd, Dublin

CONTENTS

Acknowledgements

I t would have been impossible to write this book in as much detail without the first hand knowledge of those directly involved in the Irland-Redaktion, German Radio's wartime Irish service. The author is grateful to the following for giving of their time to recollect important details relating to the period: Dr Hans Hartmann whom the author met in Cologne in 1990; Mr Francis Stuart who granted a number of lengthy interviews to the author; Dr Hilde Spickernagel who provided a mass of detail through a lengthy correspondence; and the family of the late Dr Adolf Mahr.

The author is also grateful to the directors of the many archives he was granted access to in Belgium, Germany, Britain, Ireland and the United States. These are listed at the back of the book under the heading of archival sources. In particular, the author wishes to thank the director of the Irish Military Archive, Commandant Peter Young, and his staff for their help and encouragement. In addition, a number of previously closed files at the Department of Foreign Affairs (concerning official protests over Francis Stuart's broadcasts from Berlin) were made available to the author through the good offices of the then Minister for Foreign Affairs, Mr Gerard Collins TD, and the Secretary of the Department, Mr Noel Dorr.

Thanks are also due to the following individuals who read the drafts and/or final version of this work presented as a doctoral thesis (the book was rewritten from the thesis of the same title which is available for consultation at the library of Dublin City University): Dr Hans Hartmann, Cologne; Mr Thomas Turpin, Trinity College, Dublin; Dr Colum Kenny, Dublin City University; Dr Eunan

O'Halpin, Dublin City University; Professor Ronan Fanning, University College Dublin; Mr Donal O'Donovan, Kilbride Books, County Wicklow; and Dr Pat Wallace, Director of the National Museum, Dublin.

For their help in dealing with German language texts, the author wishes to thank the following: Carola Hogreve, Monika Schlenger, Andrea Kunze-Galt, Christine Schuhmann, Deirdre Humphreys and Ursula Kopetschek. Ms Hogreve, formerly of the Goethe Institute in Dublin and now on the Institute's headquarters staff in Munich, provided much help and encouragement over a number of years to the author in his endeavours, as did Ms Schlenger.

Assistance with texts in the Irish language was granted to the author by the following, to whom grateful thanks are due: the broadcaster and translator, Seán Ó Briain; Eoghan Ó hAnluain of the Department of Modern Irish, University College Dublin; John Walsh of Teilifís na Gaeilge and Darina Ní Chinnéide of Raidió na Gaeltachta.

Finally, the help of the following is much appreciated: the staff of the Oireachtas Library and Journal Office; Dr Séamus Mac Mathuna, University College Galway; Professor Conn R. Ó Cleirigh, UCD; Professor F.J. Byrne, UCD; Mr Tomás Ó Cathasaigh, UCD; Mr Tony Eklof, UCD Law Library; Fr Ignatius, director of the Franciscan Library, Killiney, County Dublin; Mark Farrell, researcher; Nicholas Carolan, administrator of the Irish Traditional Music Archive, Dublin; Valerie Walsh of Dublin City University Library; Jim Brady, author and bookseller; Dr Seán Ó Heochaidh, Gortahork, County Donegal; Monsieur Emmanuel de Beer de Laer, Brussels, for research in Belgium and Luxembourg; and Mr Hermann Töbermann, local historian of Augustfehn, Germany; the late Mr Liam Bergin; BBC wartime monitors Lorna Swire, Maurice Irvine and Vladimir Rubinstein; Mrs Margaret Greiner; and Mrs Jean Sheridan-Healy.

Foreword

There has been frequent recrimination about broadcasts to Ireland from Nazi Germany during the Second World War. Only last year, huge publicity attached to an abortive attempt to have Francis Stuart, the most celebrated of the broadcasters, deprived of his membership of Aosdána, the assembly of savants supported by the Irish government. What has been lacking hitherto has been a detailed reconstruction of the history of the Irland-Redaktion. This is what David O'Donoghue now provides, with such a wealth of information that it is unlikely the work will ever need to be done again.

Not that it is detail alone that ensures the authority of this work. Research is often subordinated to propagandistic agendas. It can be difficult to achieve a degree of balance when dealing with so potentially emotive a subject as Nazism, or anything remotely connected with it. The normal duty of the historian, to refrain from rushing into judgement of character or motive until all the possible facts have been garnered, has to compete with a sense of revulsion at the horrors of that régime. What inspires confidence in the enduring value of this work is the combination of the massive research on which the conclusions are based with the author's scrupulous sense of fairness.

O'Donoghue has gone to enormous pains to reconstruct the historical reality. He has been indefatigable in ferreting out information in Ireland, Britain and Germany, whether from archival sources, including military and intelligence files, or oral sources. He has tracked down survivors, as well as the relatives, friends and contacts of those involved who might shed light on any aspect of the experience. As the oral part of the work will never be able to be done again, it is reassuring that one can have such confidence in the meticulous manner in which O'Donoghue has discharged his task.

Realising that the Irish broadcasts revolved around the personalities of a relatively small number of men and women, he has sought to recreate their individual biographies in sufficient detail to understand both themselves and the relations between them. What impulses drove them? How did they find themselves in Berlin? How did they respond to the changing circumstances as the war progressed? The answers naturally vary, depending on whether he is discussing the Celtic scholars, Professor Ludwig Mühlhausen and Hans Hartmann, or Adolf Mahr, still nominally Director of the National Museum in Dublin while he was also playing a key role in connection with the broadcasts in the German Foreign Ministry throughout the war, or Francis Stuart, or the often depressed Susan Hilton, heavily dependent on alcohol, who found herself in Germany as a virtual prisoner of war.

At a purely human level, the story is absorbing in its own right. One can oscillate between the hapless Hilton, on the one hand, and the frequently hilarious story of John Francis O'Reilly, who came to be in Germany in the first place by virtue of leading a group of Irish potato pickers, who happened to find themselves in Jersey when the Germans occupied it in 1940, and made their way to the Hermann Goering Works at Watenstedt by a boisterous train journey which alas did little to elevate familiar images of Irish stereotypes, their capacity for drink and destruction on the train leaving their new hosts reeling in disbelief and dismay.

The broadcasting policy itself can most charitably be described as surreal. Mühlhausen and Hartmann struck on the idea of broadcasting in Irish, on the assumption that Irish speakers were the most pro-German, or at least anti-British, to be found in Ireland. The Irland-Redaktion broadcast, in Irish, twice weekly for most of the war. Indeed, part of the German master plan for destabilising Irish-American support for President Roosevelt after America entered the war was to broadcast across the Atlantic in Irish! One may be forgiven for suspecting that this ranks among the less rewarding allocations of scarce resources in a war economy.

It wasn't until 1941 that broadcasts in English to Ireland began. The Irish broadcasts had at least the advantage of creating some employment in the BBC for Irish speakers whose job it was to monitor and translate the broadcasts, before the transcripts were passed on to MI5. O'Donoghue incidentally brings out clearly the close cooperation between MI5 and G2, Irish intelligence, which was also monitoring the broadcasts, and which frequently compared information with its British counterpart.

O'Donoghue also brings out nicely the rivalry between Goebbels' Propaganda Ministry and Ribbentrop's Foreign Ministry, as they struggled for control of even so modest a prize as the Irland-Redaktion. What comes across here is the sheer inanity of much German bureaucracy, and the blundering buffoonery of the Propaganda Ministry in 1941, as it went so far as to entrust Irish broadcasts for a brief period to Wolfgang Dignowity, who knew nothing about Ireland, and reinforced his own ignorance by recruiting colleagues who knew equally little.

The main theme of the broadcasts themselves was the importance of Ireland maintaining its neutrality, with the prospect of reunification if Ireland did not support the British war effort. The claim that neutrality would result in Irish unity was based on the premise that a grateful Germany would facilitate unification following the defeat of Britain. However naïve this may seem (or at least however much such unification would have been intended to serve German rather than Irish interests) the broadcasters seem to have convinced themselves of its validity.

That the broadcasts were generally supportive of Irish government policy makes it less surprising that William Warnock, the Irish representative in Berlin, welcomed the broadcasters, including Francis Stuart, to the legation.

For many readers, most interest in this volume will doubtless centre on Stuart himself. His very first broadcast adopted the theme that 'Ireland belongs to Europe and England does not belong to it. Our future must lie with the future of Europe and no other'. It might almost sound like a rehearsal for debates on EMU! The essential quality of Stuart's broadcasts seems to be naïvety. There is no overt anti-Semitism to be found in them, and he was actually sacked in January 1944 for refusing to follow an anti-Soviet line. By the standards of Nazi ideology, the broadcasts generally seem to have been remarkably free of anti-Semitism. On the evidence here, only Professor Mühlhausen, an odious character in several ways, purveyed anti-Semitism. The extracts produced by O'Donoghue could otherwise have been as easily broadcast from the Germany of the First World War as from the Germany of the Second World War.

But of course the Germany of the Second World War was not the Germany of the First World War. How much Stuart believed of the gloss he put on the reality of life in the Germany of his time remains an open question. But his politics seem to have had little to do with Nazism in itself, and much more with a type of tormented personality searching for some unattainable ideal of a humankind purged of the contaminating influence of materialistic liberalism through purification by suffering. Whatever demon of destruction lured him on, it was not apparently a particularly racist demon. Bourgeois society was the enemy that had to be destroyed before his version of redemption could be realised.

Stuart seems to have rather lost faith in Hitler because he was not sufficiently revolutionary for his taste. Before Germany invaded Russia, he apparently thought that Stalin rather than Hitler might be the redeemer, and his aspiration to transfer to Moscow was apparently aborted only by the inconvenient timing of Operation Barbarossa. Naïvety seems to have remained an enduring characteristic of Stuart. As late as 1989 he was assuring O'Donoghue that only Soviet Russia waged 'a really honourable war'.

While there is much about Stuart in this book, one of the many virtues of O'Donoghue's work is that it allows us see Stuart, as well as all the others involved, in the context of the entire broadcasting operation. If it is in general a sombre tale, it is lightened by episodes of low farce, particularly when the indomitable and incorrigible John Francis O'Reilly was pursuing his personal agenda with scant solicitude for Hitler's grand strategy.

Above all, it is the soundness of the scholarship and the fairness of the author that command respect throughout. O'Donoghue does not seek to browbeat his readers, but provides them with sufficient evidence to draw their own conclusions, while expressing his own in a restrained manner. The debate will doubtless continue, but it can now do so on a vastly better informed basis than ever before.

Professor J. J. Lee
Department of History, University College Cork
March 4, 1998

Introduction

This book explores in depth for the first time a little known aspect of Germany's wartime overtures to neutral Ireland: the propaganda broadcasts beamed to Ireland from Berlin during World War II by Nazi Radio's Irish service, the Irland-Redaktion.

Other books have tackled Ireland's thorny relationship with Nazi Germany — both the official and clandestine aspects — in the 1939-45 period, but most have dealt with the radio service only in passing. These published works include Enno Stephan's *Spies in Ireland*, J. P. Duggan's *Neutral Ireland and the Third Reich*, and Carolle J. Carter's *The Shamrock and the Swastika*. Robert Fisk's *In Time of War: Ireland, Ulster and the Price of Neutrality, 1939-45* allocates 27 pages to Francis Stuart and Hans Hartmann's work in the Irland-Redaktion but appears only as a minor addendum in a work devoted to a much wider topic.

In general, history books focusing on Ireland's position vis-à-vis Germany in the Second World War have dwelt on the secret links between the IRA and the Nazi regime — initiated in early 1939 with the visit of the German agent Oscar Pfaus to the republican leadership in Dublin. In exchange, one of the IRA's most senior strategists, Jim O'Donovan, travelled to Germany no less than three times in 1939, before the outbreak of war, to establish transmission codes, arrange for advisors and arms to be sent to Ireland, and to cement relations with German Intelligence. In forging such links the IRA was operating on the traditional notion that 'England's difficulty is Ireland's opportunity', the difficulty in this case being Germany's threat to the hitherto dominant position of the British empire.

This notion was consciously exploited in Germany's approach to Ireland during World War II. It is clear that the Nazis sought to use Ireland's neutrality for their own ends, and the Irland-Redaktion — always calling on the Irish public to 'keep your neutrality', while warning of dire consequences if this policy were to be abandoned — was an overt element in that strategy. In putting the Irish radio service on air in 1939 the Germans assembled a small and motley group of people to do their bidding: a few Nazi academics who were fluent in the Irish language having studied in the Gaeltacht regions before the war; other Germans with little or no experience of Irish affairs; Irish expatriates of various political views and indeed none; as well as some French, Russian and British citizens who served with the 'Irish' radio team.

None of those Irish involved had set out for Germany originally with the express intention of broadcasting propaganda back home to Ireland, yet they were easily recruited as propagandists. Among them there was no equivalent of Galway's William Joyce, also known as Lord Haw Haw, the chief announcer on German Radio's English service, who had been part of Mosley's fascist blackshirt movement in pre-war England. In addition, unlike other European language services of Nazi Radio — and in particular the Deutschland Sender or German home stations — there was little anti-Semitism on the Irland-Redaktion apart from some broadcasts Joyce himself made in 1943, under a cover name, to reach what he termed his 'Irish followers'. Of the few Irish involved, John O'Reilly and Liam Mullally were in the mercenary mould, while the writer Francis Stuart was actually sacked from the radio service in 1944 for refusing to take an anti-Soviet line in his talks.

If the main themes were not anti-Semitism and anti-Communism, what then did the broadcasts to Ireland amount to in terms of content? The overriding theme was for Ireland to remain neutral. Dispatches from the German Army's High Command were mixed with praise of Hitler and condemnation of Britain and her Allies. As the war progressed and Germany's military fortunes faded, the propaganda attempted to instil fear among Irish listeners of a take-over of Western

Europe by the Bolsheviks along with the inferred demise of the Irish Catholic way of life. Added to the mix were 'flashbacks' to British atrocities committed during the 1919-21 War of Independence, against a background of traditional Irish music, all geared to generate a hatred of England and pride in all things Irish. There was a certain irony in the fact that Irland-Redaktion programmes were introduced by the traditional Irish jig 'The Frost is All Over', arranged by the head of the Irish Army's School of Music, Colonel Fritz Brase, who as well as being a German national was also a member of the Nazi Party.

The overall tone of the broadcasts sought to convey the message that Nazi Germany understood Ireland's aspirations to unity and, pending a German victory, would support Irish neutrality. But, in fact, a dangerous double game was in play because, while Germany preached support for de Valera's neutral stance, the Foreign Office was also planning the Russell-Ryan landing operation and had drawn up a more general invasion plan, code-named Operation Green, in addition to the invasion plan for England, known as Operation Sea Lion.

There is little doubt that Germany would like to have installed a pro-Nazi 'Quisling' style government in Dublin if Operations Green and Sea Lion had gone ahead. The battle plans were drawn up and invasion handbooks had been prepared in occupied Brussels in 1940. But Hitler's decision to pursue Operation Barbarossa, the invasion of Russia, in June 1941 lifted the immediate threat of invasion and consigned Operation Green to the back-burner of history. Nonetheless Germany continued to regard Irish neutrality as important to its military strategy and while de Valera denied Churchill access to the Treaty Ports in Donegal and Cork, it was that much easier for U-boats to harrass the North Atlantic convoys bringing food and supplies to Britain. In a rare post-war interview Dr Hans Hartmann, who was in charge of the Irland-Redaktion from 1941 to 1945, confirmed that Irish neutrality was considered important in Berlin because it was 'part of the war aims'. He doubted very much, though, if the country would ever have been invaded by Germany particularly if it maintained its neutral position. In any case, Germany had no way of knowing that de Valera's version of neutrality actually favoured the Allies and all the more so as the war progressed in their favour.

Meanwhile, the Irland-Redaktion continued to put out vague promises that the best guarantee of Irish culture and sovereignty in the long run would be a German victory. In targeting Irish language speakers — the radio broadcast only in Irish from December 1939 to August 1941, after which it added English language programmes to its output — Professor Ludwig Mühlhausen and Dr Hartmann were clearly working on the belief that this community might be most open to the 'eventual unity' message. These two Celtic scholars from Germany had wide experience of pre-war Ireland and were crucial in shaping the radio broadcasts for Irish speakers whom they believed were among the most nationalist elements in Ireland at that time.

It is important to stress that this strategy was not based on widespread market research because listenership surveys did not begin until the 1950s. Thus the decision to broadcast in Irish says more of the Nazi view of Irish speakers than of the actual Irish language community at the time. It is also important to realise that the Nazis were broadcasting in no less than 54 languages during the war. As well as beaming propaganda to their adversaries, the target audiences included occupied and neutral states as well as minorities and marginalised groups within existing national boundaries, for example the Breton and Flemish nationalists. Seen in this context the Irish case was far from unique. Yet there were unusual aspects of Berlin's propaganda drive to Ireland such as the plan to target Irish communities abroad, for example, in North America and Australia. This idea was the brainchild of Dr Adolf Mahr, an Austrian Nazi whom de Valera had promoted to the post of director of the National Museum in Dublin in 1934. Mahr, who left Dublin in July 1939 and spent the war years in the Berlin Foreign Office, was also responsible for upgrading the Irland-Redaktion in 1941 from a twice-weekly Irish language service to a nightly service of both Irish and English language programmes.

Half a century on from the end of the Second World War, the story of German Radio's wartime Irish propaganda service provides a remarkable footnote to the history of Irish-German relations in the 1939-45 period.

Biographical Notes

Helmut Clissmann (1911-1997), and
Elizabeth Clissmann, née Mulcahy

Elizabeth Mulcahy, the daughter of a staunchly republican family in Sligo, met her German husband-to-be, Helmut Clissmann, when both were students in Dublin in the 1930s. Mr Clissmann joined the Nazi Party in May 1934 and, in his role as head of the German Academic Exchange Service, arranged most of the study trips to Ireland by German university students in the 1930s, including those of Hans Hartmann and Hilde Poepping. In wartime Germany he was chosen to sail secretly to his wife's native Sligo to team up with IRA men there, but the plan was dropped due to bad weather. Elizabeth Clissmann spent much of the war in Copenhagen, while her husband was reputedly involved in top secret plans for the invasion of Britain, as a member of the German Army's Brandenburg Regiment. In early 1944 Mrs Clissmann was asked to prepare a report for the Foreign Office on the feasibility of broadcasting anti-Roosevelt propaganda to Irish Americans, thus helping to prevent the US President's re-election that November. However, Mrs Clissmann felt the tactic would be counterproductive and said as much in a report to one of the the the idea's originators, Dr Edmund Veesenmeyer, Ribbentrop's coup d'état specialist.

Wolfgang Dignowity (1912-   ?)

While Ludwig Mühlhausen began German Radio's weekly propaganda talks to Ireland in December 1939, Wolfgang Dignowity was appointed first head of the proposed nightly propaganda service in June 1941. Both men worked at the behest of Goebbels' Propaganda Ministry. Dignowity knew nothing about Ireland and recruited his 'Irish' radio team in Paris. His reign was short-lived as he was ousted as section head after only five months at the instigation of Adolf Mahr in the Foreign Office. Mahr chose Hans Hartmann to take Dignowity's place as head of the Irland-Redaktion in December 1941.

Hans Hartmann (1909-   )

A rising star in pre-war European linguistic circles, Hartmann began by mastering Russian and in 1937 switched his attention to Celtic studies. In common with other German university students in the 1930s, he was obliged to join the Nazi Party to get funding. In 1937 he travelled to Ireland on a student exchange scholarship. Hartmann fell in love with Ireland and its people, mastering the Irish language in less than two years. What began for him as a one year visit turned into a two and a half year stay and only ended when the German Legation in Dublin arranged for German nationals to leave Ireland for Germany on 11 September 1939. Back in Germany, Hartmann continued studying under Professor Mühlhausen at Berlin University where he was appointed a lecturer in 1942.

Susan Hilton, née Sweney (1915-1983)

Hilton broadcast to Ireland under her maiden name of Susan Sweney. Born in India, she attended school in England and joined Mosley's fascist movement in the 1930s. After a police raid on her London flat, she left Britain on 28 May 1940 aboard a ship to join her husband in Burma. Her ship was, however, sunk by a German raider in the Indian Ocean on 13 July 1940. Along with other survivors, Hilton was taken aboard a prison ship bound for occupied France where she was put ashore in September 1940. While her fellow prisoners were interned she was granted a measure of freedom in Paris where she worked as a journalist. Hilton was asked by the Nazis to undertake a spying mission to Ireland but refused. In 1941 she moved to Berlin to work first on propaganda broadcasts to Britain and, from January 1942, with Hartmann's Irland-Redaktion. After leaving the Irish team in autumn 1942, she worked for Goebbels' Propaganda Ministry. By mid-1943 she was being shadowed by the Gestapo who suspected her of being an Allied spy. Hilton had the unenviable distinction of being imprisoned both by the Nazis from August 1944 to April 1945 on suspicion of being an enemy agent, and by the British from April 1945 to 1947 for treason (a charge strongly contested to this day by her family).

Adolf Mahr (1887-1951)

An Austrian archaeologist, Mahr left the Vienna Museum of Prehistory in 1927 to join the National Museum in Dublin as Senior Keeper of Irish Antiquities. He joined the Nazi Party in April 1933 and was promoted to the post of museum director by de Valera's cabinet in July 1934. As head of the Nazis' Auslandorganisation (foreign organisation) in Ireland, Mahr was the most powerful member of the small pre-war Austro-German community in Dublin. He spent the war years in Berlin working on the Irish desk at the Foreign Office. In effect, he controlled all Germany's radio propaganda to neutral Ireland from November 1941 to May 1945.

Angus Matheson (1912-1962)

This Scots Gaelic-speaking academic from Glasgow University was the BBC's first Gaelic monitor, hired at the behest of MI5 in mid-

1940 to translate Berlin's Irish language radio talks just two weeks after the German Army had entered Paris. Because MI5 feared an imminent invasion of Britain, the intelligence service wanted to check every Irish language broadcast from Berlin to Ireland for hidden messages and items of military value. Angus Matheson was head of the Department of Celtic at Glasgow from 1938 until his death in 1962. In March 1942 he left the BBC to undertake code-breaking work with MI5. His Gaelic translation work at the BBC monitoring service was continued by Jane Charleton and later Maurice Irvine, both from Belfast.

Ludwig Mühlhausen (1888-1956)

An accomplished linguistic expert whose post-war career foundered because of his overt links to the Nazi Party and activities as an SS officer in occupied France, Mühlhausen joined the Nazis in 1932 and used his membership to advance his academic career. In 1937 he moved from Hamburg to take over the Chair of Celtic Studies at Berlin University where other propagandists such as Hans Hartmann, Hilde Poepping, Francis Stuart, Madeleine Meissner and Norman Baillie-Stewart also later studied and taught. Mühlhausen broadcast in Irish most Sunday nights from December 1939 to mid-1941. From 1942 he worked with the SS in France where it is believed he forged links with the Breton nationalist movement.

John O'Reilly (1916-1971)

This flamboyant County Clare man was the only member of the Irland-Redaktion to have volunteered for a spying mission. He joined the radio propaganda unit in Berlin in September 1941 but left a year later to train as a spy with German naval intelligence in Bremen, and later in Hamburg. Equipped with a radio transmitter, O'Reilly was parachuted back to his native Kilkee by the Luftwaffe in December 1943 and was arrested almost immediately. He was interned for the remainder of the war, apart from a brief period of freedom when he escaped from Arbour Hill prison in Dublin before being swiftly recaptured. After the war he became a publican and hotelier and, in 1952, wrote his memoirs for the *Sunday Dispatch* in London.

Frank Ryan (1902-1944)

A leading member of the IRA's left wing republican congress faction in the 1930s, Frank Ryan fought with the International Brigade against Franco's forces in the Spanish civil war. In 1940 he was sprung from death row in a Spanish prison with the help of the Nazis who planned to send him to Ireland aboard a U-boat with IRA leader Seán Russell.

The plan, masterminded by Ribbentrop's coup d'état specialist Dr
Edmund Veesenmeyer, collapsed when Russell — who had been
trained in sabotage techniques in Berlin — died of a perforated ulcer
aboard the U-boat off the west coast of Ireland in August 1940. Ryan
returned to Berlin where he was kept in the style of a senior diplomat.
In 1944 the Nazis wanted him to help with their propaganda plan
aimed at persuading Irish Americans not to vote for Roosevelt.
Although he was against the plan, Ryan was due to visit Hartmann's
relocated radio team in Luxembourg in mid-1944 where he saw a role
for himself as an advisor/translator. However, he died in a Dresden
sanatorium on 10 June 1944.

Hilde Spickernagel, née Poepping (1916-   )

Hilde Poepping was another German exchange student whose interest
in Ireland brought her to University College Galway for a year's studies
in 1937-38. Poepping later married a fellow student at Berlin University
and, after completing her studies, as Mrs Spickernagel, joined Adolf
Mahr on the Irish desk at the Foreign Office. Her main duties involved
the preparation of propaganda material for broadcast to Ireland. In
December 1941, after six months with Mahr, she was transferred to
join Hartmann's newly formed nightly Irish radio service, the Irland-
Redaktion, where she occasionally read news bulletins. She left
Hartmann's team after a year to give birth to her son and played no
further role in the wartime Foreign Office or radio service.

Francis Stuart (1902-   )

Even in his nineties, Stuart still has the capacity to stir controversy
over his wartime broadcasts for Nazi radio, a role he described as 'a
neutral writer addressing a neutral audience'. Stuart made his first
broadcast from Berlin to Ireland on St Patrick's Day 1942 at the request
of Hans Hartmann — both men were then lecturers at Berlin University.
Stuart's talks praising the IRA and advising people how to vote in the
1943 general election prompted official complaints to Berlin by de
Valera's government. Stuart continued his radio talks until January
1944 when he fell out with Hartmann and Mahr over their demand
that he broadcast anti-Russian propaganda. For a time his passport
was withheld and he was threatened, via anonymous phone calls, with
imprisonment in a concentration camp. However, he avoided arrest
with the help of influential friends at the Foreign Office. After the war
he spent some years in exile in Paris and London before returning to
Ireland in 1958.

for

Claire, Catherine, Véronique and Áine

1

Goebbels' Gaelic Lord Haw Haw

In the closing weeks of 1939 some radio listeners in Ireland tuned into a strange evening broadcast[1] on the medium wave. The language was unmistakably Irish but the programme was not emanating from either Radio Éireann or the BBC's Scottish service — the only two radio stations in the world known to be broadcasting in Gaelic at that time.

Monitors at the Irish Army's headquarters in Dublin's McKee Barracks who had been screening radio output since the start of the war in September 1939, scratched their heads as they tried to make out what sounded like an attack on Allied propaganda. References to the Black and Tans were included by the mystery speaker who signed off with the words: 'Go mbeannaí Dia dhaoibh a chairde, agus go saora Dia Éire' (God bless you my friends and may God save Ireland). Was it, they thought, perhaps an illegal IRA broadcast from Irish soil? It certainly was not Radio Éireann which had to follow strict guidelines on impartiality in an effort to uphold Ireland's neutral stance in the conflict then beginning to spread around the globe. So where did the mystery broadcast come from?

The answer to the puzzle was as astounding as it was intriguing, for the man speaking a Kerry dialect into the microphone that night in Berlin's radio centre (Rundfunkhaus) was none other than Professor Ludwig Mühlhausen, the leading German linguist and Celtologist. Mühlhausen had spent some time in the 1920s and 1930s studying Celtic folklore and Irish dialects on the Blasket Islands, in Connemara

1

and in south west Donegal. He was one in a long line of German Celtologists who had taken an interest in Ireland's language and folklore since Franz Bopp had written his pioneering work on the Celtic languages in 1839.

As the 20th century dawned, German Celtologists continued to be fascinated by the prospect of establishing a link between Irish Gaelic and earlier tongues originating in the Middle East and India. Ireland's western seaboard, with its vestiges of a language and culture which seven centuries of Anglo-Norman influence had failed to suppress, continued to attract German language scholars. In 1907 Heinrich Zimmer's Department of Celtic Studies became an independent section within Berlin University's Indo-European language seminar. Zimmer was a tough taskmaster who insisted his students speak at least one modern Celtic language as well as having a knowledge of the earlier Brittonic languages, including Welsh, Cornish and Breton, in addition to Scots, Irish and Manx Gaelic.[2]

German-Irish scholarly links were cemented by Kuno Meyer (1858-1919), who took over the Chair of Celtic Studies at Berlin University in 1911. From 1897 Meyer was editor, along with Ludwig Christian Stern, of the *Zeitschrift für celtische Philologie* (*Celtic Philology Journal*) which still appears regularly today. In 1903 Meyer founded the School of Irish Learning in Dublin and the following year he began publishing its journal *Ériu*. This, together with his work on translating early Irish poetry and researching Irish lexicography and metrics, won him widespread recognition. He was granted the freedom of Dublin and Cork, though his name was erased from the roll of honour in Dublin's City Hall in a vote dominated by pro-British elements on the Corporation during the First World War.[3] Probing into the Celtic past, men like Kuno Meyer and his successor Julius Pokorny, who took over the Chair of Celtic Studies at Berlin in 1920, could not fail to be affected by Ireland's quest for independent nationhood.

Germany's defeat in the First World War gave rise to popular resentment at what was seen as the country's relegation to second-class status by the Treaty of Versailles. Coupled with the effects of widespread unemployment and financial collapse during the Depression, this resentment provided an incubator for Hitler's fledgling National Socialist party. After coming to power in 1933, the Nazi party sought to stamp its influence on the academic world as well as every other section of German society. Ironically, one of the Nazis' first academic victims turned out to be the pro-Irish, anti-British Professor Pokorny, who was sacked — on the pretext that he was part-Jewish[4] — from his post in Berlin in October 1935. Driven into exile, he sought refuge first in Vienna and later in Zürich. The Nazi party used its all-embracing influence to make sure that Ludwig Mühlhausen — who had joined the party in 1932 — got Pokorny's job.[5]

From an Irish point of view, Mühlhausen was an interesting choice. He had founded the Department of Celtic Studies at Hamburg University in 1928, was a fluent Irish speaker and knew Ireland well. In December 1939, at the behest of Goebbels' Ministry of Propaganda, he inaugurated German Radio's first Irish language talks.

Footnotes

1.   Joe Healy's report of Mühlhausen's first known broadcast on 10 December 1939, though not a verbatim transcript, is held at the Irish Army's Military Archive in Cathal Brugha Barracks, Dublin (MA G2/2473).

2.   Rockel, 1990, pp. 26-9.

3.   See J.P. Duggan, 'Kuno Meyer: Time to Make Amends?', *Irish Times*, 12 April 1990, p. 11.

4.   According to Professor F.J. Byrne of UCD, Pokorny always denied any Jewish connections but was kept under surveillance by the Gestapo (Byrne interview, 30 December 1991). According to Professor Conn R. Ó Cléirigh of UCD, who was a student of Pokorny's, the German professor had partial Jewish ancestry through a maternal grandparent (letter to author from Ó Cléirigh, 4 May 1993).

5.   Rockel, 1990, pp. 30-1.

2

The Austrian Archaeologist

On 15 September 1927 a dark-haired, moustachioed man, wearing pince-nez glasses, stepped off a German liner at Cobh harbour and set foot on Irish soil for the first time. For the next 12 years the newly independent Irish Free State was to be his adopted home. Adolf Mahr, then aged 40, had travelled from Vienna with his 26-year-old wife Maria, their baby daughter Hilde and son Gustav. He had worked in the Austrian capital's Natural History Museum and was now on his way to Dublin to take up a post at the National Museum in Kildare Street.

The Mahr family would join the small but growing Austro-German community in pre-war Ireland which at its peak in the 1930s would number over 500.[1] Most of its members were professionals who — at the invitation of a government anxious to distance itself by all means from British influence — held medical, teaching, administrative, engineering and other jobs in the newly emergent state. After Hitler's rise to power in January 1933, a number of German colony members chose to join the Nazi Party. As such they formed an important fascist nucleus in Ireland which, while small — they amounted to about 10 per cent of adults in the Austro-German community — could wield a certain influence. What marked Mahr out from the rest was that in the 1930s he would assume the leadership of the Nazi Party's local organisation in Dublin, becoming its Ortsgruppenleiter or local branch leader.

Adolf Mahr was born on 7 May 1887 at Trent in Southern Austria, at a time when the power and influence of the Austro-Hungarian empire was at its height. His father was a bandmaster to the Emperor Franz Josef. After studying geography and prehistory at the University of Vienna, Mahr went to work for the Linz Museum in 1913 before joining the Natural History Museum in Vienna two years later. During the First World War he enlisted for military service in Salzburg. In 1919 Mahr, then aged 32, saw his beloved native South Tyrol region ceded to Italy under the terms of the Treaty of Versailles. The prospect of reintegrating this region into Austria was one of the principal factors that later attracted Mahr to Nazism. In 1927 he was appointed Senior Keeper of Irish Antiquities at the National Museum in Dublin. Although he was technically an alien, Mahr thus became a permanent and pensionable member of the Irish Civil Service.

The rise of Éamon de Valera to power as head of a Fianna Fáil government in 1932, and the Nazis' rise to power in Germany the following year, were developments that suited Adolf Mahr whose career at the National Museum was poised to take off. Hitler was appointed German Chancellor on 30 January 1933. On 6 March 1933, the Secretary of the Department of Education in Dublin, Seosamh Ó Neill, wrote a letter[2] to his opposite number at the Department of Finance, James J. McElligott (the Minister for Finance at the time was Seán MacEntee), stating that Mahr's 'personal qualifications are such as to enable the Minister for Education [Thomas Derrig] to accept him unreservedly as a most suitable person for appointment to the post of Director of the National Museum'.

As well as advancing up the promotional ladder of the Irish Civil Service, Mahr was also applying for membership of the German Nazi Party. His party membership dated from 1 April 1933, meaning that his application was made at about the same time that Hitler was sworn in as Chancellor some two months earlier. The Irish government approved Mahr's appointment to the top museum post at a cabinet meeting on 17 July 1934 and three days later the President of the Executive Council, Éamon de Valera, personally signed the cabinet minutes[3] which included Mahr's promotion. According to Mahr's daughter, Mrs Ingrid Reusswig, de Valera knew her father personally and was aware of his Nazi Party links, although it is not clear exactly when in the 1930s the Irish leader became aware of them.

The post of director of the National Museum had been vacant for 18 years before Mahr got the job. The previous incumbent was Count George Noble Plunkett, whose services were dispensed with after the 1916 Rising in which his son had taken part. From 1916 to 1934 the job had been held in an acting capacity by one of the museum's three resident keepers.

From the time he took up his appointment at the museum on 29 September 1927, Mahr threw himself enthusiastically into his new job, reorganising the Irish antiquities section and purchasing new items to exhibit there. Former and current museum staff acknowledge that Adolf Mahr's contribution to the National Museum was a positive one.

Mahr made it his business to know his newly adopted country well and his diaries for the 1927-35 period, which pay meticulous attention to detail, show that he travelled widely around the country. In 1928 he was elected a member of the Royal Society of Antiquaries of Ireland, and in the summer of that year was photographed during an archaeological dig at Lough Crew, County Meath with his fellow Austrian, the expressionist painter Oskar Kokoschka. In 1937 the Nazis labelled Kokoschka's work as 'decadent' and his paintings were stripped from art galleries throughout the Third Reich. Mahr made a point of keeping the compromising photograph well hidden. If published, it would have led to his sacking as local Nazi Party chief in Ireland. It was eventually discovered among his papers at the museum long after the war.

In 1931 Mahr edited the first volume of *Christian Art in Ancient Ireland*, and two of his essays appeared in the second volume of the same work (edited by Mahr's protégé Dr Joseph Raftery and published in 1941, when Mahr was working at the Foreign Office in Berlin). Mahr was also a member of the Royal Irish Academy and wrote for its *Proceedings*, as well as contributing to the English quarterly *Antiquity* and many German publications. Mahr was president of the Prehistoric Society and also authored a 1939 book entitled *Ancient Irish Handicraft*.

If Mahr had worked solely as a museum director he might never have attracted the publicity which after the war would see him named as a Nazi in heated Dáil exchanges and which led effectively to his being barred from resuming museum work in Dublin. But during the 1930s Mahr's role as local Nazi Party leader gave him an influence far beyond that of a humble museum director.

Footnotes

1. Duggan, 1975 (p. 58) puts the German population at 529 in 1936, and 460 in 1946. Carroll, 1975 (p. 36) estimates it at approximately 400 in 1939. Nazi records held by the Bundesarchiv in Berlin indicate that over 30 of the pre-war Austro-German community in Ireland were party members (i.e. approx. 25 per cent of adult males). A handful were on the state payroll and held high-ranking positions in the public sector.

2. Ó Neill to McElligott, 6 March 1933 (DoF E53/3/33, document no. 348-32F).

3. Minutes of the 7th Cabinet, pp. 339-41 (NA, 1/5, S6631). Mahr appears to have been tipped off about his impending promotion almost a week before the cabinet meeting. His diary entry for 11 July 1934 reads: 'Zum Director ernannt [appointed as Director]'. Mahr frequently mixed English, German and Irish spellings in his diaries. (NM, Mahr diaries 1927-35. Mahr's diaries from 1927-35 are held at the National Museum in Dublin. His 1936-39 diaries, which are thought to contain details of his trips to London and elsewhere, were removed from the museum after the war by members of the Mahr family who are believed still to have possession of them).

3

Guinness und Gespräche at the Red Bank Restaurant

Ten years after Adolf Mahr had arrived in Ireland, another Nazi Party member set foot on Irish soil who was to have almost as much influence as the Austrian archaeologist in shaping German radio propaganda to Ireland in the war years. Hans Hartmann arrived at Cobh on 3 April 1937 to study the Irish language and the folklore of Gaeltacht areas. In common with many other German students who visited Ireland in the 1930s, his trip had been arranged by the German academic exchange organisation whose representative in Dublin was Helmut Clissmann, a former TCD student.

Hartmann, then a 27 year old Berlin University student, immediately made his way to Dublin to work at the National Museum with Mahr. Hartmann's alien registration card shows a young bespectacled scholar with dark hair cut short, back and sides. The secret file kept on Hartmann by the Irish Army's Intelligence section, G2, indicates that, despite the apparently innocuous nature of his study trip to Ireland, he was kept under close surveillance during his two and a half year visit which ended on the outbreak of the Second World War.

Staying in a flat at Dartmouth Square, Hartmann's attendance at German social functions was noted on his secret file.[1] He enjoyed meeting his fellow countrymen at soirées in the Red Bank restaurant in Dublin's d'Olier Street as well as the Gresham Hotel in O'Connell Street and Kilmacurragh Park Hotel in County Wicklow (run by a

German named Charles Budina). But the Red Bank was a favourite spot where, on Wednesday nights, Hartmann would join Helmut Clissmann and Adolf Mahr over pints of Guinness, ignoring the German beer that had been specially imported by the restaurant's owners, Mr and Mrs Schubert.

In the late 1930s Irish Army intelligence had no way of knowing it, but the Red Bank's German gatherings contained personnel who would soon play important roles in the Nazi war effort as it related to Ireland. During the war Clissmann, for example, was an agent for Abwehr II, the German counter-intelligence division responsible for contacts with discontented minority groups in foreign countries — in Ireland's case, the IRA. He was involved in the preparation of operation Sea Lion, Hitler's plan to invade England, as well as being privy to the top-secret, but ultimately aborted, 1940 plan to land IRA leaders Seán Russell and Frank Ryan on the Dingle peninsula from a U-boat. In addition, Mahr worked at the wartime Foreign Office in Berlin, while Hartmann broadcast to Ireland under the aegis of Goebbels' Ministry of Propaganda and, later, Ribbentrop's Foreign Ministry.

If, however, G2 had hoped to net a leading German spy in the person of Hans Hartmann, they were to be disappointed. Hartmann's mission was purely academic. He wanted to master the Irish language — which he amazed everyone by doing in less than two years — as well as gather folklore material for a doctoral thesis, to be supervised by Ludwig Mühlhausen. The thesis led, in 1942, to a lecturing post in Mühlhausen's Department of Celtic Studies at Berlin University.

In Dublin, Hartmann was assigned to work under Adolf Mahr at the National Museum, but Mahr soon realised Hartmann was not cut out for museum work and arranged for his transfer to the Folklore Commission at University College Dublin in Earlsfort Terrace. Professor Séamus Hamilton Delargy from Antrim, a friend of Mühlhausen's, had been director of the Commission since it was established in 1935. At UCD, Hartmann was in his element, working with Máire MacNéill and Seán Ó Súilleabháin, a native of Kenmare, County Kerry, who formed a close friendship with the German. Together with Ó Súilleabháin, Hartmann drew up a questionnaire seeking details of Gaeltacht folklore including superstitions, beliefs and fairytales. Copies of the questionnaire were sent to people in the Kerry, Connemara and Donegal Gaeltachts, and the results were collated by Hartmann who used them as the basis of his thesis (presented at Berlin University in 1941) entitled 'Sickness, Death, and Concepts of the Hereafter in Ireland'.[2]

Foreign exchange students were supposed to stay in Ireland only for one academic year but thanks to Professor Delargy, who supported his application for an extension, Hartmann was able to stay much longer — two and a half years, in fact — during which time the Garda Special Branch noted his continued attendance at gatherings of the German colony at the Red Bank restaurant as well as his regular visits to Adolf Mahr's house at Waterloo Place. On 17 September 1938, detectives followed Hartmann to a showing at the Olympia Theatre of a German film which, they reported, featured coverage of Hitler's visit to Rome. Hartmann was accompanied by a TCD student, Hans Garlach. In addition to following Hartmann to social events, the police also followed him to work at the Folklore Commission in Earlsfort Terrace. Police reports noted that Hartmann was often accompanied by the German Legation's typist, Helen Neugebauer, whom he later married.

But who was the man whom Irish police spent so much time following and where did he come from? Hans Hartmann was born on 18 November 1909 in the small village of Rustringen, near Oldenburg in northern Germany. At university he opted to study philology, a subject that was to dominate his life. Hartmann's love of languages would mark him out later as one of Germany's leading linguistic experts. When Hitler took power in Germany, Hartmann, like many others of his generation, was put under pressure to join the Nazi Party. He recalled:

> I became a member of the National Socialist Party in 1933. The reason was that my studies had been paid for by the Studienstiftung [student foundation] whose members were told that since the Reich had done so much to promote their studies they should show some gratitude and that the least they could, and should, do was to enter the party. That I did in order to be left undisturbed further on.[3]

Hartmann deliberately avoided the mainstream of German academic life. The path of chemicals or engineering would have meant a lucrative job in the Third Reich's expanding industrial and armaments sector, but it was not for him. In the 1930s Hartmann was at his happiest wandering the remote boreens of Connemara and Donegal. In those Gaeltacht areas he tried to get to grips with the dialectical maze of a language which had, at that time, few written guidelines for students. In 1936, at the age of 27, the scholar from Rustringen graduated from Berlin University after completing a paper entitled 'Studies on the stress pattern of adjectives in Russian'.[4] He never actually visited the Soviet Union but 'learnt Russian in 1930-31 from a well educated, bilingual German-Russian emigré who had been evicted from a flourishing estate situated in the area of Saratov, the principal town of the German Volga Republic, and who was, naturally, strongly opposed to Soviet communism'.[5]

Within a short time of his graduation Hartmann was to switch his attentions westwards to Ireland and the Celtic world; hence his exchange visit to Ireland which lasted from April 1937 to September 1939. The war years would see Hartmann contributing increasingly to German Radio's Irish service broadcasts.

Footnotes

1.   MA, G2/0071 (Hartmann file).

2.   The work appeared in book form under the title *Über Krankheit, Tod und Jenseitsvorstellungen in Irland* (Halle, 1942). Hartmann dedicated it to Ireland's first President, Douglas Hyde, whom he admired for his earlier work as president of the Gaelic League (Conradh na Gaeilge). Hartmann recalls: 'I never met Hyde but Delargy was his assistant so we heard a lot about him almost every day. I highly appreciated his *History of Irish Literature*, which I used very much. I think he was a great man. I did not have the honour of meeting him but when I dedicated my first book to him I asked Hempel to go to Douglas Hyde and ask him whether he wanted to accept the dedication, and he did so. Hyde let me know he was very pleased and grateful that I had done this kind of work' (Hartmann interview, 21 October 1990).

3.   Hartmann interview, 21 October 1990.

4.   Hartmann, *Über die Betonung der Adjektiva im Russischen* (Berlin, 1936).

5.   Hartmann's letter to author, 16 August 1993.

4

Ludwig Mühlhausen:
Scholar and Spy

L udwig Mühlhausen, the man chosen to launch Goebbels'
Irish language propaganda broadcasts from Berlin in
December 1939, was widely recognised as an accomplished
linguist; as well as mastering Irish, he spoke Welsh, Dutch, French,
Breton, Flemish and English. But the German's cold academic
exterior hid another altogether more sinister person. According to a
secret intelligence profile, drawn up by G2 in mid-1943,[1] Mühlhausen
was an 'enthusiastic Nazi' and a spy. This unflattering portrait claimed
the German Celtologist was a member of pre-Nazi fascist groups
such as the German National People's Party and the Steel Helmet
organisation. During the First World War he had worked as a spy in
Wallonia, Southern Belgium.

Mühlhausen joined the Nazi Party on 1 May 1932, some nine
months before Hitler came to power. Mühlhausen's wife Else was a
native of Leipzig. They married in 1914 after he had taken a doctorate
in philosophy at Leipzig University. Mrs Else Mühlhausen had been
active in extreme right-wing political organisations even before
joining the National Socialists. By 1932 she had become a member
of the inner circle of the Nazi Party in Hamburg where she and her
husband were then living. Hitler's rise to power as Reich Chancellor
gave Mühlhausen's career a boost. Firstly, the Nazis sacked the Jewish
director of Hamburg's Commerce Library, Dr Rosenbaum, to make
way for Mühlhausen. Then, in October 1935, the Nazis removed
Professor Julius Pokorny from the chair of Celtic Studies at Berlin

University where he had worked for 15 years. Mühlhausen filled the vacancy in 1937.[2]

Mühlhausen's interest in Ireland and the Irish language had been stimulated by a number of summer visits to Cork and Kerry in the late 1920s. He gave a series of lectures at UCC in the summer of 1929 when he stayed with the parents of a Cork language student, Joe Healy, at Springfield in Cobh. Healy, who ten years later was called in by G2 to monitor Mühlhausen's initial radio talks, stayed with the Mühlhausen family while studying at Hamburg University from 1927 to 1929. Healy, and his UCC colleague Séamus Kavanagh, spent some time in Germany teaching Mühlhausen Irish, while they perfected their German.

Healy's younger brother Louis remembers the German professor's summertime visits to his parents' home in Cobh and recalls that the younger Healy children did not get on with him.

> Mühlhausen came from Hamburg and my father had to meet him coming off the liner in Cobh. He was a tall, spare, bespectacled man. I suppose in a way he was arrogant and had absolutely no sense of humour, so as youngsters we did not care for him very much. He moved on down to Kerry and spent some time on the Blasket Islands speaking Gaelic to the natives. Joe was still in Germany at that time. The professor spent more time with us on his way back.

The following summer, Mühlhausen was back staying with the Healys again but relations with the younger children had not improved.

> Mühlhausen made himself very much at home. The family laid on a nice meal with a good bottle of wine. At the end of the meal Patsy and I brought in a bottle of Joe's home-made wine and said, 'Try this, professor'. He held it up to the light, sniffed at it, rolled it around and eventually tasted it, spat, and said, 'Das ist cat's piss'. We said, 'We know that, but which one? We have two cats'. My father had an awkward explanation to make in difficult circumstances and we got a mild parental admonition. We could never relax with Professor Mühlhausen. He seemed arrogant and easily offended.[3]

Mühlhausen returned to Ireland in July 1932 where he studied the local Irish dialect and folklore of Cornamóna in County Galway.

There he met Professor Delargy, director of the Folklore Commission. Mühlhausen was accompanied by a German professor of geography who took a great number of photographs of Lough Corrib and the Aran Islands. In January 1937, Delargy stayed with the Mühlhausen family in Hamburg and recalled that the German professor showed him 'thousands of photographs, plans and drawings' he had made in Ireland. In late summer 1937 Mühlhausen was back in Ireland again, this time, ostensibly, to study Irish dialects in Donegal. Delargy had put the German in touch with a Donegal folklore specialist named Seán Ó Heochaidh. In July 1937, shortly after taking up his new post at Berlin University, Mühlhausen wrote to Ó Heochaidh, in Irish, saying: 'I would like to stay in a fisherman's house. The most important thing for me is to be among the people, among the hills and by the sea'.[4] So it was that on 25 August 1937 Seán Ó Heochaidh met Mühlhausen in Killybegs as he descended from the Galway train. He had arranged for the German to stay with a Teelin fisherman, Hugh Byrne. Byrne recalls that the German,

> spent six weeks in my parents' house and never spoke anything but Irish. His Irish was very good; he had learned it on an earlier visit to the Blaskets. However, at first I could barely understand him because of the Kerry Irish. After a while we got on fine and were able to speak together. For the first week he was there, Mühlhausen shared a room with León Ó Broin [a distinguished historian and civil servant who later became Secretary of the Department of Posts and Telegraphs]. They had fierce arguments about religion. Mühlhausen kept a large picture of Hitler in his room, while Ó Broin kept a crucifix next to his bed.[5]

Many years later Ó Broin recalled the time he shared that room in Teelin with Mühlhausen.

> When he woke the first morning we were together, he took out his Nazi song book and sang a verse or two. I responded by kneeling down and provocatively blessing myself. He then put on his dressing gown, walked with me to the pier head nearby and dived into the bleak sea. Not to be outdone I did the same and nearly died of the cold. I gave this morning exercise up; the Nazi, a man of tougher breed, did not.[6]

Hugh Byrne remembers the German paying for his board in advance. Mühlhausen spent the entire six weeks in Teelin taking photographs and visiting elderly people to record their old folk tales. According to Byrne, Mühlhausen never went out in a fishing boat and never touched a drop of drink.

> He idolised Hitler and thought he was a god. I don't think he had any religion. He smoked cigars and spoke of the 1914-18 war which he had fought in. He told me Germany would get the Rhineland back without firing a shot, and they did. He was very anti-British and said he would not set foot on British soil. When he left Donegal for Dublin [in October, to stay with Delargy] he deliberately went through Sligo so he wouldn't have to go through the North.

According to local people who remembered his visit to Teelin, Mühlhausen was a direct and humourless character. He boasted that his daughters were working for the Reich on a German pig farm and enjoying every minute of it. But Teelin folk could not figure out whether the German was having them on or not when he claimed that Germany would run Ireland far better than either the British had done or the Irish were doing — even to the extent of levelling the local mountain, Slieve League![7]

Seán Ó Heochaidh took the German around the area introducing him to the best Irish speakers so Mühlhausen could work on the South West Donegal dialect. But as well as studying the language, the local man noted that Mühlhausen 'took hundreds of photos'.[8] Local people in Teelin were convinced he was spying because he took so many pictures, including ones from the summit of Slieve League from where he had a clear view across Donegal Bay to the coast of Sligo.[9]

During the war, de Valera secretly granted permission for RAF flying boats based on Lough Erne to overfly the Bundoran air corridor to the Atlantic. This was one of the areas photographed in detail by Mühlhausen. Some of the German's photographs of County Donegal and surrounding areas, including three taken in Teelin, appeared in a German military handbook produced in occupied Brussels, and published in Berlin in 1941. This was intended to assist with a top secret invasion plan for Ireland code-named Operation Green. When Hugh Byrne was shown copies of the three Teelin photographs he was sure Mühlhausen had taken them. León Ó Broin's son Éimear says his father 'reported Mühlhausen's spying activities to an Irish Army friend, but nothing was done since he was not breaking the law in any way'.[10] Adolf Mahr's son, Gustav, comments: 'It would appear that Mühlhausen actually had carried on espionage in Ireland'.[11]

As well as containing scores of photographs, the 1941 handbook, entitled *Military Geographical Data on Ireland,*[12] included maritime charts, coastal profiles, and aerial photographs of harbours and inlets, as well as one picture of the County Donegal fishing village of Bunbeg where Hans Hartmann stayed at the beginning of 1939. Also in the handbook was a list of approximately one hundred Gaelic words and their German equivalents. Some pictures in the handbook are thought to have been taken in the summer of 1939 by the German photographer Joachim Gerstenberg. He toured the country taking scores of pictures for his book *Éire, ein Irlandbuch* published the following year in Hamburg. It included pictures of Lough Swilly in County Donegal — one of the three Treaty Ports — and Cobh Cathedral overlooking another Treaty Port, as well as Killary Harbour and Bantry Bay, two of the deepest inlets on the west coast. Photographs of Tramore strand in County Waterford and Killiney strand in south County Dublin were also featured.

As the 1930s drew to a close in Ireland, the pieces of a jigsaw were being put into place which would lead to the creation of a unique radio service — Dr Goebbels' Irish propaganda unit, known in Berlin as the Irland-Redaktion.

Footnotes

1.   MA, G2/2473 (Mühlhausen file).

2.   Rockel, 1990, pp. 30-1.

3.   Letter to author from Dr Louis D. Healy, Mandurah, Western Australia, 14 January 1992.

4.   Mühlhausen to Ó Heochaidh, 29 July 1937 (copy of letter supplied to author by Dr Seán Ó Heochaidh, Gortahork, Co. Donegal).

5. Byrne interview, Teelin, Co. Donegal, 15 January 1992.

6. Ó Broin, 1985, p. 132.

7. Mühlhausen was probably not joking. According to an undated memorandum written for G2 during the Emergency period, Mühlhausen 'has a very sincere regard for Ireland and its people, but thinks that German culture would be good for us, and our country better run by Germans than by either the British or ourselves'. (Memo to G2, undated. MA, G2/2473. The anonymous memo is handwritten under the heading 'Correspondence Clissmann re Exchange Students'. It was probably written by either Helmut Clissmann or Professor Séamus Delargy).

8. Ó Heochaidh interview, Gortahork, Co. Donegal, 14 January 1992.

9. In the event of a German invasion, the north-west region could have played a critical role as a gateway to republican areas in Northern Ireland. As it was, Sligo did feature in the Abwehr's plans. In February 1940, the German spy Ernst Weber-Drohl was landed off the Sligo coast from a U-boat (Stephan, 1963, p. 66; Fisk, 1983, p. 138). Despite confusion over the landing site, a wall map in the Irish Military Archive pinpoints the Sligo coast as the agent's place of arrival. In September 1940, Helmut Clissmann set sail from Brest bound for Sligo Bay. He was to liaise with IRA men and accompany them to Britain to assist in Operation Sea Lion — Hitler's plan to invade the United Kingdom. But the trip to Sligo was called off after only four days due to heavy storms (Stephan, 1963, p. 154). Clissmann had close ties with the area. His wife Elizabeth Mulcahy was a member of a staunchly republican family from Sligo. Mrs. Clissmann's father had been a judge in the Sinn Féin courts during the 1919-21 War of Independence. In addition, Ludwig Mühlhausen had already reconnoitred the Sligo area. Donegal fisherman, Hugh Byrne, recalls that in October 1937, when Mühlhausen left Teelin for Dublin, 'he went on by Sligo and Leitrim. He did not take the shorter route through the North of Ireland because he would not put his foot on British soil. He hated the English because of Germany's defeat in the First World War'. Seen in retrospect, Mühlhausen's explanation to his Donegal host for travelling to Dublin via Sligo appears as a pretext for covertly photographing the region.

10. Éimear Ó Broin interview, Dublin, 10 June 1992. Ó Broin adds: 'My father said Mühlhausen went back to Berlin with photographs of some of the inlets on the south and west coasts of Ireland, possibly with a view to enabling U-boats to shelter in these inlets or to make possible landings of agents... My father was certain that Mühlhausen was a spy'.

11. Letter to author from Gustav Mahr, Berlin, 28 November 1990.

12. Cox, 1975, pp. 83-96.

5

Dr Mahr's Departure

As Christmas 1937 approached, members of the German colony in Ireland had every reason to be confident. Hitler had been in power for almost five years and Germany's star was rising in world affairs. That November, Hitler's plans to dominate Europe were outlined at the Hossbach Conference. A year earlier, both Italy and Japan had signed pacts with Nazi Germany.

Members of the German community in Dublin booked the Gresham Hotel for their annual Christmas party on 19 December. The balconies of the hotel's Aberdeen Hall were decorated with swastika flags and tricolours. Under a large portrait of Adolf Hitler and a world map of Germany's international shipping lines, German children acted out a scene from *Der Weinachtstraum* (the Christmas Dream) to the delight of their parents looking on. Piano accompaniment was by Colonel Fritz Brase, the head of the Irish Army's School of Music, who during the 1930s had sought permission from the Army Chief of Staff to set up a branch of the Nazi Party in Dublin; he was curtly told to choose between the Nazis and the Irish Army, and chose the latter.

The festive proceedings had been set in motion by the president of the German Society, Oswald Müller-Dubrow, a director of the giant Siemens-Schuckert group, which in the late 1920s had won the contract to build the Shannon hydroelectric scheme — the jewel in the crown of Ireland's post-independence drive towards modernising an economy that had until then been largely based on agriculture.

19

German Society members and their guests were treated to three Christmas songs by Frau Erni Ritter, as well as a choral rendition of the seasonal hymn *Stille Nacht* (Silent Night).

The highlight of the evening came when the German Minister to Ireland, Dr Eduard Hempel, asked all present to 'rise and salute the Leader and Chancellor of the Reich'. A contemporary report[1] noted that 'with right arms raised in the Nazi salute, the gathering sang *Deutschland, Deutschland über Alles* [the German national anthem], the *Horst Wessel Lied* [a Nazi song], and *A Soldier's Song* [the Irish national anthem]'. Whatever their personal feelings, the Germans assembled in the Gresham could hardly have refused to join in the Nazi salute and singsong since leading members of the local Nazi Party were present. They included Adolf Mahr, Robert Stumpf (a radiologist at Baggot Street Hospital), and Helmut Clissmann. As the Germans made their way home from the city centre that winter evening they could not have guessed that in less than two years they would have to leave their peaceful host country, rallying to the call of the Third Reich at war.

Adolf Mahr continued his work as director of the National Museum, but as a leading Nazi Party member, he also had other functions to attend to. In May 1937, for example, he was an official guest at the coronation of King George VI in London.[2] The invitation to attend that event demonstrates the high rank Mahr held in the pre-war German colony. In fact, Mahr's powers within the Austro-German community far outweighed those of the German Minister, Dr Hempel, Berlin's top diplomat in Dublin. This situation came about not only because of Mahr's party post as Ortsgruppenleiter but also because he was head of the Irish section of the powerful Auslandsorganisation or AO, the Nazi Party's foreign organisation (Müller-Dubrow was the AO's local deputy leader). With the backing of the AO, Mahr left no one in any doubt that he was in charge and proved as much by getting two diplomats recalled to Berlin in the 1930s. They were Georg von Dehn-Schmidt (posted to the German legation from 1923-34) and Erich Schroetter (1936-37).[3]

The AO was not a secret organisation but it was far more than just an umbrella group for Germans living abroad. Its functions spanned everything from the promotion of Irish-German trade links, to keeping an eye on Germans outside the Fatherland, monitoring political developments in the host country, and providing suitable candidates for espionage. It sent agents abroad to propagate Nazi doctrines and extend party discipline over German nationals. It was also given the task of maintaining contacts with subversive organisations in various countries. Founded in 1931 by Ernst-Wilhelm Bohle, the Auslandsorganisation was the most important Nazi agency for gathering foreign information. By 1939 it had over 50,000 members world-wide and Bohle had been rewarded with a post as State Secretary in the Foreign Office.

As AO chief in Ireland, Mahr would have been responsible, as was every AO district leader, for drawing up a monthly report on the local political situation. These reports, which sometimes included economic and military information, were forwarded to Bohle and then scrutinised by senior Nazi Party figures like Hess, Bormann and Himmler. Internationally, the AO provided a pool of potential spies and, in 1937, was liaising with German counter-intelligence, the Abwehr.[4]

Irish Military Intelligence records for the period reveal that Adolf Mahr's enthusiasm for his museum work was paralleled by his activities on behalf of the Nazi Party. According to G2, 'Germans arriving in Dublin were supposed to report to Mahr... There is a record of a man called Plass (an exchange student) being reprimanded for failing to do so'. In the late 1930s G2 was convinced that Mahr was using his position in Ireland to rally both Irish and Germans to the Nazi cause. In fact, as early as 1936 or 1937, the Secretary of the Irish Department of External Affairs, Joe Walshe, had complained about the 'Nazi organisation in Dublin' to the German representative, Dr Schroetter. Whether or not Walshe passed on these concerns to his Minister, de Valera (who held the portfolio of External Affairs as well as being head of government), the latter continued to enjoy good relations with Mahr. One anecdote from the Scottish archaeologist Dr Howard Kilbride-Jones, makes the point that Mahr and the Taoiseach knew each other well. In June 1938, Mahr and Kilbride-Jones went to de Valera's office to seek extra funds to complete an excavation at Drimnagh. After a half-hour discussion the two archaeologists left with Dev's personal cheque for £400 [£16,000 in late-1990s values]. As we left, Mahr turned and asked, 'Is this coming out of your pocket?' 'No', replied Dev, 'I shall get Mr Mac Entee [Minister for Finance] to reimburse me'. We left laughing. Next morning I walked into the Bank of Ireland in St Stephen's Green and presented the cheque. The cashier looked at me as though it were a hold-up.[5]

Mahr was apparently unaware that his activities were attracting the attention of the Special Branch, Army Intelligence and the Department of External Affairs, so life continued much as normal in the German colony. Dr Joseph Raftery, a young colleague of Mahr's at the National Museum, knew his boss was a Nazi supporter but described Mahr's wife as the 'active Nazi' of the family. Raftery remembers Maria Mahr at a social occasion in Dublin 'standing like Joan of Arc, reciting a poem about the Munich putsch, and shouting at the top of her voice the last line, "Und ihr habt doch gesiegt" (And you have conquered nevertheless)'.[6]

Another friend of Mahr's, Helmut Clissmann's wife Elizabeth (née Mulcahy), agrees that Mahr was active in the Nazi Party in Ireland before the war. Mrs Clissmann put this down to,

> the sort of enthusiasm that we Irish find in our American exiles. A kind of 'green hills far away' exile's enthusiasm... Dr Mahr had that kind of idealistic, impractical admiration for developments in Germany; Germany's escape from the conditions of the Treaty of Versailles and the reunification of Germany and Austria. He had a great feeling for Austria.[7]

On 12 March 1938 German troops marched into Austria bringing about the Anschluss or union between both countries. According to Mahr's daughter Ingrid, the Anschluss was the main reason for her father's attraction to Nazism. Mahr also wished to see the Anschluss carried to what, for him, would have been its logical conclusion; the reintegration of his native South Tyrol region into Austria from Italy. But as events unfolded, this was never to happen.

On 18 December 1938 members of the German Society gathered once more at the Gresham Hotel for their annual Christmas party. But this occasion, coming less than a year before the Second World War, was to be the last of its kind. Once again the ballroom walls were decked out with swastikas, and German children put on a play entitled *Eine Nacht im Kyffhauser*. Musical accompaniement was provided by Colonel Fritz Brase and Maria Mahr. Hans Hartmann dressed up as Santa Claus to distribute the children's presents — an event he recalled during a broadcast to Ireland on Christmas Eve 1943 — and Paul Schubert of the Red Bank Restaurant presided as acting president of the German Society.[8]

As 1938 drew to a close, the Irish authorities were beginning to be as worried as local Nazi Party members about the possible consequences of Adolf Mahr's double life — as a civil servant and Nazi Party boss — becoming public knowledge. In December a senior Auslandsorganisation director, Admiral Menske, visited Ireland to ensure a smooth transition of power in the local party should Mahr's ambiguous position be revealed. Menske named Heinz Mecking to be Mahr's successor as AO chief in Ireland should trouble arise for the museum director. Mecking was chief adviser with the Turf Development Board and a member of the Nazi Party. In 1936 he had come to Ireland from the German bog drainage equipment manufacturer Klasmann but a contemporary account assessed his bog drainage advice as 'disastrous' because of the vast differences between German and Irish boglands. Mecking 'set himself up as a Nazi intelligence agent, photographing railway stations, river bridges, sign posts and reservoirs'.[9] After being named as Mahr's potential successor in December 1938 he attended a Nazi Party conference in London.

Nazi members in Dublin had every reason to be concerned as the net was beginning to tighten around their hitherto unfettered activities on behalf of the party. On 22 February 1939, Joe Walshe decided to put his earlier reservations about Mahr in writing[10] for de Valera so that the Taoiseach would be under no further illusions about how he felt. Walshe was blunt in putting forward his concerns, and wrote that:

> The existence of a Nazi organisation in Dublin, having as its chief member and organiser an employee of our State, was not calculated to improve relations between our two Governments.

Walshe had made the same point verbally the same day, 22 February, when he met German Legation official Henning Thomsen who was a member of the SS. Further on in his memo, Walshe forecast unrest if Mahr was unmasked:

> ... our Catholic people and clergy would begin to make public protests and the [Irish] Government would be placed in a very awkward situation when the position of Dr Mahr, Director of the National Museum, as head of the Nazi cell in Dublin, became a matter of public controversy.

In the same memorandum, Walshe revealed that he had frequently complained about the 'Nazi organisation in Dublin' both to Dr Hempel and his predecessor, Dr Schroetter. This confirms that Walshe's worries about Mahr dated back at least to June 1937 when Schroetter left Dublin or, even earlier, to 1936 when he had first been appointed to Ireland. After Walshe's blunt missive, de Valera could no longer claim to be ignorant of Mahr's activities or their possible effects. The result was predictable. Although he had been shadowed beforehand, by the spring of 1939 Mahr was under constant scrutiny by the Garda Special Branch and Army Intelligence. In addition, the authorities ordered the surveillance of all mail destined for the Mahr family home at 37 Waterloo Place. This revealed a mixed bag of anti-Jewish newsletters from Germany, an invitation to a Nazi old boys' reunion in Vienna, letters from academic colleagues abroad and a detailed list of arrivals and departures of German nationals sent to Mahr from the German Legation in Dublin.[11] One of the last letters he received before leaving Ireland came from Ludwig Mühlhausen in Berlin, addressed to 'Dear Party Comrade Mahr'. Mühlhausen told Mahr that his book *Ten Irish Folktales*, based on his sojourn in Donegal two years earlier, had been sent to the printers that day, 4 July 1939. The professor signed off 'Heil Hitler, ever yours'.

But luck was running out for Adolf Mahr who scarcely had time to reply to Mühlhausen. In any case he would see the professor shortly in Berlin. No doubt bearing in mind what had been decided at the secret AO meeting with Menske six months before — and perhaps having been tipped off by someone in the know — Mahr packed his bags and left Dublin for Cork. At Cobh harbour he sailed for Hamburg on 19 July 1939. He would never return to Ireland. His colleagues at the museum must have guessed something was up. Of his decision to leave, Joe Raftery said, 'Mahr could not have been expected to do otherwise, given his loyalty to the [Nazi] party and the advent of war'. In fact, the museum director had the perfect cover for a summer trip to the Third Reich having been appointed official Irish representative to the Sixth International Congress of Archaeology due to be held in Berlin that August. No sooner had Mahr sailed for Germany than his place as local head of the Auslandsorganisation was taken over by Heinz Mecking, as planned.

Three days after Mahr left, G2 officers were busy copying one of the most suspicious letters ever to be mailed to his Dublin address. Signed by SS officer Friedrich von Weinertsgrün at the Nazis' topographical office in Wenzelsplatz, Prague, it indicates that Mahr may have supplied maps, reports or other sensitive material which could have assisted in drawing up part of Germany's battle plans — particularly the top secret Operation Green, the invasion blueprint for Ireland. The letter, dated 11 July 1939, contained the following:

> Many thanks for last letter... I have become a head official of the SS since the 1st June and am with the Reserve Command of the R.u.S. Head Office of the Prague Topographical Office. The questions referred to are therefore now of greater importance than ever. At all events, thank you sincerely for your efforts... Heil Hitler. [signed] Friedrich Maier (Edler) von Weinertsgrün.[12]

The Prague letter was one of the factors which later prompted G2's Dan Bryan to inform Frederick Boland at External Affairs that,

> Mahr approached one of the German intelligence sections which dealt with matters concerning a landing in Ireland, with a long report and was, as a result, employed in that section for a year or two [as] was Dr Otto Reinhard of our Forestry Department.[13]

In the 1930s, Reinhard had fought off 65 other candidates for the job of Forestry Director with the Department of Lands. But at the outbreak of war in 1939, after registering 'only a moderate success' in the post, he left Ireland for Germany.[14]

Perhaps Mahr alone knew the destiny that awaited him in wartime Berlin. He would, arguably, have been of far more use to the Third Reich had he remained in neutral Ireland during the war. It was clear, however, that his cover as a museum director was about to be blown and, as such, his effectiveness — if not that of his colleagues in the local Nazi Party — would have been much reduced. As things turned out the Austrian archaeologist, who had spent the previous 12 years in Ireland, was to prove an asset in Ribbentrop's Foreign Office, where he would work on the Irish desk. He had established a rapport with Ribbentrop during several visits to London when the senior Nazi was ambassador to the Court of St. James, from 1936 to 1938.[15]

Footnotes

1. *Irish Times*, 20 December 1937.

2. Author's interview with Mrs Ingrid Reusswig (née Mahr), Dublin, 28 July 1994.

3. Duggan, 1975, pp. 23-4.

4. Kahn, 1978, pp. 98-100; Hoehne, 1979, pp. 230-1. The AO's influence was demonstrated by the fact that its agents were instrumental in securing Hitler's backing for Franco in the Spanish civil war.

5. Kilbride-Jones, 1993, p. 3.

6. Author's interview with Dr Joseph Raftery, Dublin, 20 May 1991. Raftery was encouraged by Mahr to study in Germany and, in 1935, he was awarded a prestigious Humboldt Fellowship by the German government. In 1937, Raftery took his PhD at Marburg University with a thesis on the Early Stone Age in Ireland. Adolf Mahr's wife, Maria, was Dutch. Her father, Professor Van Bemmelin, taught zoology at Leiden University.

7. Author's interview with Mrs Elizabeth Clissmann, Dublin, 19 October 1990.

8. 'German Colony's Christmas Party', *Irish Times*, 19 December 1938, p. 6; *Irish Press*, 19 December 1938, p. 15. The Gresham party was for the German colony's children. The annual German Society dinner dance took place on 27 December 1938 at the Portmarnock Hotel. Hans Hartmann and Adolf Mahr were followed there by Special Branch detectives (MA, G2/0071).

9. Andrews, 1982, pp. 162-3.

10. Walshe to de Valera, 22 February 1939 (FLK, de Valera Papers, file no. 953 'Anglo-Irish Relations' in J.P. Walshe's memoranda, 1932-39). The fact that Walshe's memo was filed, by de Valera's own staff,

under 'Anglo-Irish Relations' — and not, for example, 'Irish-German Relations' or 'Internal Affairs' — suggests that de Valera was more worried about a negative British reaction to Mahr's being unmasked than about the 'public protests [by] our Catholic people and clergy' that Walshe warned of. Walshe's memo may well have been prompted by the political fallout from the IRA's S-plan bombing blitz of Britain which had been declared just six weeks earlier on 12 January. The S-plan campaign continued until March 1940 (see Coogan,T.P., 1970, pp. 164-71).

11.   Mahr letters file (MA, G2/130). But was Mahr anti-Jewish? The anti-Semitic newsletters found in his post may have been unsolicited. Mahr's museum colleague, Joe Raftery, says Mahr 'though a Nazi supporter, was not anti-Jewish' (Raftery interview, 20 May 1991). Raftery based this opinion on his belief that Mahr's housekeeper, Gretel Spiegelfeld, was Jewish. Mahr's daughter, Ingrid, concurs in part with Dr Raftery's comments: 'My father was pro-Nazi but not anti-Jewish. He had many Jewish friends whom he warned to flee Austria in the 1930s'. She says Raftery was wrong, however, about the housekeeper being a Jewess: 'Although she had curly hair and a hook nose, she was not Jewish. She was, in fact, an Austrian countess who had lost her estate in the carve up of the Austro-Hungarian empire after World War I'. (Ingrid Reusswig interview, 28 July 1994). But according to Mahr's friend, the Scottish archaeologist Dr Howard Kilbride-Jones, Gretel Spiegelfeld was 'a Jewess who had fled her native Austria' (Kilbride-Jones, 1993, p. 30). Whatever the true story about Mahr's housekeeper, when, in 1939, Mahr got a chance to help a Jewish doctor — who had known him in the 1920s — to flee Vienna, he was not able to assist. This may have been because Mahr's own position in Dublin was rapidly becoming untenable (see this chapter and Epilogue). Whether or not Mahr realised the net was tightening on his Nazi *Ortsgruppe*, the passage into law of the draconian Offences Against the State Act — on 14 June 1939, just a month before he left Ireland — would have served to remind Mahr of the possible danger of internment. The OAS Act was used by de Valera to crack down on his former IRA comrades (Lee, 1989, pp. 221-4). It could, however, just as easily have been turned against Nazis but for the fact that most party members in Ireland left for the Fatherland on 11 September 1939 (see Chapter 6).

12. Von Weinertsgrün to Mahr, 11 July 1939 (MA, G2/130. Letter no. 10/ A 136/39). The initials RuS stand for Rasse und Siedlung (race and resettlement) — one of five branches of the SS 'responsible for organising the settlement and welfare of SS colonists in the conquered and occupied countries in the east' (Snyder, 1976, p. 281). Mahr was in an ideal position to supply detailed maps and photographs to Germany, as his diaries for the 1927-35 period, held at the National Museum, make clear. A diary entry for 20 December 1933 notes: 'Army Air Corps made aerial photos [of excavation site at Duleek, Co. Meath]'. Another diary entry for 9 August 1934 reads: 'Dank Ordnance Survey für zahllose maps für Jessen's Ausgräber' (thank Ordnance Survey for countless maps for Jessen's excavation).

13. Bryan to Boland, 4 May 1946 (MA, G2/0245).

14. MacLysaght, 1978, pp. 222-4.

15. Ribbentrop was appointed German ambassador to Britain on 11 August 1936 and remained in London until he was appointed Reich Foreign Minister on 4 February 1938. During that 18 month period, Ribbentrop was visited several times by Mahr. Mahr's daughter, Ingrid, recalls that in 1937 (on 12 May) her parents were official guests at the coronation of King George VI in London (Ingrid Reusswig interview, 28 July 1994). This emphasises the point that Mahr's standing in the pre-war Austro-German community in Ireland was far higher than that of the Minister (ambassador) who did not attend the coronation, although Mahr — who presumably went as part of Ribbentrop's entourage — may have taken advantage of the hiatus caused by Dr Schroetter's departure and Hempel's appointment to Dublin on 22 June 1937, some six weeks after the coronation (Duggan, 1975, p. 35).

6

By Mail Boat to the Fatherland

As the storm clouds of war gathered over Europe in August 1939, the Mahr family was on holidays at the Hotel Lindenhof in Millstatt-am-See, an alpine lake resort in southern Austria near the border with Italy and Slovenia. It would be the last peacetime summer Europe would witness for six years. Back at the Mahrs' homestead in Dublin their Austrian housekeeper, Gretel Spiegelfeld, picked up a letter[1] as it dropped through the mail box. Dated 18 August, the note from her mistress Maria Mahr spelled out Adolf Mahr's travel plans: 'My husband is going to Berlin, Stettin, Kiel and then, in September, to the Parteitag [Nazi Party rally]'. What Gretel Spiegelfeld did not know was that the letter she was reading had already been opened and copied by the Irish authorities who continued to monitor Mahr's mail after he had left the country.

The final destination mentioned in Maria Mahr's letter is the most revealing of all. It confirms that, as well as carrying out his museum director's duties by attending the International Congress of Archaeology in Berlin in August, Adolf Mahr was intent on fulfilling a key function for party members by attending the annual Nazi rally at Nuremberg. The Parteitag, a major focal point for the party, had been held every year since 1923. The 1939 rally, which Adolf Mahr planned to attend, was scheduled to take place from 2-11 September.[2]

With Mahr in Berlin, the German colony's members back in Dublin were in a quandary. Should they stay in neutral Ireland or return to Germany? In which place could they best serve the Third Reich?

Even if they wished to return home, could they do so now that Britain had blockaded Germany's ports? These and other questions were uppermost in the minds of the small community as it pondered its next move. Some Germans had reservations about throwing in their lot with the Nazi regime. They included Heinrich Becker, an exchange student at UCG, who chose to stay in Ireland. During the war, while taking photographs in Galway, Becker was apprehended by the Gardaí who thought — mistakenly as it turned out — that he was signalling a U-boat.[3]

It took no fewer than three meetings at the German Legation to decide the fate of the German colony, such was the uncertainty over what to do. According to Mrs Margaret Greiner (née Beirne from Frenchpark in County Roscommon) — whose husband Harry, a German engineer, helped start the Solus light bulb factory in Bray in the 1930s — what swung the German colony in favour of returning home was the fear that they would all be interned should Britain invade Ireland.[4] This was a very real prospect since Churchill and others wanted the Royal Navy to re-occupy the three Treaty ports at Cobh, Berehaven and Lough Swilly, which had been handed back to de Valera in 1938.

On foot of their decision to return to the Reich, Hempel sought the Irish Government's assistance in arranging for all the Germans to leave Ireland. Against the odds — German ports were blockaded and nearly all cross-Channel sailings to the Continent had been halted — the Department of External Affairs reached a special agreement with the British authorities to let the Germans travel home. So it was that on the evening of Monday, 11 September 1939, an excited group of adults and children gathered at Dún Laoghaire harbour to board the mail boat *Cambria* for Holyhead in North Wales. The trip had been so hastily arranged that quite a number of German nationals living outside Dublin were unable to avail themselves of this safe passage home through enemy territory.

Hempel was at the harbour to bid farewell to the 50 strong group, and Professor Friedrich Herkner of the National College of Art told an *Irish Times*[5] reporter that 'several of the party were of military age and were returning to Germany to join the colours. They had all been advised by their Legation to leave. One never knew how long the trouble would last and several of them had to return for economic reasons'. Amid shorts of 'Auf Wiedersehen' and Nazi salutes, the *Cambria* slipped into the night carrying its unusual cargo of souls to Britain with whom they were now at war. As well as Professor Herkner, the passengers included Dr and Frau Dr Robert Stumpf, Hans Hartmann, Helen Neugebauer, Harry and Margaret Greiner, Karl Krause, Karl Kuenstler, Herr and Frau Niemann, Herr Lohmeyer, Charles Budina, Herr Schubert, Otto Reinhard, Herr Stecker, Hans Boden and Heinz Mecking. Mrs Greiner recalls that her husband 'had to jump aboard the *Cambria* at the last minute as he was organising things to the last'. She also remembers Mecking — a Nazi Party member — giving the fascist salute, while Budina — who was not in the party — 'said he needed a change of air and did not think the war would last long'.

The journey home proved something of a nightmare for the Germans who arrived around midnight at Holyhead to be met by British troops. Ordinary Irish passengers were allowed to board the train to London but the Germans were kept aboard the mail boat for some hours while their papers were checked. In the early hours of 12 September the adults and children were made to run through a gauntlet of 20 policemen — ten on each side — onto three buses with blacked out windows. The convoy of buses made its way through the night to London where the German colony was put up in the German ambassador's residence. Unfortunately for them, the ambassador had already left along with every stick of furniture, so they had to sleep on bare floorboards. There they stayed for three days, guarded by a police cordon outside the residence which they were not allowed to leave. Food was provided from local hotels.

On the evening of 14 September the Germans were again put aboard a number of buses and taken to a railway station in London. From there they went by sealed train to the port of Gravesend. There they were taken off the train, five at a time, to be searched 'from top to bottom' before being put aboard a Dutch ship bound for Rotterdam. From neutral Holland they were taken by train to Germany thus accomplishing a wartime trip through enemy lines to the Fatherland, courtesy of de Valera and numerous British bobbies!

Footnotes

1. Maria Mahr to Spiegelfeld, 18 August 1939 (MA, G2/130).

2. Hitler's invasion of Poland on 1 September 1939 put paid to the rally. In fact, a secret decision not to go ahead with the Parteitag was taken on 26 August 1939 (Burden, 1967, pp. 164-5); According to Shirer (1960, p. 628) the decision to cancel the rally was made even earlier, on 15 August.

3. Author's interview with Seán Ó Súilleabháin, Dublin, 30 November 1991.

4. Details of the German colony's departure are based on the author's interviews with Mrs Margaret Greiner, Dublin, 25 May 1993 and 26 June 1993.

5. 'Fifty Germans Leave for Fatherland', *Irish Times*, 12 September 1939, p. 7.

7

Berlin Rundfunkhaus, 1939: the War of Words Begins

As the so-called phoney war, or Sitzkrieg, got under way in the autumn of 1939, life continued much as normal in Berlin. Germans with Irish connections, including former members of theGerman colony in Ireland who had made it back to the Fatherland, were gradually assigned tasks to help the war effort. Among them, Professor Ludwig Mühlhausen, whom the Propaganda Ministry approached shortly after the outbreak of war. Because of his competent Irish, Mühlhausen was asked to set up the Irland-Redaktion or Irish service of German Radio, which he managed to get up and running by December 1939.

At the same time he was also asked to handle radio propaganda to Brittany via a French language station called La Voix de la Bretagne (the voice of Brittany) which stayed on air until the fall of France in June 1940. At that point the Germans saw no further use for the Breton station, which makes one suspect that the Irland-Redaktion would also have been axed had Ireland been similarly occupied.[1]

From the Nazis' point of view there was nothing unusual about broadcasting in relatively obscure minor European languages; Goebbels wanted the Nazi message to reach every corner of the world and he felt radio was the best way of achieving that.[2] Although, public television broadcasts had begun in Germany and Britain in 1936, their range was strictly limited to major cities like London and Berlin (many had viewed the 1936 Berlin Olympics on closed-circuit TV screens in the Reich capital, but international TV transmissions did not become technically possible until the 1950s).

Consequently, the Reichsrundfunkgesellschaft (RRG or Reich Broadcasting Company) was the jewel in Goebbels' propaganda crown as it could reach a much wider audience than either Nazi newspapers or cinema newsreels. By December 1939, RRG was putting out programmes in 19 European languages, including Irish, and by 1941 this number had leapt to 29 European languages.[3]

Mühlhausen's talks in Irish were limited to only 15 minutes on Sunday nights, yet initially they had a wider audience than one might imagine, principally because they 'piggybacked' onto the end of the Lord Haw Haw broadcasts which were popular in the 26 Counties as well as in nationalist areas of Northern Ireland. At this time Mühlhausen still held the chair of Celtic studies at Berlin University as well as doing his radio propaganda work for Ireland and Brittany.

In the late 1930s he had toured Germany lecturing on his pet subject of 'Ireland: Land and People', using dozens of slides he had taken in Gaeltacht regions to illustrate his talks. The Irish Chargé d'Affaires in Berlin, William Warnock, was keeping an eye on Mühlhausen and reported to G2 that he was a member of the SA or Sturmabteilung (storm detachment) of the German Army. By 1939 the SA was declining in importance as a result of a purge of its leaders, including Ernst Roehm, in 1934. This may have explained Mühlhausen's later decision — in 1943 — to join the more powerful and influential SS.

Mühlhausen's first talk from the Berlin Rundfunkhaus, on 10 December 1939, was heard by his former student Second Lieutenant Joseph G. Healy at McKee Barracks in Dublin. Healy noted that

in good Irish, a mixture of Kerry and Western dialects, Mühlhausen said it was a pleasure to talk over the air to his Irish friends, imagining himself seated 'cois na tine agus boladh na móna im' shrón' [by the fire and the smell of the turf in my nose]. He characterised as lies, statements about the persecution by the Germans of Czechoslovakian and Polish Catholics, and reminded his listeners of the atrocities committed in Ireland by the Black and Tans and the Auxiliaries.[4]

The following day's *Irish Press* carried a headline, 'Talk in Irish from German Radio Station', and described Mühlhausen as being 'well known in Irish university circles'. In an uncensored story — that amounted to the finest advertisement for his talks Mühlhausen could have hoped for — the newspaper reported the professor's account of pre-war conditions in Poland, which included a passing reference to the Anglo-Irish struggle: 'Is cuimhin libh fiche bliain ó shin na Black and Tans [You remember the Black and Tans 20 years ago]'.[5]

At Army HQ in Dublin that Sunday night, Joe Healy could scarcely believe what he was listening to. Here was the German professor he had befriended, using the native tongue as a weapon of Nazi propaganda. It is small wonder that Healy immediately provided a full and unflattering profile of Mühlhausen for G2, or that both men were destined never to meet again. The first Mühlhausen talk monitored by the Irish Army in Dublin was on 10 December 1939. At 8.25 p.m. that Sunday night, Dublin time (9.25 p.m. Berlin time) the German professor was on air via RRG's Hamburg and Bremen transmitters as well as the Berlin shortwave station DXB (on 31.22 metres). But if Healy and other pre-war acquaintances of Mühlhausen's in Dublin, including Delargy, were taken aback by the ferocity of the professor's Nazi talks, it was nothing to the effect they had on one of the German's 'Irish friends' in Donegal. As Christmas drew near, Mühlhausen used his Sunday night talk to send seasonal greetings to Seán Ó Heochaidh, the Teelin man he met in 1937.

Within days of the broadcast being monitored in Dublin, Ó Heochaidh had an early morning visit from the police:

> There was a knock on my bedroom door and I said, 'Tar isteach'(come in). The first person to stick his head around the door was the Garda Superintendent followed by a detective and one of the local guards. It frightened the guts out of me. I thought someone must have been killed in a road crash, but the Superintendent said, 'Cool down, Seán, there's nothing wrong. We were asked to interview you and find out what connection you had with this famous German man who's broadcasting from Berlin.'

According to Ó Heochaidh, the Irish authorities thought he was 'a fifth columnist' for the Germans and, consequently, kept a close eye on him (de Valera was worried at the time that Germany might occupy nationalist areas in the North as a prelude to invading Britain through the 'back door').[6] The Garda surveillance on Ó Heochaidh was only lifted when Professor Delargy intervened to explain to the Department of Justice the innocent relationship between Mühlhausen and the Donegal man.

In addition to his audience in the Gaeltacht and at Army HQ in Dublin, Mühlhausen had another important and no less critical listener. At the German Legation on Dublin's Northumberland Road, Dr Hempel was tuning his radio set and picked up the 10 December talk. In a telegram to the Berlin Foreign Office on 13 December, he reported that the Irish language broadcast had 'an outstanding effect. Received widespread recognition. In particular, the government has been pleased because of this "first international recognition" of the Irish language'.[7]

Hempel then spelt out his recipe for success with Irish listeners:

> With a view to the propaganda content, I recommend a careful and gradual approach; initially rather an overall view of our cultural relationship to Ireland, old Irish culture and the altruistic interest and activity of German research for its revival. Furthermore, descriptions of German life style, through which a better opinion of today's Germany can be fostered by means of unobtrusive direction to known focus points. Avoid the expression Gaelic language rather than Irish language which is preferable here [William Joyce (Lord Haw Haw) was introducing Mühlhausen with the words 'Presently, you will hear our usual Sunday evening service in Gaelic...']. Mühlhausen's knowledge of the language and expressions which represented the local ethnic character very well, were indeed acknowledged.

But it seems little or no attention was paid to Hempel's advice at the Foreign Office, since Mühlhausen, who worked for the rival Propaganda Ministry, was intent only on repeating standard Nazi propaganda which he personally translated from German into Irish.

As 1940 approached, Mühlhausen could content himself with the thought that his talks had, at least, attracted some listeners. His bland repetition of Nazi war propaganda would continue into the new year when he would be joined on air by a colleague who knew Ireland as well as if not better than himself, Hans Hartmann.

Footnotes

1. German Radio's service for Slovenia was also dropped when the area came under German control. Since Radio Paris came under Nazi control after the fall of France in June 1940, it is logical to conclude that Radio Éireann would also have been taken over in the event of a German occupation of Ireland. There would, thus, have been no further need for the Irland-Redaktion to remain on air.

2. For Goebbels, radio was the 'chief instrument of propaganda' (Shirer, 1960, p. 307). Less than two months into the war, Hitler's Propaganda Minister planned new radio services to target Irish listeners and French Communists. 'On 30 October 1939 Goebbels instructed [Alfred] Berndt (then head of the RMVP [Propaganda Ministry] radio division) to set on foot the necessary discussions with the AA [German Foreign Office] and OKW [Defence Forces' Supreme Command] to enable a French Communist and an Irish station to be started up' (Balfour, 1979, p. 465, quoting from Boelcke's study of the minutes of Goebbels' daily meetings with his staff). The basic idea, repeated throughout the war, was to beam the Nazi message to discontented minority groups in enemy, occupied or neutral states, including areas targeted for invasion. Thus, radio stations were designed to target niche listenerships such as Communists in France (Radio Humanité borrowed the title of the French Communist Party's daily newspaper *l'Humanité*) and Breton nationalists (La Voix de la Bretagne). Similarly, Irish listeners could be classified as a 'discontented minority' in the context of republicans in Northern Ireland or Britain, as well as IRA members and sympathisers in Britain and Ireland generally. But Goebbels failed to reach a mass audience with his Irish radio station idea; the most he could achieve was Mühlhausen's weekly Irish-language talk, the first of which was broadcast on Sunday, 10 December 1939. Ironically, two years later, it was Adolf Mahr — the museum director from Dublin — who succeeded, where the mighty Propaganda Minister could not, in launching a nightly bi-lingual (Irish and English) radio service tailor-made for neutral Ireland.

3. According to the political archives of the German Foreign Office (AA political archive, file R27188, document 'Foreign language news service of German Radio', 1 December 1939), the following languages were being broadcast by German Radio at the end of 1939: English, Irish, French, Italian, Spanish, Portuguese, Dutch, Swedish, Lithuanian,

Romanian, Serbo-Croat, Slovenian, Hungarian, Bulgarian, Greek, Turkish, Iranian, Hindustani, Arabic and Afrikaans. By 1941 a further nine European languages had been added. According to Schwipps (1971, p. 75), from 1941 to 1944, German Radio's European services were broadcasting in 29 languages, as follows: German, English, French, Spanish, Portuguese, Italian, Swedish, Danish, Norwegian, Finnish, Icelandic, Faeroese, Flemish, Dutch, Irish, Hungarian, Slovakian, Croatian, Romanian, Bulgarian, Serbian, Greek, Russian, Ukrainian, Belo-Russian, Latvian, Estonian, Lithuanian and Polish. According to Pohle (1955, p. 456) by 1943 German Radio was broadcasting in 53 foreign languages (i.e. 54 including German). By the end of 1942, the BBC was broadcasting in 45 languages, 22 of them European (Mansell, 1982, pp. 122-3).

4.   Healy report for G2, 11 December 1939, MA, G2/2473. Although the German Foreign Office's file R27188 of 1 December 1939 (see note 3 above) lists Irish as one of the languages being broadcast as of that date, there is no record of a talk by Mühlhausen until Sunday, 10 December 1939. It must be concluded that this was the first talk in Irish ever broadcast on German Radio.

5.   *Irish Press*, 11 December 1939, p. 9.

6.   Bowman, 1982, p. 207 and Fisk, 1983, pp. 262-3 regarding de Valera's emergency evacuation plan. Ed Slowey from Portadown was Radio Éireann's chief engineer in the war years, and a personal friend of de Valera, whose speeches he always recorded on an acetate disc cutting machine (advanced technology for those years). According to Slowey's widow, Eileen — who worked as a secretary in the GPO — 'in the event of an invasion, Ed had to go with de Valera to Hazelhatch station on the railway line from Kingsbridge (now called Heuston) to Limerick Junction. He went there a few times [without de Valera] to do rehearsals. They were supposed to climb telegraph poles but he would not do that in a million years. He had no head for heights whatsoever — but would not admit that he could not do it — so he asked another man, Mr. Carroll, who was an inspector, to go up the pole wearing grips around his ankles. That poor man was terrified as well, but Ed said: "You'll have to do it", so he did. There was a secret hideout from where Dev was supposed to broadcast to the nation. It was fairly near Straffan in county Kildare, at a railway bridge with telegraph poles. The evacuation plan was top secret and Ed was not even allowed to tell his family until after the war. It never arose, thank God. We were

very lucky' (author's interview with Eileen Slowey, Dublin, 15 November 1990). Mrs Slowey's recollections suggest that the emergency government headquarters chosen by de Valera was, in fact, Ardcaen House near Naas (see Fisk, 1983, p. 263), which is equidistant from Slowey's transmitter system at Straffan and the Curragh military camp.

When asked why he thought the Germans had bothered to broadcast in Irish at all, Seán Ó Heochaidh replied: 'Because they intended to invade Ireland and they wanted as many people behind them as possible' (Ó Heochaidh interview, 14 January 1992).

7.   Sturm, 1984, p. A111. Was Hempel exaggerating things by telling Berlin that the Irish government was 'pleased' with Mühlhausen's talk? It is unlikely that any member of the Fianna Fáil administration would have departed from the strict neutrality line by expressing favour for a belligerent's radio service. Hempel may have misread the *Irish Press* article as a token of government approval since the newspaper was owned by de Valera. Alternatively, the German diplomat may simply have based his reports to Berlin on approving nods and winks expressed privately to him by Walshe and/or Boland at External Affairs.

8

Berlin University's Radio Team

In January 1940 Ludwig Mühlhausen continued teaching as head of the Celtic Studies department in Berlin University, although he had few students since most able-bodied men had been called up for military service. Among those not called up was Hans Hartmann, recently arrived back from his two and a half year stint in Ireland. Under Mühlhausen's supervision, Hartmann got to work on his doctoral thesis on Irish folklore which would take another two years to complete.

In the same month of January, a tall thin 37 year old Irishman arrived to take up a lecturing job at Berlin University's English department. He was the writer Francis Stuart. Among his mostly female students was a 24 year old girl from Danzig named Madeleine Meissner. She was studying Arts, English and Philosophy and the following year pupil and teacher would become lovers. Another of Stuart's students was Hilde Poepping who had spent the 1937-38 academic year as an exchange student at UCG. After the war, Poepping recalled that Francis Stuart 'stressed wherever he went that he had come on a mission for the IRA, though he never explained to which group inside the IRA he belonged'.[1] In Galway, Poepping had gathered material for a thesis on the Irish writer James Stephens, which was published in 1940 by Mühlhausen's Institute of Celtic Studies. On her return to Germany in 1938, Poepping met Mühlhausen for the first time (his move to Berlin in October 1937 coincided with her trip to UCG) at Berlin University 'and tried to improve my Irish with his help'. She recalls that even at that time, the German professor 'did not have many students'.

The war was already well under way when Stuart left Ireland in December 1939 to take up his teaching post. It was not his first working visit to Nazi Germany; he was offered the job as a result of a lecture tour taking in Berlin, Munich, Hamburg, Bonn and Cologne in mid-1939. The tour came about after Stuart's wife, Iseult,[2] sought Helmut Clissmann's help in arranging it. Professor Walter F. Schirmer, head of Berlin University's English Department, was impressed by the Irish writer and offered him a full time job in Berlin starting in January 1940. By the time Stuart got to the Reich capital, Schirmer was also working at the Foreign Office as deputy head of the section dealing with German Radio's foreign language transmissions. In the circumstances it was inevitable that Stuart would be roped into the propaganda business. Perhaps that was what Schirmer had in mind all along. But if the Nazis had planned to use the Irish writer to their own ends, Stuart had his own agenda and, as Hilde Poepping had spotted early on, there was far more to him than the outward image of a humble university lecturer. Of his decision to go to Nazi Germany, Stuart says: 'When the war looked like breaking out, I didn't want to be caught here [in Ireland]. I mean, for a writer to have been all those years where nothing had ever happened, it was necessary for me to get away'. He might have added, but didn't, that he was fleeing an unhappy marriage.

As well as taking up his lecturing post, Stuart was acting as an IRA courier to Berlin. Before leaving Dublin he had been summoned to a meeting with the IRA's chief of staff, Stephen Hayes, and Jim O'Donovan who masterminded the IRA's 1939 bombing campaign in England. The IRA wanted Stuart to contact the Abwehr in Berlin and ask for a new radio transmitter as the previous one had been seized in a police raid. They also wanted him to request that a German liaison officer be sent to Ireland. Stuart was given half a piece of paper to take to Berlin where the other half would help to identify him as a genuine IRA messenger. Dismissing what he saw as the IRA's 'playacting like you read about in the old spy books', Stuart got rid of the torn piece of paper when he reached London. He continued on to Berlin, via Switzerland, with no means of identifying himself to German counter-intelligence: 'Either they believed me when I got to Germany or they didn't. I couldn't care less really'.

In the event, the Abwehr did not believe Stuart until he insisted they telephone Professor Franz Fromme who knew Stuart from a 1939 visit to Dublin.[3] The eccentric German Abwehr agent enjoyed dancing jigs on table tops and spoke Irish. Eventually, Fromme came along and vouched for Stuart who would otherwise have been placed in a very awkward situation. Stuart wisely decided not to ask his new employer, Professor Schirmer, to vouch for his identity as this would have tipped off the university authorities that he was more than just a lecturer.

The devastating results of Jim O'Donovan's S-plan to bomb England had not escaped the notice of Goebbels. On 8 February 1940, the German Propaganda Minister recorded in his diary the execution of IRA men Peter Barnes and Frank McCormick in Birmingham the previous day for their part in the Coventry bombings (in which five people died in August 1939), commenting:

> We seize on this with all our might. This gives us ammunition for several days. I keep impressing my people with one basic truth: repeat everything until the last, most stupid person has understood.

Early in 1940 it was decided to double the Irland-Redaktion's output to two talks per week. Rather than undertake the task himself, Mühlhausen asked his student Hans Hartmann to contribute a 15 minute talk on Wednesday nights to complement his own Sunday night broadcasts. With the war on, Hartmann could hardly refuse the request, especially as he was depending on Mühlhausen to supervise his doctorate from which he hoped to get a teaching job at the university (he did just that, two years later). But why did Hartmann only broadcast in Irish? He recalls:

> It was quite natural... my aim was to promote the Irish language and Irish culture as much as I could from the German side. That was the reason I used the Irish language.[4]

At the same time as Hartmann was beginning to write his first weekly talks, Francis Stuart was also writing radio scripts but not for broadcasting by himself— that would come later. Stuart's recruitment as a propagandist came as a result of a visit he made on 4 February

1940 to present a letter of introduction from Hempel to Ernst von Weizsäcker,[5] State Secretary at the Foreign Ministry.

> Von Weizsäcker asked me if I had listened to William Joyce's broadcasts at the beginning of the war when I was at home in Ireland. I said — partly as a joke but there was some truth in it — 'He's winning the war for you single handed with his propaganda'.[6] Von Weizsäcker said 'Really?'. I think that remark of mine was repeated to the Propaganda Ministry because shortly after that I was asked if I would write some talks for Joyce.

In fact, it was the Foreign Office that requested Stuart to write some talks for Lord Haw Haw. Stuart's diary entry for 18 February 1940 noted:

> Was asked by Dr Haferkorn of the Foreign Office if I would write some talks for William Joyce... I agreed and wrote three, the first of which Joyce will broadcast tonight and, as I have no radio, have arranged with William Warnock to spend the evening with him at our legation and listen to it there. The theme of my contributions, which I know is not exactly what either the Germans nor Joyce want, is a recollection of some historic acts of aggression on the part of the United Kingdom, similar to those which British propaganda is denouncing the Nazis for.

Stuart recalls meeting Joyce at the Berlin Press Club and comments that 'he was a man of extraordinary courage'. But Stuart's role as Lord Haw Haw's scriptwriter was destined to be shortlived:

> As it turned out, the talks I wrote were not what Joyce wanted. Above all they were not what the German propaganda people wanted — there was naturally nothing anti-Semitic and nothing in great praise of Hitler — because they had no interest in British atrocities throughout the ages.

Despite being dropped as a scriptwriter, Stuart was settling well into his new life in wartime Berlin. Having collected back pay from the university which had accumulated since the autumn of 1939, he decided to throw a party to celebrate St Patrick's Day, 1940. Stuart's guests that night at the Hotel Kaiserhof, not far from Hitler's Chancellery, included diplomats, writers and a national newspaper editor. They also included Herr Hauptmann, the head of the German Red Cross and, last but not least, William Warnock, from the Irish Legation. Stuart and Warnock became friends, sometimes making up a threesome for golf along with the Irish diplomat's secretary, Eileen Walsh. She had also worked for Warnock's predecessor Charles Bewley, a Quaker convert to Catholicism whom de Valera sacked from the diplomatic corps in 1939 because of his overt fascist beliefs.[7]

While Stuart and his friends were drowning the shamrock in Berlin, de Valera was all too aware of German Radio's efforts to find an audience in neutral Ireland. On 30 April 1940, the Irish leader was asked in the Dáil if he knew about 'unfriendly references to this country by certain German radio stations and, if so, whether he has made or proposes to make representations to the German government in the matter'. De Valera's reply was off-hand:

> I know there is a report in circulation of alleged unfriendly references to Ireland in recent German broadcasts. But I have not been able to discover anyone who claims to have actually heard the references...

Perhaps wisely, de Valera did not bother to inform the Dáil that Army Intelligence was supplying his government with transcripts of German broadcasts relating to Ireland. Among the recipients in cabinet was Frank Aiken who had been interned in the Curragh camp with Francis Stuart during the civil war almost 20 years earlier. In his dual role as Taoiseach and Minister for External Affairs, de Valera would have been informed of Stuart's scriptwriting and other activities by Joe Walshe via Warnock.

At the same time, April 1940, Franz Fromme got back in touch with Stuart to introduce him to Hermann Goertz, an Abwehr agent who was in training for a secret spy mission to Ireland to make contact with the IRA. Stuart gave Goertz his wife Iseult's address at Laragh Castle in County Wicklow for use as an emergency safe house. Later, Stuart regretted doing so as Iseult was arrested by the police when Goertz made straight for her house after parachuting into Ireland in May 1940. Despite many close shaves with the Special Branch, Goertz remained on the run and evaded capture for 18 months.

Footnotes

1. Letter to author from Dr Hilde Spickernagel (née Poepping), Hanover, 9 February 1992.

2. Iseult was the daughter of Maud Gonne MacBride and the French political activist, Lucien Millevoye. Stuart converted to Catholicism before marrying Iseult in 1920 (Elborn, 1990, p. 36). Maud Gonne MacBride's first husband, Major John MacBride, was executed for taking part in the 1916 Rising. The couple's son Seán was briefly IRA chief of staff in 1936 (Cronin, 1980, p. 64). He later entered mainstream politics and, as head of the Clann na Poblachta party, became Irish Minister for External Affairs in 1948 (Rafter, 1996, p. 100).

3. Fromme first visited Ireland in 1932 to research a book on the country. It was published in Berlin in 1933 under the title *Irlands Kampf um die Freiheit* (Ireland's Struggle for Freedom). The eccentric German professor returned to Ireland in April 1939 when he met Francis Stuart. Another Abwehr agent, Oscar Pfaus, had been in Dublin two months earlier to establish links with IRA leaders. Fromme was the best man at Pfaus' wedding in Hamburg in August 1939 (Stephan, 1963, pp. 20-1, 26).

4. Hartmann interview, 21 October 1990.

5. Ernst von Weizsäcker's son, Richard, was President of Germany from 1984 to 1994. Following the collapse of Communist East Germany in autumn 1989, von Weizsäcker presided over the reunification of West and East Germany on 3 October 1990.

6. Stuart borrowed this phrase from his friend and fellow writer Liam O'Flaherty who — in late 1939 on a visit to the Royal Hotel in Glendalough, Co Wicklow — told Stuart that William Joyce 'was winning the war for Germany single-handed' (Stuart, Francis, 1984, *States of Mind*, p. 31).

7. Bewley believed the Western powers should back Hitler to halt the spread of communism — a key theme of Nazi radio propaganda from mid-1941 to the end of the war — and he 'saw an active role for Ireland in this context' (Duggan, 1975, p. 65).

9

MI5 and Others Lend an Ear

Goebbels' fledgling Irish radio team was up and running, producing twice-weekly talks in Irish during 1940; but was anybody in Ireland listening to this Nazi message? The answer is yes, though not in the substantial numbers that would have made Propaganda Ministry officials smile. In any case, the size of the audience must remain a 'guesstimate' since no precise figures are available for the period. This is mainly due to the lack of precise audience research techniques in the early years of radio and the fact that in the 1930s many people flaunted the law by refusing to buy a licence. In 1938 the Irish authorities discovered 25,000 unlicensed radios and there were probably many more.[1]

Nevertheless, the 166,275 radio licences held in the 26 Counties at the outbreak of war provide an indication of the potential audience for Berlin's Irish radio service. One in 17 of the population had a radio, more if unlicensed sets were included: a healthy target figure for the Nazi propagandists. Forty per cent of licensed radios were in the Dublin area, while Connacht and Donegal — prime target areas for the Irish language broadcasts — had only a sprinkling of sets.[2]

One wartime listener to the Irland-Redaktion was Tomás de Bháldraithe — later to become the distinguished Professor of Modern Irish at UCD — who lived at Cois Farraige in Connemara for two years from September 1939. He recalled:

> It was difficult to hear the Irish talks of German Radio because there were practically no radios. People in the Gaeltacht were

46

desperately poor and could not afford to buy radio sets. You would
have to be a parish priest or a teacher to afford one. People would
gather outside the window of the local post office trying to listen
to one of the few radios in the locality. I heard Mühlhausen, I
knew the thing was going on.

De Bháldraithe also heard some of Hartmann's broadcasts, and
had already met the German scholar when travelling to Galway by
train before the war. But in the post-war years he never mentioned
the radio talks to Hartmann, wishing to spare him any embarrassment.
In the 1960s, both men worked together on recording Irish dialects
in Gaeltacht areas along the West coast.[3]

By 1941 when German Radio launched its nightly, bilingual (Irish
and English) service, there were 183,303 licensed radio sets in Éire.
But radio sales fell in the war period due to a shortage of batteries;
many households had no mains electricity. In 1941, one in nine people
in Dublin had a radio, but only 1:12 in Waterford, 1:15 in Limerick
and 1:16 in Cork. In the Gaeltacht regions, where Mühlhausen and
Hartmann were personally known, there were even fewer radios,
1:26 in County Donegal, 1:30 in Galway and 1:32 in Kerry.[4]

On top of these factors, Nazi radio's Irish service was up against
stiff competition in the war years. In addition to Radio Éireann and
the BBC, William Joyce (Lord Haw Haw) was also a big attraction
to Catholic nationalist listeners, north and south of the border, who
wanted to see Britain beaten by Germany. Ironically, the same
listeners failed to realise that Hitler's top English-language announcer
was a fascist who had no time for the idea of a united Ireland.[5]

Just how many people were listening to Joyce? In April 1940, *Life*
magazine reported that half of all English radio listeners were tuned
to Lord Haw Haw. But BBC estimates for the same period gave
Joyce less: 15.7 per cent of the English audience; it was reckoned the
Galway man had a similar following in neutral Ireland.[6] This would
put Haw Haw's Irish audience at approximately 60,000 — assuming
two adult listeners per radio set and including a minimum of 25,000
unlicensed sets in the total. Since Mühlhausen's weekly talk went
out immediately after Joyce's *View on the News* programme on
Sunday nights, it might be assumed that the German academic had a
similar audience. The reality, however, was very different. Seán Ó
Lúing, the noted historian and biographer of Kuno Meyer, remembers

hearing one of the first Mühlhausen broadcasts at the end of 1939 while in the house of a neighbour, Pádraig Búlaeir, at Gortmore, Ballyferriter in the Kerry Gaeltacht.

> The young people of the parish held card sessions there. The radio was turned on in anticipation and the young people, all locals who would enjoy the English language broadcasts of Lord Haw Haw, expected something in the same style. We were all disappointed. Mühlhausen was anything but an effective speaker. He was laborious, ineffective, with a slow and poor delivery of words, giving out official German propaganda. He was dreary. After a few minutes, interest vanished and someone said, 'Sea, roinn amach na cártaí' [Right, deal out the cards].[7]

In Galway a local university student, Seán Mac Réamoinn, who became head of RTE Radio in the 1960s, heard Mühlhausen's talks and recalls that 'during a student rag week I did a skit on the professor, sending him up and calling him Doctor Fullhausen. But Lord Haw Haw was listened to with greater interest locally as a Galway man'.[8]

Mühlhausen and Hartmann had a better following in the Donegal Gaeltacht. Both men had studied local dialects there — Mühlhausen in Teelin from August to October 1937, and Hartmann in Bunbeg from mid-January to mid-February 1939, and in Teelin in April the same year. Local folklore specialist, Seán Ó Heochaidh, knew the Germans well. Commenting on their broadcasting abilities he says: 'They were really good and I assure you that they had a great audience in these Gaeltacht areas'.[9] This view is partly confirmed by Sligo woman, Elizabeth Clissmann, who returned home to Ireland from Denmark after the war to find that Hartmann had had 'a very big audience in the Gaeltacht areas'.[10]

Éimear Ó Broin, whose father León briefly shared a holiday cottage with Ludwig Mühlhausen in Donegal in 1937, regularly listened to the Irland-Redaktion as a teenager in Dublin throughout the war. He puts Berlin's Gaelic broadcasting efforts down to 'German thoroughness'. He found the Irish language broadcasts

> wasteful because very few people listened to them and the audience was not very regular... it wasn't very subtle or well prepared propaganda, it was more a projection of the presence of Germany into Irish-speaking Ireland. Most people here listened to Joyce and the other English speakers on German Radio.[11]

Hans Hartmann himself learned from Hempel's reports to the Foreign Office in Berlin that his radio service had 'a fair number of listeners'.[12] One of his main speakers, however, Francis Stuart, got the opposite impression. When he eventually returned home to Ireland in the late 1950s, he found his wartime radio talks were 'not only forgotten but almost unknown' and 'the signal was feeble and difficult to hear'.[13]

After listening to Germany's Irish output for 18 months at the BBC's monitoring service, Maurice Irvine from Belfast felt Hans Hartmann's broadcast material

> was cleverly slanted to gauge reactions of support among people who were strongly influenced both by the Irish nationalist and traditional Catholic social, teachings. If the propaganda had been at all widely listened to, it would have tended to ensure that Irish sympathies did not veer too much to the Allied cause.

Irvine also thought that Hartmann's 'Flashback' feature about Black and Tan atrocities during the Irish War of Independence could have been moderately effective with staunch Irish nationalists 'since it linked up British misdeeds in the past with their current activities, thus alienating any sympathy there might have been for the British cause in Ireland'.[14]

Despite having a following in the Donegal Gaeltacht, German Radio's Irish service was at a distinct disadvantage to its sister English service which broadcast for 15 hours a day, compared to Mühlhausen's 15 minute talk on Sunday nights. Even later in the war, when the Irish ration was increased to one hour a night, it was still dwarfed by the total of 204 hours of programmes broadcast daily in 1943-44 by German Radio's European services in no less than 29 languages.[15] Nonetheless, it is remarkable that German Radio bothered to broadcast in Irish at all.

Germany's Gaelic broadcasts were not only attracting an audience, albeit a small one, in Ireland. In early May 1940 the Dominions Office in London was expressing concern about Germany's Irish radio propaganda programmes and asked the BBC if Nazi broadcasts to Ireland could be jammed.[16] In the event, no attempt was made to jam them and this may have been to avoid counter-jamming measures by Berlin. At that stage of the war, however, Nazi propaganda was riding the crest of a wave with the German war machine sweeping away all in its path. On 9 April 1940 the Germans seized Denmark and invaded Norway, capturing the capital, Oslo. A month later on 10 May, Germany invaded the Netherlands, Belgium and Luxembourg. With the Dutch Army surrendering on 14 May and Belgium capitulating on 27 May, the German Army continued its advance westwards, entering Paris on 13 June 1940.

Despite the wave of conquests which gave Nazi Germany control of most of the European mainland from Poland to the Atlantic coast, the weekly Irish language talks from Berlin had little to say, apart from exhorting Irish listeners to 'keep your neutrality' (Coinnígí bhur neodracht). On 28 June 1940 an instruction was issued to the German Army High Command that 'in order to mislead the enemy, all available information media should spread the word that we [the Germans] are preparing a landing in Ireland... '.[17] There is no evidence that the Irland-Redaktion complied with this instruction, but the following day, 29 June 1940, German Radio's short-wave German-language service to North America carried a commentary on the naval war, by Vice Admiral Friedrich Luetzow, which mentioned Ireland's refusal to join the conflict.[18]

Until the Fall of France, the only people bothering to monitor Mühlhausen and Hartmann's talks were Irish Army Intelligence officers and Dr Hempel at the German Legation in Dublin. Germany's military advances caused such concern in Britain, however, that MI5 (Britain's domestic intelligence service) began to take an interest in the Irland-Redaktion's material. As a result, MI5 requested the BBC monitoring service to add Irish Gaelic to the long list of foreign languages it was already listening to. In the course of the war the BBC engaged three Gaelic monitors to listen to Berlin's Irish language output. The first such monitor arrived at the BBC's secret monitoring centre (at a stately home in Evesham, Worcestershire) on 1 July 1940. Angus Matheson had travelled from Glasgow University where he worked in the Department of Celtic Studies.

At the same time in Berlin, Francis Stuart was back in contact with German counter-intelligence. Helmut Clissmann introduced him to Kurt Haller, a close associate of the Foreign Office's coup d'état specialist Edmund Veesenmayer. The latter had arranged the return in May of IRA leader Seán Russell from America to undertake a secret mission to Ireland.[19] Calling at Stuart's Berlin flat one evening in early August, Haller asked the Irish writer if he would sail secretly to Ireland aboard a Breton fishing boat to set up advance links with the IRA prior to Russell's return. Stuart agreed, but that part of the plan was abruptly dropped before Russell set sail for Ireland a short time later. The ultimately aborted episode became the stuff of republican legend with Russell teaming up with another IRA man, Frank Ryan, to sail aboard a U-boat to Ireland. The Nazis had persuaded Franco to release 38 year old Ryan from death row in a Spanish prison following his participation with the International Brigade in the Spanish civil war.

Abwehr II's war diary did not specify the nature of Russell's trip, although since he had been trained in sabotage methods near Berlin it is thought the most likely possibilities were to stage attacks on British installations in Northern Ireland and/or to force a coup d'état against de Valera, thus installing a pro-Nazi government in Dublin. Whatever the ultimate objective it was not to be achieved, since Seán Russell died of a perforated ulcer aboard the U-boat on 14 August 1940, just 100 miles west of Galway.

Despite the setback, Veesenmayer still harboured a desire to get Frank Ryan back home to take over the secret task originally assigned to Russell. Back in Berlin, Ryan sought out Francis Stuart and the two men began a daily routine of lunching together and poring over Irish newspapers which Ryan brought to Stuart's flat in Westfälischestrasse. But even though both men had come from active IRA backgrounds, they were not destined to become wartime friends. Stuart recalls that

> Ryan was in a very ambiguous position; starting off fighting for the International Brigade and ending up as an adviser to the SS Colonel Veesenmayer, a Jew exterminator. I never liked Ryan, we didn't really get on... As long as the Germans were planning an invasion of England, Ryan was treated like a VIP... He got diplomat's rations and facilities, and he used to share them with us. He was a generous person but very, very touchy. I remember one day we were both walking down to the university where I had a class. We disagreed over something. He said to me, 'When' — not 'if', mind you — 'Germany wins the war I will be a minister

in the Irish government'. I took this as some sort of threat to me to
keep in with him. I took that very much amiss. I didn't like this
'When Germany wins the war.'[20]

Ryan's comment about becoming a member of the Dublin
government is the clearest indication that what Veesenmayer had in
mind was, in fact, a coup d'état against de Valera.[21]

At the Rundfunkhaus, Mühlhausen and Hartmann together provided
the only German Radio commentaries being specially targeted at
neutral Ireland at that time. All their talks, without exception in Irish,
were being monitored and translated by G2 for the attention of the
Dublin government, and by the BBC for MI5 (if important military
material was included) and the Northern Ireland government.

As 1940 drew to a close Hartmann was still pumping out standard
Nazi propaganda with an Irish angle for his listeners in the Gaeltacht
and elsewhere. For example, one of his talks on 10 November 1940,
included a potted history of the Nazi party and Adolf Hitler's rise to
power:

> Hitler has remained faithful to his promise to remove the injustice
> of the disgraceful Treaty of Versailles. He was prepared to do that
> peaceably but England and France did not allow him. They declared
> war on Germany in order to carve up Germany completely.

Then, making a pitch at his Irish audience, Hartmann summarised
the exchanges between Churchill and de Valera over the Treaty Ports
and Ireland's neutral stance, adding: 'I am sure that you have heard
of the great number of English ships that are being sunk by German
U-boats to the west of Ireland'. He signed off with the customary
slogan 'May God bless and save Ireland'.

Discussing his style of propaganda long after the war, Hartmann
insisted that he tried to keep military dispatches and anti-Semitic
references to a minimum, although under strong pressure from the
radio's management to include such items from a central reporting
pool.[22] To avoid having to fill his 15-minute slot with anti-Jewish
material and war communiqués, Hartmann opted for current and
historical Irish angles. In contrast to his own style, Hartmann
categorised Mühlhausen's talks as 'aggressive propaganda'. For
example, a talk by Mühlhausen on 20 November 1940 was
characterised by anti-English invective. Citing examples of what he

termed England's lack of regard for smaller nations, Mühlhausen added: 'The English do not like to place their own precious lives in danger. The English do not like to make use of their own soldiers in war. They prefer to sacrifice other peoples and nations for the glory of the Empire'. Mühlhausen then countered an RAF statement about unlimited warplane production in England saying:

> That is of no consequence. A few days ago, Coventry, the great centre for the production of aeroplanes and motors, was reduced to a pile of scrap iron [Coventry had been blitzed by the Luftwaffe on 15 November]. Bombs weighing altogether hundreds of millions of pounds are dropped every night on the English cities. There is no counting the number of armaments and munitions factories, etc., which have been destroyed in London and other places.

After warming up his audience — the target listeners were presumably ardent nationalists, since over 250,000 Irish people[23] were aiding the British war effort through factory work or military service at the time — Mühlhausen hammered home the Irish angle:

> The English have not abandoned their claims to the Irish ports. It would be tantamount to a second annexation of Ireland if the English succeeded in obtaining the Irish ports again. I am sure that the Irish nation, though it is indeed a small nation, is sufficiently strong to resist this move. Ireland would never again be free from English control if she willingly handed over her ports to the English. The English already deeply regret that they gave Ireland sufficient liberty to be able now to remain a neutral state. May God bless Ireland, and may Ireland save herself.

It is not clear what Mühlhausen meant by his last four words. Perhaps '... with Germany's help' was the unspoken message he meant to convey. In any case, the fear of Britain seizing the ports by force was very real among Irish government ministers, not to mention the public at large, so the German professor knew he was touching a raw nerve.

A month later, on 15 December 1940, Mühlhausen was again indulging in his 'aggressive' style, peddling fear among Irish speaking listeners as he spelt out Ireland's fate in the event of an English victory:

> If England succeeds in defeating Germany, Ireland will be lost sooner or later. The English would take revenge on Ireland because she was neutral in this war instead of sacrificing her life for the Empire. There would be then no one in the world who would

prevent the English from bringing Ireland once more under subjection and from destroying Irish freedom. On the other hand, if we succeeded in defeating the Empire, Ireland, the whole of Ireland, Ireland from Belfast to Cork, would be free forever from English control. We only smile when we hear the English say that we would swallow up Ireland. There is no doubt whatever that we will succeed in defeating England this time. Stand firm then against the English now, and the whole of Ireland will at last be free. God bless and save Ireland.

That particular broadcast was considered sufficiently strong by the BBC monitors for it to be telexed just two hours after transmission to the relevant authorities in London.

In effect, Mühlhausen was calling on Catholic nationalist Ireland to back Nazi Germany. The stick was the fear of British re-occupation, while the carrot was the promise of a united 32 county state. However tantalising this prospect might have seemed to nationalists — and Churchill was to make a similar offer to de Valera[24] — doubters could point with good reason to the fact that despite Germany's defeat of France, no steps had yet been taken to grant independence to Brittany. There would be little Christmas cheer in either Dublin or London that winter.

Footnotes

1. Radio Éireann did not begin official audience research until 1953, although in 1939 the station's director, Thomas Kiernan, had made the first attempt at some listener research. But his questionnaire, sent to 2,575 householders, only drew an 11 per cent response (Gorham, 1967, pp. 115-6. For figures on unlicensed radio sets see Brown, Terence, 1981, p. 153).

2. Gorham, 1967, p. 181.

3. De Bháldraithe interview, Dublin, 15 November 1990.

4. 'Geographical distribution of radio licences, 1941' *Radio Éireann Annual Report,* Dublin, 1941, appendix A, table III.

5. As a teenager in Galway, Joyce had acted as an informer for the British during the Black and Tan war (Cole, 1964, pp. 23, 40-6). In 1942, Hans Hartmann — then head of the Irish service of German Radio —

turned down Joyce's offer to broadcast to his 'Irish followers'. The German academic knew full well that Joyce's political message — for Britain to join with Germany in an anti-Bolshevik alliance — would not fit in with the green, pro-neutrality line of his Irish radio service (Hartmann interview, 21 October 1990). One wartime listener who appreciated Joyce's talks was the spy Günther Schütz who tuned in every Friday night while interned in Custume Barracks, Athlone. Schütz had parachuted into County Wexford on 12 March 1941 and was arrested almost immediately. He recalled listening to all the news programmes in English from German stations: 'Every Friday night there was a transmission based on a newspaper edited by Dr Goebbels including his leading article. That was the event on Friday nights. We switched on William Joyce, Lord Haw Haw, and I think that was one of the most delightful transmissions to listen to. He was witty and, in German we would say, geistreich [clever], sharp, intelligent and sophisticated. Lord Haw Haw had a brilliant mind and I still despise what the British did to him. It is despicable that they could have hanged such a brilliant man' (Schütz interview, Shankill, County Dublin, 6 September 1990). While Joyce's radio talks had a loyal following among Irish nationalists, they did not go down too well with the Northern Ireland Protestant establishment. Ulster's prime minister, Lord Craigavon, worried about 'the effects on working men of the Haw Haw broadcasts' and advised Downing Street to counter-attack the Nazi propaganda using 'speakers recruited from the ranks of the labouring classes such as young farmers and shipyard workers' (Briggs, 1970, p. 154).

6.   Cole, 1964, p. 149.

7.   Seán Ó Luing letter, 9 March 1993.

8.   Seán Mac Réamoinn interview, Dublin, 8 August 1991.

9.   Ó Heochaidh letter, 20 June 1991. Ó Heochaidh interview, Gortahork, Co. Donegal, 14 January 1992.

10. Elizabeth 'Budge' Clissmann interview, Dublin, 19 October 1990.

11. Éimear Ó Broin interviews, Dublin, 10 and 15 June 1992.

12. Hartmann interview, 9 July 1990.

13. Fisk, 1983, p. 407; Stuart interview, Dublin, 17 November 1989.

14. Maurice Irvine interview, Brighton, 31 January 1992.

15. Schwipps, 1971, p. 75.

16. Cathcart, 1984, p. 111.

17. Fisk, 1983, p. 224.

18. Roller, 1987, p. 222.

19. Franz Fromme was assigned to meet Russell as he stepped off a transatlantic liner in Genoa in May 1940. He accompanied the IRA leader to Berlin (Stephan, 1963, pp. 98-9).

20. Author's interview with Stuart, 17 November 1989. In an article entitled 'Frank Ryan in Germany', *The Bell*, November 1950, p. 38, Stuart wrote of meeting Ryan in Berlin a decade earlier in 1940: 'It was then that I got to know him well and that we became close friends'. Either Stuart revised his opinion of Ryan in the 40 odd years between both statements or Stuart had, in 1950, deliberately painted a rosy picture of his relationship with Ryan for an Irish audience. This could have been to ingratiate himself within republican circles in Ireland. More likely, it was to win favour with his brother-in-law, the then Foreign Minister Seán MacBride, who was angry ('understandably', according to Stuart) with the writer for having abandoned his wife Iseult (MacBride's half sister). At the time he wrote *The Bell* article — at the insistence of veteran IRA man Peadar O'Donnell who had been a close associate of Frank Ryan (Elborn, 1990, p. 229) — Stuart was stranded in Paris without a valid passport. Effectively, with MacBride blocking him, Stuart could not return home.

21. As a target country, Ireland represented one of Veesenmayer's few failures. He successfully engineered coups d'état in Croatia in 1941, Serbia also in 1941, Slovakia in 1943 and Hungary in 1944 (Cronin, 1980, pp. 252-3). His nickname as Ribbentrop's 'coup d'état specialist' was justifiably earned. Long after the war, Veesenmayer appeared to regret that he had not chosen Mrs Elizabeth Clissmann to spearhead his coup d'état plan in Ireland (see footnote no. 6 for chapter 22).

22. Author's interview with Hartmann, Cologne, 28 December 1990.

23. Duggan, 1975, p. 162; Lee, 1989, p. 226.

24. Fisk, 1083, p. 323; Lee, 1989, pp. 248-9.

10

Dr Mahr's Blueprint

The winter of 1940 saw Francis Stuart working as a translator at German Radio's Drahtloser Dienst (wireless service), assisted by Madeleine Meissner who did secretarial work there in the late afternoons. Stuart explains: 'I worked at translating German news bulletins into so called "BBC English". It passed, in a German sense, as excellent BBC English but I don't think it was that expert.' It was while translating German news bulletins for transmission to England that Stuart met William Joyce's wife Margaret. Despite Stuart's view of Joyce as being 'courageous' the two men did not get on and Stuart never exchanged more than a few words with Lord Haw Haw.

> Something about Joyce I didn't like was his deeply anti-Irish background, as indeed all these Mosleyites had. He was very anti-Irish in his early days in Galway and had collaborated with the Black and Tans.

Perhaps understandably, given Stuart's republican credentials, he kept his distance from Joyce during the war, despite broadcasting from the same radio building in Berlin. As winter 1940 turned to spring 1941 Stuart shared cups of tea with Margaret Joyce, 'a very pleasant, ordinary Englishwoman', and Madeleine during bouts of translation work in the editor's office at the Rundfunkhaus.

But it wasn't all cups of tea and harmless banter. On his own admission, Stuart was dancing close to the flame. His acquaintances included senior members of the Nazi Party. The point is well illustrated by his recollection of a visit, with Frank Ryan and Helmut Clissmann, to a Berlin night-club in 1941.

> In the club, off the Kurfürstendamm, we drank two or three bottles of champagne. We met two of Ryan's friends. One was wearing his party swastika badge on a little gold plaque, which meant he was a founder member of the Nazi Party. I thought it was funny — because these were rare and extremely influential people — that Frank Ryan, who had come from the International Brigade in Spain, had such a friend. Towards the end of the evening, this friend of Frank Ryan said to me: 'I suppose you'll stay on here in Germany when the war is over?'. He meant, of course, when Germany had won, because in 1941 it looked to most people as if it would. I replied: 'Well, no I won't, because I write in English and I want to live where English is spoken', and he said: 'But if, as I understand, your readers are in England or America, perhaps after being in Germany you will lose some of them'. And I said: 'Do you know what? When this war is over, wherever I am I hope it will be the losing side, because if it's the winning side it will be intolerable for me. I hope I'll be among the losers and the guilty'.

The top Nazi then turned to Frank Ryan and asked if Stuart was joking. Ryan replied: 'I don't know what he means, but he's certainly not joking'.[1]

Stuart continued lecturing at Berlin University, but events beyond his control or knowledge ensured that he would eventually be sucked more deeply into the Nazi propaganda machine. At the start of 1941 Mühlhausen and Hartmann were still holding the Irland-Redaktion fort alone. It is one of the anomalies of the German propaganda drive that while key events of Irish interest — such as the Luftwaffe raids on Belfast in April and May 1941, the accidental bombing of Dublin's North Strand by the Luftwaffe on 31 May 1941, and Frank Aiken's failed arms-buying mission to America, also in May — passed off without comment on German Radio's Irish service, they were mentioned in dozens of languages by German Radio announcers broadcasting to the rest of the world.

The controversy over Britain's attempt to introduce conscription in Northern Ireland provided German propagandists with valuable material. In fact, Radio Éireann had given the Germans all the ammunition they needed on the conscription issue by broadcasting an anti-conscription statement from the Catholic Primate of All

Ireland, Cardinal MacRory, on 22 May 1941, which said any attempt to impose conscription in Ireland 'would be disastrous'. Goebbels himself could not have done better than the cardinal who went on:

> To compel them [the Irish] to fight for their oppressor would be likely to rouse indignation and resistance... an ancient land made by God was partitioned by a foreign power against the vehement protests of its people. Conscription was an old trick to compel those who still lie under this grievous wrong to fight on the side of its perpetrators.

Just six days after the cardinal's statement was broadcast, Hans Hartmann — who regularly monitored Radio Éireann broadcasts for suitable propaganda material — jumped on the anti-conscription bandwagon, commenting:

> A few days ago, Irishmen gave the governments of the Six Counties and Great Britain to understand that they had resolved to resist conscription in the Six Counties by every means at their disposal. I hope that in the end they will have their reward for their bravery and steadfastness.

At the end of this talk Hartmann treated his listeners to a lecture on the history of the United Irishmen. In the event Britain did not introduce conscription in Ulster; Churchill thought it would be more trouble than it was worth.[2]

Meanwhile, Hartmann's old friend from the National Museum in Dublin, Adolf Mahr, had joined Ribbentrop's team at the Foreign Office.[3] He was fully aware of the talks format that both Hartmann and Mühlhausen were putting out and he did not like it. Mahr did not get on with Mühlhausen and thought that devoting so much effort to Irish language talks was a waste of time. In March 1941 he began to draw up a blueprint[4] for Ribbentrop which, by the end of the year, would transform the Irland-Redaktion's two 15-minute talks a week into a much bigger unit broadcasting to Ireland every night.

Mahr believed that Germany could tap into a huge worldwide anti-British audience by tailoring programmes for the international Irish community which he estimated at 10 million people, not including what he termed 'half breeds, totally absorbed in Anglo-Saxon culture'. He wanted 'declarations by Catholic bishops from the recent past' and 'statements by de Valera' to be used on air to bolster claims to

Irish unity and eliminate 'the Ulster injustice'. In addition, his proposed propaganda menu would include such delicacies as 'horror propaganda' including 'English cruelty', 'Cromwell's scandalous deeds', 'the persecution of Catholics' and 'the epic Irish War of Independence'.

As well as targeting nationalists in Ireland and republicans in British cities like London, Liverpool and Glasgow, Mahr wanted to set up secret transmitters to target 'people with an Irish ethnic identity' in the United States (to lobby against US entry into the war) and in Australia. Mahr felt that suitable speakers for the secret stations could be recruited from among 'Irish inmates of prisoner of war camps' in Germany.[5]

At the end of his 15-page report for Ribbentrop, Mahr concluded:

> The overthrow of British imperialism is unavoidable since it has afflicted Ireland with so many crimes. With it, it will bring Ireland's reunification so that it can sever all remaining connections to the British Empire. Then Ireland will see the fulfilment of its indefeasible right to total sovereignty. Only then will the reconstituted sovereign Irish nation be able to fully contribute, in friendship with all peoples and without link to other powers, to the rebuilding of the true international community of peoples which has been destroyed by England's plutocratic and unChristian imperialism.

The blueprint was a mixture of Nazi dogma and Mahr's personal vision of a united Ireland which was heavily coloured by his contacts with the Irish republican ethos from 1927 to 1939.[6] In effect, it amounted to a clarion call to the IRA which at that time was being ruthlessly put down by de Valera's government. IRA leaders saw a major opportunity to be gained from a Nazi victory over the old adversary, England, that had now become a common enemy.

Mahr's report — only one of several up for decision — was discussed at a top level Foreign Office conference in Berlin, presided over by Ribbentrop himself, on 22 May 1941. Ironically, the official title of the conference was 'Meeting about propaganda for countries standing under the yoke of Great Britain'. In effect, this revealed that Foreign Office mandarins were not aware Ireland had gained her independence in 1922. As far as they were concerned, Éire was lumped together with India, the Arab world, South Africa, Canada and Australia.

Although Mahr was not present at the meeting his Foreign Office superiors, to whom he had submitted the blueprint, were. They included: Gerhard Rühle who, as well as being a member of the Reichstag, was head of the Foreign Office's radio section (Rundfunkabteilung); Markus Timmler, in charge of Section Ru Xb dealing with radio propaganda to the British colonies; and Ribbentrop's Under-Secretary of State, Paul Woermann. The latter's attendance was significant, not just because he was director of the political division in the Foreign Office but also due to his inside knowledge of secret attempts to influence events in neutral Ireland, including the failed Russell escapade nine months earlier and the Goertz espionage mission. As early as 10 February 1940, Woermann had backed the idea of covert operations in Ireland, telling Ribbentrop that 'by reason of its militant attitude towards England, the IRA is a natural ally of Germany'.[7]

After one and a half hours of discussion at the Wilhelmstrasse, Ribbentrop gave the go ahead for Mahr's propaganda plan. But getting the Nazi Foreign Minister's approval would prove to be the least of Mahr's problems as he struggled to launch his revamped radio service for Ireland. Just nine days later, on 31 May 1941, the German war machine spectacularly shot itself in the foot when the Luftwaffe accidentally bombed Dublin's North Strand, killing 28 people and damaging up to 1,000 homes.[8] With copious amounts of egg on their faces, the Germans had some serious explaining to do. In the most brutal and unexpected way, the North Strand bombing had lent weighty support to Adolf Mahr's plan for a new bilingual Irland-Redaktion, the need for which was now more urgent than ever.

Luckily for the propagandists, Churchill's decision not to pursue conscription in Northern Ireland coincided with the Luftwaffe's gaffe. Thus, at the beginning of June 1941, German Radio's foreign services were telling the world: 'It is impossible that the Germans bombed Dublin intentionally', as well as reporting that 'London has abandoned the proposal of introducing conscription in Northern Ireland'. In the first week of June, audiences from Spain to Norway were kept abreast of Irish affairs — though not including the North Strand bombing —

by the Germans whose radio reported that while Ireland's request for US arms had been refused, 'the USA has agreed to ship 500,000 tons of petrol to Éire'.

But these broadcasts were at odds with Berlin's weekly Irish language talks for the same period, during which listeners were offered no explanation for the Dublin bombardment. To avoid having to explain to his Irish listeners why the Luftwaffe had bombed a neutral city with the same alacrity as British cities like Coventry and London, Ludwig Mühlhausen carried on as if nothing had happened, forecasting that 'The Celtic race will come into its own again if England collapses'. In the same broadcast he called on Irishmen to stand united 'to free the island'.

As Éamon de Valera and Frank Aiken stood among the ruins of the North Strand, they must have wondered what more misfortune might befall their small neutral state and, above all, whether things could be much worse if Ireland was at war. Meanwhile, the Irland-Redaktion had conveniently sought refuge from an embarrassing situation deep in the Celtic mist. But even more embarrassing moments lay ahead for the propagandists as the focus shifted from an invasion of the British Isles and the German war machine swung off at top speed in an easterly direction.

Footnotes

1.   Stuart interview, 17 November 1989.

2.   Fisk, 1983, p. 521.

3.   Despite his visits to see Ribbentrop in London in the 1936-38 period, Mahr did not manage to join the German Foreign Office until 1940. From late 1939 until early 1940 he worked as an academic assistant at the museum of pre- and early history in Berlin. From there he moved to the Foreign Office as an assistant and by 1942 had become head of the Irish subsection of the political broadcasting department. By 1944, Mahr was head of section Ru 9 dealing with political broadcasting to the USA, England and Ireland (Mahr's curriculum vitae supplied to author by German Foreign Office, Bonn, 7 August 1991).

4.   Mahr, 'Rundfunkpropaganda nach Irland' (Radio Propaganda to Ireland), 18 March 1941 (AA, R67483). An English translation of this 15-page report appears as an appendix to this book.

5. In fact, attempts were made to recruit Irish prisoners in Germany to the Nazi war effort. One such prisoner, Tim Ronan of Rosscarbery, County Cork, recalled: 'It is likely that Irish POWs were approached about propaganda work. To my knowledge nobody took up the offer. I spent approximately two years in Friesack [camp]. During that time I was approached once to assist the Germans — they did not specify the type of work — I refused. Sometime afterwards a number of us were transferred to a camp near the Polish border where we remained for approximately one and a half years. There were approximately 150 POWs in Friesack' (Ronan to author, 1 March 1994). The IRA leader Seán Russell wanted to recruit 200 POWs for an Irish brigade to fight with the Germans — presumably as part of an invasion force to topple de Valera, had his August 1940 landing plan succeeded. (For more details of the Irish brigade plan and the Friesack camp, see Carter, 1977, pp. 124-35).

6. While little is known about Mahr's views on the IRA in the 1927-39 period, he did shelter an IRA man, Michael Heany, who was on the run in 1937. Mahr allowed Heany to hide out in the National Museum just a stone's throw from the Taoiseach's office. Mahr and the IRA man were photographed together in the museum in 1937 during a visit there by the Folklore Commission. (Author's interview with Professor Tomás de Bháldraithe, Dublin, 15 November 1990). Photographs of Mahr and Heany together at the museum are held by the National Museum and the Department of Irish Folklore at UCD.

7. Fisk, 1983, p. 340.

8. O'Farrell, 1981, pp. 283-4.

11

Dr Mahr versus Dr Goebbels

The German-Soviet non-aggression pact, signed on 23 August 1939, ensured that no anti-Soviet broadcasts were heard on German Radio — including the Irish service — until Hitler attacked Russia on 22 June 1941. From then on, the radio propagandists in Berlin got the green light to play the anti-communist card. A week later, on 29 June 1941, Mühlhausen tried to rally Irish support for Operation Barbarossa: 'I am sure that the Irish people are well pleased [with the invasion of Russia] for I have had many occasions to learn of the Irish hatred of Bolshevism'. Then, after listing Germany's military successes against Russia in the preceding week, Mühlhausen praised the Führer as the man 'who succeeded in bringing about German unity and in giving the whole of Europe the hope of unity and happiness'. Mühlhausen conceded that it would be 'difficult for many people to forget their own ways and to acquire a common European feeling, just as it took the German people many years to understand the aims of Adolf Hitler'.

On 9 July 1941 it was Hartmann's turn to relay the new anti-Soviet attitude to Irish listeners, repeating the German Army High Command's line justifying Barbarossa, namely that Russia had been planning an attack on Germany. As well as accusing Stalin of putting hundreds of thousands of homeless children to death, Hartmann commented:

> The fate of Russia under Bolshevik rule is comparable to the fate of Ireland under English sovereignty, and it is to be noticed that these two powers have now entered into an alliance.

But behind the occasional Irish language broadcast from Berlin a fierce internal power struggle was going on between the Propaganda Ministry and the Foreign Office for control of the Irland-Redaktion. Unknown to Adolf Mahr — whose plan to revamp the Irish service had been accepted by Ribbentrop in May 1941 — the Propaganda Ministry had pinched his ideas and had picked their own appointee to launch the service as soon as possible.

The man chosen by Goebbels to head up the new-look service was Wolfgang Dignowity, a 28 year old graduate of the Nazis' Reich Presse-Schule (national college of journalism). Dignowity was from Chemnitz in Saxony and had joined the party in July 1933. In mid-July 1941 Dignowity set off for Paris to recruit his 'Irish' radio team. Not surprisingly for a man who knew little or nothing about Ireland, none of his new team was Irish. They included a 24-year-old Breton nobleman, Count Alain Keroer, another Frenchman called Jacques Piche who had worked as a journalist in America, and a multi-lingual Russian émigrée, Sonja Kowanka from Leningrad, whose family had fled the October Revolution of 1917 and settled in France. The nearest Dignowity got to a genuine Irish recruit in Paris was James Blair whose father was Scottish and mother Irish. Since 1918 Blair had been proof-reading for an American newspaper in the French capital as well as writing for US papers. Unfortunately for Dignowity, Blair had not visited Ireland since he was a child.

The circumstances surrounding Dignowity's blundering and the background to his appointment by the rival Propaganda Ministry came to light in a memorandum written by Adolf Mahr for his Foreign Office superiors on 9 September 1941. In the memo Mahr revealed that another meeting concerning the setting up of an expanded Irish radio service was held under the aegis of the Propaganda Ministry in Berlin on 27 May 1941, just five days after Ribbentrop's conference. That meeting was attended by representatives of Goebbels' Ministry, German Radio's shortwave service (DKW), and Kult R, the Foreign Office's cultural/political division dealing with broadcasting matters. As soon as he found out that the 27 May meeting had taken place, Mahr arranged a meeting with Walter Kamm, then in charge of German Radio's European programmes section. Mahr already knew Kamm from his daily visits to the secret Concordia propaganda unit.

On 5 June, Mahr sought an assurance from Kamm that the Foreign Office's own broadcasting section would be involved in establishing the new Irish radio service. But Kamm told Mahr that the Propaganda Ministry was appointing Dr Dignowity as head of the Irland-Redaktion. Mahr then tried to arrange a meeting with Dignowity 'as quickly as possible' but Dignowity appears to have kept him at bay since the earliest appointment date arrived at was 16 July. On 15 July Dignowity cancelled the meeting telling Mahr he was ill, but two days later, on 17 July, Dignowity travelled to Paris to put together his own broadcasting team. The new 'Irish' team assembled for the first time in Berlin on 22 August 1941 at a meeting that was also attended by Mahr's Foreign Office boss, Dr Kurt Georg Kiesinger.[1]

According to Mahr, whose records were incomplete, the nightly Irish programmes began either on 26 or 28 August 1941. Mahr finally managed to meet his rival on 5 September when he had what was euphemistically termed a 'working session' with Dignowity. Another so-called working session followed on 8 September which was also attended by the British journalist, James Blair, and Mahr's assistant, Hilde Poepping. Mahr was less than impressed with the team Wolfgang Dignowity had put together to broadcast to Ireland and he spared little time in letting his Foreign Office superiors know about what he saw as the shortcomings and unsuitability of the entire staff. With a detectable tinge of sarcasm, Mahr told his bosses: 'This international team contains only one person who knows Ireland a bit from his own experience, namely Dr Dignowity himself'. Yet, according to Mahr, Dignowity had never even visited Dublin. When questioned, Dignowity vaguely told Mahr that he had spent some time on an Irish farm. However, although all foreign visitors were obliged to complete an alien's registration form on arrival, the Irish Military Archive has no record of Dignowity ever having visited Ireland. Mahr also noted that while Dignowity had studied languages and economics in Germany and Geneva, his knowledge of French and Swiss affairs far outstripped his limited knowledge of Irish matters.

A short time after Mahr penned his sharp criticism of Dignowity, a genuine Irishman appeared in the Berlin studios and began broadcasting home to Ireland. John Francis O'Reilly hailed from

Kilkee, County Clare and had arrived in Berlin via a hotel job in London and potato picking in the Channel Islands. When the Germans invaded the Islands in July 1940 O'Reilly acted as an interpreter. At the behest of the German military commander on Jersey, Prince Von Baldeck, O'Reilly persuaded no fewer than 72 fellow Irish labourers to take up factory work at Watenstedt in Germany to help the Third Reich. But the Kilkee man soon tired of factory work and after answering an advertisement, he was interviewed in September by a Herr Bock at the Propaganda Ministry in Berlin. The interview led to a voice test at the Rundfunkhaus on 24 September 1941 during which O'Reilly had to read part of a speech by Winston Churchill. With a dearth of Irish people in wartime Berlin, O'Reilly was snapped up by the radio service but, no sooner was he installed at the microphone than he began to share Adolf Mahr's view of his new colleagues in the so-called Irish team whom he bluntly summed up as follows:

> Dignowity was affable and an accomplished linguist but, like the other members of his staff, his knowledge of Ireland was purely geographic. Resentment was shown to me by the two Frenchmen [Piche and Keroer] and the Englishman [Blair]. They regarded me as an interloper in the Irish section. But within a few weeks, having found my feet, my Irish spirit of independence asserted itself and I did not hesitate to point out that they, in fact, were the intruders. This was the Irish section and I was an Irishman. All the artistry in the world could not make a shamrock out of the fleur-de-lys or the English rose. If they were not prepared to co-operate with me, well, the English section was next door and the French section was just down the corridor. Dr Dignowity supported me in my attitude and I also won the approval of the Russian girl, Sonja [Kowanka].

From his desk at the Foreign Office, Mahr continued to put pressure on Dignowity but it took some time for his critical report to be acted upon by the Foreign Office. Dignowity survived as head of the service for only five months, until the end of October 1941, when he and the two Frenchmen were removed.[2]

At the BBC monitoring centre in Evesham, Angus Matheson was still translating the twice-weekly Irish language talks but, on 8 September 1941, BBC monitors noted for the first time a talk 'In English for Ireland' on the Zeesen transmitter at 8 p.m. on 28.45

metres. The broadcast quoted a report in *The Times* that more US 'technicians' were arriving in Northern Ireland. A week later, monitors at McKee Barracks in Dublin discovered that not only was Berlin devoting nightly English-language talks to Ireland but one of the speakers had a name, Pat O'Brien. Try as they might, Army Intelligence could not discover who O'Brien was and G2 had no way of knowing that it was just a cover name chosen by the Germans to convey the 'ordinary Irishman in the street'. The voice behind the cover name belonged to none other than James Blair whose talk themes were supplied by Mahr at the Foreign Office. Some of the Pat O'Brien scripts were later written for Blair by John O'Reilly.

Meanwhile, Professor Mühlhausen was in the process of being axed by Dignowity. Later, Mahr and Hartmann did not want Mühlhausen on their team either but he continued putting out anti-Bolshevik propaganda in August and September as the new nightly service was being phased in. On 10 August, the German professor boldly predicted that 'Bolshevik Russia will soon lie prostrate before us and there will remain nobody in Europe then to prevent us defeating England, as Poland, France, Yugoslavia, Greece and Bolshevism were defeated'. On 24 September he warned his Irish audience that Stalin and Churchill had made a pact to destroy Germany, adding:

> If they do, Bolshevism will spread through Europe and throughout Ireland. From the monasteries of Ireland, Christianity came to the continent of Europe. There is a close tie between Ireland and Germany, yet England and America in union with Russia want to bring Ireland into the war against Germany.

On 27 October 1941, G2 reported that a new commentator, John O'Reilly,

> has been making short announcements for the past week. He is definitely Irish and speaks with a southern accent... The subject of his broadcast was a talk on Russia in respect of religious matters; comparison being drawn between Russian anti-religious activities and the Penal Law era in this country. The commentator spoke with a thorough knowledge of the facts as regards this country and the broadcast was one of the most effective made to this country to date.

As well as impressing the Army monitors in Dublin, O'Reilly was also making an impression on his employers in Berlin who had offered him a one year contract to stay.[3]

By early November 1941, BBC monitors were picking up the first in what was to become a regular series of items on British atrocities during the Irish War of Independence. While Francis Stuart had pioneered the idea of recollecting 'historic acts of aggression on the part of the United Kingdom' in the small number of scripts he wrote for William Joyce early in 1940, the idea was refined by Adolf Mahr for delivery on air by O'Reilly under the title 'Flashback into Irish History'. Mahr had got hold of an official US Congress document entitled *The Struggle of the Irish People* which was first adopted at a January session of Dáil Éireann in 1921. The document proved a useful propaganda tool for Mahr's radio team as it detailed dates and locations of British actions in Ireland in the 1919-21 period. BBC monitors recorded the first such example on 6 November 1941 under the heading 'Anniversary item dealing with incidents of 6 November 1919, 1920 and 1921 during the troubles in Ireland'. Though listeners in Ireland did not know it, the decision to use O'Reilly's real name in broadcasts, along with the introduction of the 'Flashback' series marked the departure of Dignowity and his two French recruits. Mahr was determined to put an extreme Irish nationalist slant on the Irland-Redaktion and so began shaping it in the likeness of the Ireland he had first encountered in 1927 after arriving from Vienna.

If there was an obvious flaw in Mahr's approach it was that his image of Ireland had become somewhat dated. Over 20 years had passed since the War of Independence, yet Mahr's propaganda continued as if that conflict was still in full flight, as if the Treaty granting Ireland partial independence in 1922 had never been signed, and as if the subsequent Civil War had never occurred. More importantly, Mahr's propaganda turned a blind eye to the fact that most of the anti-Treaty forces had long since abandoned armed struggle to join de Valera in the Dáil. In addition, the absent Dublin museum director could not have known that de Valera's neutrality policy would favour Britain over Germany.

Wartime Berlin held a certain attraction for nationalists of all sorts, including IRA men, who saw obvious opportunities to be gained from a Nazi victory in Europe. With Irish, Indian, Breton, Flemish, Ukrainian and other nationalists gathered in Berlin, and many of them working in close proximity in the Rundfunkhaus, it was natural that propaganda ideas would be exchanged as the broadcasters mixed socially. William Joyce, for example, occasionally played chess with Subhas Chandra Bose then living in Berlin as leader of the 'Indian freedom fighters' and who broadcast anti-British propaganda to India. The Indian nationalists' radio propaganda sometimes echoed similar themes on the Irland-Redaktion, such as on 19 November 1941, when Pat O'Brien, alias James Blair, told listeners that

> Ireland and India are akin in their relations to England. Both have been robbed and have fought desperately and persistently for independence. In the 18th century the Ulster wool industry was ruined. Identical measures were taken in India to stifle her industries. British products were substituted for Indian ones, and Birmingham and Manchester were built on the ruins of Indian trade. Recurrent famines followed. Ireland was turned into a charnel house during the artificially created famine of 1845-1848. England did nothing to alleviate the hardship. She continued to import food from Ireland and prevented Ireland from importing food from elsewhere.

A few months later, Chandra Bose was telling his listeners that: 'If India had been allowed to remain neutral, like Ireland, there would have been no possibility of India coming within the arena of the present war'.

While Mühlhausen's talks had by this stage been dropped altogether, Hartmann was allowed to continue broadcasting and, in fact, Mahr had even greater plans in mind for him than simply contributing weekly Irish talks. On 30 November 1941, Hartmann contributed a 15-minute talk in Irish entitled 'Germany, the Saviour of Europe' in which he said:

> England declared war on Germany and allied herself to the devil. Ribbentrop recently said that England is paying dearly for the war. Her allies have one by one been defeated. Russia, her last friend, is doomed and her naval blockade has failed while Germany has gained lands, mines, factories, all the raw materials that she and Europe need. It is Hitler who has saved Europe, and England will go on sinking lower.

The reference to Ribbentrop was proof that Goebbels had now lost his bid for overall control of the Irland-Redaktion.

The Japanese attack on Pearl Harbour, on 7 December 1941, brought America into the war, yet, while it merited a passing comment, the Irish service seemed more interested in the events of over 20 years before. On 17 December John O'Reilly's 'Flashback' item was introduced thus:

> As usual we are beginning our programme this evening with a flashback into the history of British terrorism in Ireland. Exactly 21 years ago today, that is to say on Thursday, December 17th 1920, British Crown forces waging war upon the civil population of Ireland, committed more acts of savage terrorism. At midnight, British auxiliary police walked into the home of Michael Edmonds of Tipperary town. He was taken from his bed to some hills nearby where his British abductors shot him through the brain in cold blood. Further to this typically ruthless murder, Black and Tans burned down homes in Tipperary town, where the murder had taken place, and in Swanlinbar, Co. Cavan. Twenty one years ago, the British were prepared to stoop to the lowest form of murder and brutal intimidation. They did not care because they thought they were triumphant. Today, however, they would prefer to have these atrocities forgotten because they realise they are now being beaten themselves and they fear retribution.

Shortly before Christmas Hans Hartmann was installed, at Mahr's behest, as the new head of the Irland-Redaktion. Mahr and Hartmann shared a common interest in Irish affairs. They had known each other since 1937 at the National Museum in Dublin. Mahr had effectively picked his own man to run the Irish radio service and their dual mandate would run for the remainder of the war. On 28 December 1941, as if to demonstrate his new found position of influence, Hartmann launched forth with a hard-hitting speech praising Ireland for her neutral stance but warning of dire consequences should that policy be abandoned:

> Ireland stands alone in the midst of great nations who are engaged in war to the bitter end and it might appear that she will never be able to maintain her neutrality, especially as the USA, on whom she placed all her hopes, is participating in the war... As regards Mr Roosevelt and the capitalists and Jews in America, it is difficult to discern any nobility or sense of honour in their conduct... but the man in the street in America, the workers, the poor, the Irish and others, have not changed their opinion. Roosevelt and his friends have led them into a war against their will. They are in it now and there is no remedy.

Forecasting that Roosevelt might send troops to Northern Ireland, Hartmann warned his listeners:

> The fine edifice of the Republic would collapse immediately if the Irish government did not succeed in avoiding war and maintaining neutrality. In addition, it is likely that in such a case the war would be fought on Irish soil despite the long-standing friendship between Germany and Ireland. This means that there is no other course open to the Irish people, if they have sense and do not wish to commit suicide, but to defend their neutrality at any cost. As for the Irish living in the USA, I am sure that they fully understand the conduct of Ireland, though a great part of them are at present on the side of the government in the American war. I should not like to see Ireland completely destroyed and to see everything achieved after the last war brought to nothing again... The greatest vigilance is called for. God bless and save Ireland.

Some 45 years after the war, when Hartmann was asked why Irish neutrality was considered to be so important by the authorities in wartime Berlin, his reply had an uncanny resonance with that broadcast of 28 December 1941. He commented:

> It was a part of the war aims. One can start from the assumption that Hitler did not actually want to attack England. He favoured a solution, or a distribution of the world, leaving the East to him and the seas and the West to England and America. Then, when de Valera declared his neutrality, Hitler said to himself that that was the best thing for him too. He really wanted to respect Ireland's neutrality if Ireland was not foolish enough to make some move to make that difficult for him; to force him into another attitude. Irish neutrality was really one of the objectives which was in conformity with German policies.

Hartmann also added this personal view of Ireland's neutrality:

> When I took over the broadcasts I told my superiors that I would back up the Irish neutrality policy as strongly as possible, and they had no objection to that... I felt a strong obligation towards Ireland and the country's neutrality policy. I did not want to do anything to endanger this policy and the policy of Hempel who was a very cautious and considerate man'.

Did Hartmann feel his Irland-Redaktion's programmes were serving some useful purpose? 'Yes, certainly. My whole work was focused on selecting news and making programmes to fit the Irish neutrality policy. We were very much engaged in and intent on doing so'.[4]

As 1941 drew to a close Hartmann's team comprised Kowanka (who broadcast under the name Linda Walters), Blair, O'Reilly and Poepping (who occasionally read the news bulletins), as well as Hartmann's sister-in-law, Gertrud Neugebauer, who worked for him as a typist. Adolf Mahr, of course, was providing support from the Foreign Office. On 31 December 1941, Hartmann and his team put out an end of year programme for Ireland at 12.30 p.m. The *Irish Press* reported the broadcast as follows:

> In a special New Year's Eve broadcast from Germany, over the Oslo Radio, greetings were sent by former members of the German colony here. The broadcast opened with a recital by Fräulein Mona Brase, daughter of the late Col. Fritz Brase, Director of the Army School of Music. Dr Hans Hartmann, speaking in Irish, referred to the folklore he had collected in Ireland, and Dr Robert Stumpf, formerly a radiologist in the Royal City of Dublin Hospital, followed. Engineer Karl Künstler said that Herr Krause, who has married since leaving Ireland, and Harry Greiner joined with him in sending greetings. Fräulein Dr Hilde Sütter, who had been an exchange student in Galway, said that all the other exchange students are well, except Martin Fluss who was killed in Russia. Charles Budina, formerly of Kilmacurragh Park Hotel, Co. Wicklow, who said that he is now a soldier in Paris, sent greetings to his wife, other members of his family and friends, and added that Kurweis, Arano and Kurt are well and are at home on leave. The announcer then read a message from Mrs Esther O'Sullivan to her father, relatives and friends in Kilkenny saying that she is well; and the broadcast ended with a message of greeting in Irish from Dr Ludwig Mühlhausen, the well known authority on folklore and phonetics.[5]

The regular nightly programme to Ireland also went out on the Zeesen transmitter at 8 p.m. starting with a 'Flashback' feature covering British atrocities in the year 1920. That was followed by a detailed talk on 'Neutrality in British Eyes' aimed at warning Irish listeners against American attempts to occupy the Treaty Ports. The anonymous speaker noted that:

> England has toyed with the idea of occupying the Irish ports for a long time, but even her crazy politicians admit that the idea is too

dangerous. It doesn't really matter to England whether she or one of her Allies does the occupying. England would actually prefer that one of her Allies should do the dirty work. What ally would do England's dirty work in this case? England remembers that the USA has a large Irish population who were forced to emigrate there owing to the criminal effects of English policy. England now thinks that were America to occupy Southern Ireland, the native Irish would not object because of their relatives in the States. Ireland would, in fact, welcome Mr Roosevelt's soldiers who would then come, not in the name of England, but in the name of the American Irish. It is all part of the neutrality game as played by England. Were the Irish to object to this skilful procedure they would of course be in the wrong since anyone not participating in England's war is immoral and suicidal.

The night's programmes concluded with a 25-minute broadcast of New Year's greetings at 9.30 p.m., which may have been a recording of the earlier transmission, along with some additional material put out live from the Berlin studios. BBC monitors noted that Hartmann's new assistant, Hilde Poepping, 'said that all her friends who had spent some time in Ireland sent their greetings, except her friend Martin Klot who was killed in action in Russia fighting to protect the women and children of Europe from Bolshevism'.

As Hitler's blitzkrieg against Russia failed and became instead a far more costly engagement, anti-Bolshevik themes would become all too familiar to the Irland-Redaktion's audience.

Footnotes

1. Mahr, 'Englischsprachige Sendungen nach Irland' (English-language programmes to Ireland), 9 September 1941 (BA Potsdam, file VA 62407, document no. 168). In his memo Mahr refers to his 'daily official visits to Concordia', which suggests he was a designated Foreign Office representative at the secret centre for black propaganda broadcasts. Kiesinger was Federal Chancellor of West Germany from 1966 to 1969. During the upheavals of 1968, German students embarrassed him by digging up details of his Nazi past.

2. Dr Hilde Spickernagel (née Poepping), who attended the key meeting on 8 September 1941, describes Mahr's takeover bid for the Irland-Redaktion as only a 'partial' success since a number of Dignowity's

Propaganda Ministry appointees remained with the Irish service (i.e. Blair, Kowanka and O'Reilly). Commenting on Mahr's memo of 9 September 1941, Dr Spickernagel said: 'The situation described was just one part in the well known and long drawn out struggle between Ru/Auswärtiges Amt [Foreign Office broadcasting section] and ProMi [the Propaganda Ministry]. The conferences of 27 May 1941 and 22 August 1941 were obviously won by ProMi. I dare say nobody at Ru/ AA was happy about that. I suppose Mahr felt that he should have been included earlier in the proceedings, and that — if he did not utter loud protests — he might be left out of more proceedings to come. He, therefore, tries hard to make a laughing stock of Dignowity, all Dignowity had arranged, and of the people he picked up... I am sure Mahr felt he had to prove that he could find more suitable people for running the Irland-Redaktion. But I do not think that he could have managed a change (if only a partial one, after all) without the pressure of the Auswärtiges Amt [Foreign Office] to back him up. The whole story goes to prove that his personal influence was not as far reaching as he would have liked'. (Dr Spickernagel's letter to author, 31 December 1993).

3. O'Reilly's family in Kilkee, Co. Clare, heard his broadcasts from Germany. But even 50 years after the war, his brother Bernard O'Reilly was unwilling to discuss John O'Reilly's wartime activities; author's interview with Mr Bernard O'Reilly, Glasthule, County Dublin, 15 November 1996.

4. Author's interview with Hartmann, 21 October 1990. In fact, British military chiefs agreed with Hitler's view of Irish neutrality, as described by Hartmann. On 30 May 1940 military commanders advised the British War Cabinet that 'a neutral Éire assists Germany in the general prosecution of the war, and denies to us the use of important naval bases' (Éire, report by the Chiefs of Staff Committee to War Cabinet, 30 May 1940, p. 3. PRO CAB.66/8).

5. 'Former German Colonists Send Greetings', *Irish Press*, 2 January 1942. While some of Hartmann's Irish friends thought he was in Norway, the programme was actually transmitted from Berlin via the Oslo transmitter (to obtain a stronger signal for Ireland). Oslo Radio had been in Nazi hands since the German invasion of Norway on 9 April 1940. Mona Brase has no recollection of taking part in the broadcast and suggests her piano recital was a recording (author's interview with Brase, Dublin, 8 October 1991). The *Irish Press* reporter

misheard the name Plass as Fluss. A BBC monitor also misheard the name as 'Klot', in a broadcast later the same day. Poor radio reception was probably to blame. Martin Plass came to Ireland in the late 1930s as a student via Helmut Clissmann's academic exchange programme. Plass was reprimanded for not reporting directly to Adolf Mahr — as local Nazi Party leader — on his arrival in Ireland. Plass' thesis on the writer George Russell (Æ) was published in Berlin in 1940 (Dickel, 1983, p. 173). Charles Budina made one other broadcast from Berlin on 13 June 1942 (PRONI CAB 9CD/207 BBC MR). This was Mühlhausen's last broadcast to Ireland.

Left to right
(seated in foreground):
Adolf and Maria Mahr,
their son Gustav, and
the famous Austrian
expressionist painter,
Oskar Kokoschka,
at an archeological
excavation, Lough
Crew, Co. Meath,
July 1928.

Cork student, Joe Healy (rear left) with Ludwig Mühlhausen (right) and family in Hamburg, 1928. During the war Irish military intelligence used Healy to monitor Mühlhausen's Irish language talks. Healy was later appointed Professor of Spanish at University College Cork.

Adolf Mahr's alien's registration card.
He was born in Trent, Austria (now part of Italy) in 1887.
Mahr lived in Ireland from 1927 to 1939.

Ludwig Mühlhausen pictured with some of his Celtic language students in Hamburg, 1931. Mühlhausen's wife Else (fourth from left) joined the inner circle of the Hamburg Nazi Party in 1932. In 1937 Mühlhausen took over the chair of Celtic studies at Berlin University.

341

The Taoiseach Éamon de Valera personally signed
the Cabinet's decision to appoint Mahr as
Director of the National Museum in July 1934.

Professor Ludwig Mühlhausen
in Hamburg, 1931.

Adolf Mahr (extreme left) at a party in Dublin to mark the 60th birthday of Colonel Fritz Brase (seated, centre) on 4 May 1935. Brase, who joined the Nazi Party in April 1932, was Director of the Irish Army's school of music from 1923 to 1940. Mahr joined the Nazi Party in April 1933.

Dr. Adolf Mahr on his appointment as Director of the National Museum in Dublin, 1934.

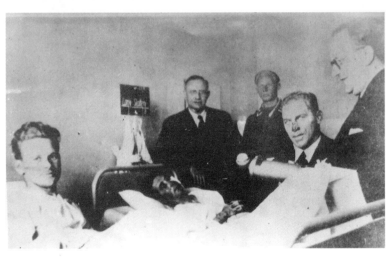

Larry Slattery (centre, in hospital bed) from Thurles, Co. Tipperary, being interviewed for German Radio's English service in September 1939.
Slattery's RAF plane was shot down over Germany in the first week of the war.

Pictured at a 1938 reception at the German Legation's garden in Dublin's Northumberland Road, left to right: Heinz Mecking, Herr Fäsenfeld, Herr and Frau Müller, and Frau Erni Ritter. Mecking was Mahr's deputy in the Nazi Party and worked for the Irish Turf Development Board.

Adolf and Maria Mahr at the Giant's Causeway, Co. Antrim, 12 July 1930.

Left to right: Dr. Eduard Hempel, the German Ambassador to Ireland (1937-45),
Dr. Vogelsang, and Dr. Adolf Mahr at the German Legation's garden party
in Dublin, 30 April 1938.

A group portrait taken during the Irish Folklore Commission's visit to the National Museum, Dublin, in 1937, provides a rare photograph of Adolf Mahr and Hans Hartmann together.

Left to right: Professor James Delargy, Séan Forde, Fr. Eric Mac Fhinn, Dr. Adolf Mahr, Osborn Bergin, Liam Price, Peadar McGinley, Eamonn O'Donoghue, Leon Ó Broin, Hans Hartmann, Louis Maguire, Rev. John G. O'Neill. Ake Campbell and Michael Heany.

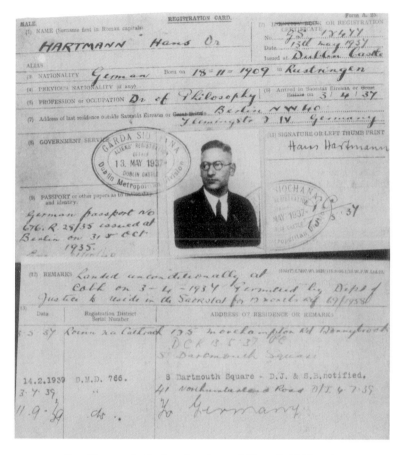

Hans Hartmann's alien's registration card. He studied Irish and folklore from April 1937 to September 1939. Hartmann and other Germans were shadowed by the Special Branch.

The Berlin Rundfunkhaus (Radio Centre) in Masurenallee retains its original 1930's format. The Irland-Redaktion (Irish Service) operated from two rooms at the rear of the building (arrowed).

A 1936 photograph of Susan Hilton

Friedrich Weckler worked for Siemens on the Shannon hydroelectric scheme in the late 1920s. He later joined the ESB as its chief accountant from 1930 until his death in 1943. Weckler joined the Nazi Party in June 1934 and was one of six Nazis working for Irish state companies.

Friedrich Herkner (pictured here in 1969) was appointed Professor of Sculpture at the National College of Art, Dublin, in 1938. He joined the Nazi Party ten days before leaving Ireland for Germany in September 1939. Unlike Adolf Mahr, Herkner was allowed to resume his Irish state job in 1947.

The Hotel Lindenhof in Millstadt-am-See, Austria,
where the Mahr family spent their last pre-war holidays in July/August 1939.

Schweizerische Gesandtschaft in Deutschland

Abteilung Schutzmachtangelegenheiten

Application for $\frac{\text{issuance}}{\text{extension}}$ of passport

(To be filled out in letters)

Surname HILTON

Christian name Susan Dorothea

Place and date of birth 2nd. Feb. 1915

Trichinopoly. South India

Marital status married
(single, married, divorced)

Present address Ilag Liebenau

Schloss 11. Zimmer 15. Germany

Occupation none

Employed by no one

Nationality British

Native or naturalized Native

Original nationality British

Any additional nationality none

Description

Height 5 ft. 3 ins.

Eyes brown

Hair brown

Distinguishing marks

Legal home residence Chetnole. Nr. Sherborne
Dorset. England

Number of last passport

Issued at F.O. London on 7/9/36

Valid until 1941

Nationality of parents both British

Present address of parents 42, Parkhill Rd.

Hampstead. London. N.W.3

Remarks Passport lost at sea 13/7/40

when British ship "Kemmendine" was

captured by German Raider "Atlantis"

in the Indian Ocean.

Two signatures of the applicant

Susan D. Hilton

Susan D. Hilton

The undersigned authority declares that
above description of the applicant is true ;
correct and that the photograph as well
the two signatures affixed below are genu

Liebenau 20 X. 19

Seal and signature of the authority

C/0594

A Swiss Legation passport application for Susan Hilton (née Sweney). Hilton was
found half-starved in the Nazi camp at Liebenau when it was liberated in April 1945.
While other prisoners were released, Hilton was detained for a further eight months at
Liebenau before being returned by MI5 for trial in London for 'assisting the enemy'.
She spent 18 months in Holloway Prison. Hilton broadcast to Ireland in 1942.

Angus Matheson was recruited by the BBC in July 1940 to monitor and translate German Radio's Irish language broadcasts.

Heinz Mecking in German Army uniform, c. 1940. From 1936 to 1939, Mecking worked in Ireland as chief advisor to the Turf Development Board. He joined the Nazi Party in 1931.

12

Hartmann's Biggest Coup

Consolidating his position as head of the Irland-Redaktion in early 1942, Hans Hartmann added a few new members to his team of announcers. The first of these was Mrs Susan Hilton (née Sweney) who, although born in India of British parents (her father, Cyril Edward Sweney, was superintendent of railway police in Madras), had Irish connections through her brother Edward who lived in County Meath. Using her maiden name of Sweney, she began broadcasting for the Irland-Redaktion on 2 January 1942. Earlier, Hilton had done some broadcasts for the Rundfunk's Scottish service, Radio Caledonia, where she used the name Ann Tower (her mother's name was Dorothy Tower-Barter). In a series of talks entitled 'Germany speaks to Ireland', she warned listeners against allowing Ireland to be turned into a battlefield following America's entry into the war:

> Many millions of Irishmen in America will be with Irishmen at home in resisting Roosevelt's aggression, should it come openly or through Britain as the back door to Ireland.

Four days later Hilton was back on the airwaves warning that 'Irish bases given to the USA would be bases given to England and would be, quite justifiably, targets for German bombers'.

On 7 January Hartmann told Irish listeners that the British Empire was

> falling to pieces and I am certain that many of the dead generations of Irishmen would envy the lot of those living at present because

they may be fortunate enough to see England broken one day.
God bless and save Ireland.

Mahr's carrot and stick approach towards Irish neutrality can clearly
be seen in the broadcasts of this period — if Ireland remained neutral
the prize of reunification would be hers once England was defeated,
but if England or America occupied the Treaty Ports or elsewhere in
the 26 Counties, Ireland would immediately become a legitimate
target with all the terror and destruction that implied.

American troops were not, in fact, heading for Castletownbere or
Cobh, but they were en route to Ulster. The arrival of US troops in
Northern Ireland on 26 January 1942 provided a prime propaganda
topic for the Germans. But Hartmann's service was slow to use the
story and was pipped at the post by a German 'black propaganda'
station called Workers' Challenge, pitched at working class audiences
in London's East End which had been a pre-war stronghold of
Mosleyite support. Workers' Challenge was scripted by William
Joyce who worked for Sir Oswald Mosley in the 1930s. The station
broke the news as follows:

> Well, workers, there's great news for us today. The Yankees have
> come. Now we're on the hog's back. All we have to do is to cheer
> like hell. But it seems that not many Yankees have come after all,
> and, just by a sort of funny misunderstanding, they haven't gone
> on to Europe. They aren't in France yet. In fact, they're in Northern
> Ireland. Just a few of them... to show that the good old Stars and
> Stripes are doing something. Stick them in Ulster. Against who?
> Good Lord, surely they don't think that Ulster needs defending
> against the Southern Irishmen today! It's all very queer. They
> seem to have gone to a place where there isn't any war going on.
> Now that's a remarkable thing, because in most wars the great and
> wise generals like to send their troops where they can meet the
> enemy. But, perhaps cunning politicians like Mr Franklin D.
> Roosevelt don't. Anyhow, don't be taken in with any propaganda
> about the Yanks who are in Northern Ireland. Roosevelt didn't
> mean them to be soldiers. He meant them to be tallymen, to make
> sure we pay as much as we can to the American capitalists.

BBC wartime monitor Lorna Swire, who recorded some of the
Workers' Challenge broadcasts, recalls them as 'a ghastly attempt to
ingratiate themselves with the "working classes"... with all the
dreadful swearing which they thought the workers would like. They
didn't, and in any case the station was badly received'.[1]

It took five days for the Irland-Redaktion to respond (probably because they had to await the official line from Mahr at the Foreign Office), with new arrival Susan Hilton telling Irish listeners that

> American troops are now on Irish soil. It has been reported that millions of Irish in America have sent messages to President Roosevelt affirming their loyalty to the United States... What is far more to the point, however, is that the Irish in America should not be false to their mother country... Ireland has managed to remain strictly neutral up to now in this war and it certainly would be tragic if through selfish and brutal interference from Roosevelt or anyone else that neutrality, which has been guarded so jealously, should be lost... The Irish in America cannot but remember that those left behind expect from them loyalty and understanding in these days when the things for which the patriots fought may so easily be lost through the selfish greed of one warmongering individual and his evil crowd of reckless followers on either side of the ocean. Never before has it been more necessary to keep calm and watchful.

With so much emphasis placed by the Irland-Redaktion on Ireland's struggle for independence, it was natural for the service to focus at Easter on the 1916 Rising. For the three and half years that he was in charge of the Irish service, Hans Hartmann always made sure that the anniversary of the Easter Rising received due commemoration. On 5 March 1942 he gave a special talk in Irish on 'The spirit of Easter Sunday, 1916', telling his listeners:

> There is an old custom in Ireland to climb to the top of the hills on Easter Sunday to watch the rising of the sun... in 1916, on the morning of Easter Sunday or the 'Sunday of the sun', they made an attempt to break the bitter darkness of English tyranny and to reach the light of the sun. Instead of going to seek the rising of the sun on the top of the hills, as was the custom of their forefathers, the Irish rose early on Easter Sunday [sic] morning and gathered in the streets to make another attempt to smash the bond between England and themselves. They were ready to give their lives for the cause of Irish freedom, and from that uprising came the freedom and independence of the Irish nation.[2]

After translating the 13-minute programme, a new BBC Gaelic monitor, Jane Charleton (a Belfast woman, she had just taken over from Angus Matheson, then transferred to MI5 for code breaking work) noted:

This was a special broadcast to the people of Ireland for Easter
Sunday and consisted of a short talk by Dr Hartmann (in Gaelic),
followed by the reading of three poems in English and of the
proclamation made on Easter Sunday 1916 by the Irish Republican
Army [sic], interspersed with selections from Bach.[3]

By contrast, the following day's broadcast to Ireland contained an
anti-Jewish talk based on William Bulfin's tale of a Jewish pedlar in
Rambles in Eirinn. The commentator, who remained anonymous,
noted Bulfin's 'reference to the connection between British
aristocracy and the Jews. This reference is all the more remarkable
as it was made in the year 1907 when the link up between British
Imperialists and Jewry was by no means so apparent as it is today'.
Part of Bulfin's story was quoted as follows:

> I was given to understand that these Jewish pedlars are to be met
> with in many parts of Ireland. I was sorry to hear about it. I was
> told that some of them, out of the profits of their trade, have already
> established themselves in Dublin and other cities as wholesale
> merchants and moneylenders, and, added the Ballymahon man
> who gave me the information, they have two patron saints, Moses
> and the Duke of Norfolk. 'The Duke of Norfolk?', I asked in some
> surprise, 'what has he got to do with the Hebrew race?' 'Oh you
> see', he explained, 'the Duke is a soft hearted man and his pity
> always goes out to the landlords and the Jews and the police and
> the Lord Lieutenants of Ireland, and all the other poor downtrodden
> wretches'.[4]

Adolf Mahr may well have chosen this segment from his collection
of Irish books, but there is another possible explanation for the talk.
In 1942, Hans Hartmann and Francis Stuart were both working at
Berlin University — Hartmann was finishing the doctoral thesis which
would soon gain him a lecturing job there, while Stuart was lecturing
in the English Department. Through his marriage to Iseult, Stuart
was related to her half brother Seán MacBride, who had been IRA
chief of staff for a brief period in 1936. Seán MacBride, who made
the transition to constitutional politics via Clann na Poblachta in
1946, was married to Catalina, the daughter of *Rambles in Eirinn*
author William Bulfin. It is possible that Stuart furnished the anti-
Jewish extract to embarrass MacBride who was known to be angry
that Stuart had left Iseult for another woman. Stuart, however, strongly
denies any such ploy.

That talk based on Bulfin's *Rambles in Eirinn* had nothing to do with me. I did not suggest it and have never hidden behind anonymity. Though related by marriage to Bulfin, I don't know where this scurrilous piece came from. As for wishing to score off Seán MacBride, my own situation was far too precarious to take time off for personal scoring. Anyhow, his deploring my adulterous relationship with another woman was very understandable.[5]

In addition to his talks about 1916, from 1942 to 1945 Hartmann made an effort to put out special programmes to Ireland on St Patrick's Day. The talks were linked by Irish records, some of which Hartmann had brought with him from Ireland and some he had found in the Rundfunkhaus music library. One wartime listener, Éimear Ó Broin, recalls hearing

> a German male voice choir singing Irish songs phonetically. They had obviously been drilled thoroughly although they didn't understand a word of what they were singing. It was amazing to listen to and showed the dedication of the programme makers. The theme music chosen to introduce the Irish section's normal programming was a Fritz Brase arrangement of the traditional jig *The Frost Is All Over*.[6]

Apart from serving to identify the station to listeners, the repeated use of the same songs was due to a shortage of Irish records in the Rundfunkhaus, as one Irish service contributor, Nora O'Mara (aka Róisín Ní Mheara-Vinard) recalls.

> I reluctantly inveigled a shy Irish housewife who was married to a German to participate in [Synge's] *Riders to the Sea*. She agreed for Ireland's sake but her effort failed when she broke down in tears upon hearing the beautiful melody *Slievenamon* played as background to Yeats' play, *The Pot of Broth*. There were six or seven old 78s of Irish music to choose from.[7]

A distinct pattern was now beginning to emerge in the broadcasts devised by Mahr and Hartmann for Irish audiences. Fritz Brase's musical arrangement was followed by the regular 'Flashback' feature, an English-language news bulletin, Hartmann's talk in Irish and, also in Irish, extracts from Wolfe Tone's diary. Another traditional Irish tune would round off the broadcast. All in all it was an Austro-German attempt to sound more like the Irish than the Irish themselves, but Hartmann was about to pull off a coup which would lend much needed authenticity to his radio service. For his first St Patrick's Day programme as head of the Irland-Redaktion, Hartmann persuaded Francis Stuart to contribute a special talk. Although Stuart had written some talks for Joyce at the English service in 1940, this was the first time he had broadcast anything himself.

Stuart says he only agreed to do the talk on the basis that he would have a free hand in writing it and would not be under any influence as to its contents. Despite this, his first talk reflected the Irland Redaktion's twin themes of early 1942: support for Irish neutrality and opposition to the arrival of US troops in Northern Ireland. Under the heading 'Ireland's place in the new Europe', Stuart told his listeners:

> I am not trying to make propaganda. You have had plenty of it and I only hope that you have now a good idea of what is true and what is false. Had I wanted to make propaganda I could have done so during my two years in Germany. I only want to put forward my idea of Ireland's place in the world and her future, which I am perhaps able to view with greater clarity from a distance. What a blessing it is that we are celebrating this day at peace, not having escaped war by dishonourable and cowardly means, but by refusing — as far as lay within our power — to waver from a strict and fearless neutrality. As an Ulsterman[8] it is galling to me that a large number of foreign troops are today occupying that corner of our country. But though we have escaped the war, and I hope may be able to do so until the end without sacrificing anything of our national integrity, we cannot nor do we desire to escape taking our share in building the new Europe... Ireland belongs to Europe and England does not belong to it. Our future must lie with the future of Europe and no other.

Stuart's initial talk used an Irish angle to lean heavily on a standard Nazi propaganda line of the time — Hitler's New Order, or the new Europe, as the Irish writer called it. Even if Stuart had scripted the entire speech himself it would have been hard for him to avoid being influenced by his hosts in wartime Berlin both at the University and at the Rundfunkhaus. Hartmann and Mahr must have been pleased with what they heard for Stuart was soon to be asked to contribute a weekly talk to Ireland. Later that St Patrick's night there was a convivial atmosphere as members of the Irland-Redaktion, including John O'Reilly, joined Adolf Mahr and other former members of the German colony in Dublin, as guests of William Warnock at the Irish Legation in Berlin's Drakestrasse.[9]

Two days later an anonymous talk entitled 'American Catholics and the war' summed up Mahr and Hartmann's chosen angle on Irish neutrality.

> American Catholics realise the dangers and possible complications which may arise for the American people when Uncle Sam sends his soldiers overseas. They know very well that the president is playing a very dangerous game with dynamite. They know furthermore that every soldier on Irish soil for instance, may be the yet slumbering spark to the fuse which may blow Ireland's so long safeguarded neutrality and independence to bits. Remembering the fact that the cradle of an overwhelming majority of America's Catholics stood in Donegal, Cork and Mayo, we understand their anxieties to keep America out of the war, and their opposition to President Roosevelt's hypocritical imperialistic war aims.

Such talks were, of course, of little use in so far as America was by then fully committed to the conflict both in Europe and elsewhere. But, in as much as the broadcasts might have helped, in however small a way, to tilt the balance against Ireland becoming involved in the war, Mahr and Hartmann probably felt they were more than justified as suitable propaganda material.

Francis Stuart gave his second talk, 'Ireland and the new Europe', on 29 March and his third, entitled 'Easter 1916: Ireland's safety in 1942', on 5 April in the course of which he said:

> As this evening I walked about the Berlin streets as a neutral, I remember the country [Ireland] has nothing to do with the war being forced by Britain. I know that had those few men not barricaded themselves into a few buildings in Dublin that day 26 years ago our position now would be a very different one. The spirit of Easter Week is the one thing which will bring us safely through this crisis. Please God, we shall be able to remain neutral to the end... I hope and believe that the end of this war will give us back our national unity, and that the struggle which began in its latter phase on that Easter morning in Dublin will then be, at last, at an end.

A fourth talk by Stuart, 'Ireland's obligation to Europe' was broadcast on 25 May.

By the end of March 1942 the Irland-Redaktion had moved house from two rooms at the rear of the Rundfunkhaus in Berlin to two smaller rooms nearby at 77 Kaiserdamm. The Kaiserdamm premises had no studios, so broadcasters from the Irish team had to cross the narrow Brettschneiderstrasse to broadcast their material from the Rundfunkhaus. The Irish service occasionally departed from its regular programme formula to allow personal messages like the one relayed by Mona Brase (daughter of Colonel Fritz) to her mother in Dublin on 4 May 1942. BBC monitors noted Brase 'played three of her father's compositions for piano forte' to mark the anniversary of his birth.[10]

As the year went on, Allied bombers stepped up their raids on German cities. On 30 May the RAF mounted a 1,000 bomber raid on Cologne, but even before that Hartmann was admitting to Irish listeners: 'it is true that they [the British] can destroy a certain number of German towns'. On 10 May, Hartmann commented:

> The British are trying to terrorise the German people by bombing their towns in preference to carrying out any major war operations against the German Army. But the German people are not to be frightened so easily. They understand that they have behind them a fine army which has fought effectively on various battlefronts from Narvik to Crete in Europe and under Rommel in North Africa. For a whole winter too, the German generals have held their lines against incessant Russian attacks on the Eastern front.

This was the first admission on the Irland-Redaktion that the invasion of Russia, launched just a year before, was not going well.

Hartmann continued his talks throughout that month, telling listeners on 17 May that the Six Counties was

> an armed camp, filled with American and British soldiers, tanks and aeroplanes out of the province of O'Neill. It is time that the Protestants of the province and, indeed, the whole people of Ireland, realised that no prosperity or peace is in store for them except through union with their Catholic brethren.

Two days later, German home stations reported that US troops stationed in Northern Ireland

> have been further reinforced. The part of the island stolen from the Irish, which was terrorised by the Britons until a year ago, is now under US control. Among the Americans in Northern Ireland there are many Jews dressed up as officers.

On 20 May Hartmann said:

Irish partisans must have watched with bitterness and rancour as America sent millions of soldiers to the Six Counties... some partisans do not agree with their government, and would be glad to be rid of foreign troops, for I am sure that in recent years their esteem for their Catholic countrymen in the South has increased... but, alas there is still in the Six Counties a party as hard as nails, who are afraid of losing some of their hoarded wealth if they yield to general Irish opinion. They would rather send the whole country to hell than surrender a single privilege.

These last two talks by Hartmann were beamed to North America as well as Ireland but the practice of targeting US listeners in the Irish language was not widely used. These talks may have been put out to North America simply to test the strength of the Zeesen facility where seven 50 kW shortwave transmitters had been built for the 1936 Berlin Olympic Games.

After taking charge of the Irland-Redaktion, Hartmann had begun regularly quoting extracts from Wolfe Tone's diary in Irish. His first recorded use of the diary was on 28 January 1942. After the war, Hartmann said he used the Tone diaries on air 'because they were far back in history, had no direct contact with present day politics but, on the whole, conveyed the idea that Ireland was entitled to be a free and independent nation, and particularly that the Catholic part of the country had the right to self-determination. I selected mostly those parts of the diaries in which Wolfe Tone urged, supported these views'.[11] On 24 May, he prefaced a diary quotation by disclosing the source of the material as follows:

I have had to give my talk in Irish this time [in fact, he never broadcast in English]. I apologise to listeners who may not know Irish. On the other hand I hope that those people who have known Gaelic from the cradle or who learned it at school will be glad to hear this language broadcast sometimes from Germany instead of our English news. Personally I should be very glad if I could in this way persuade those people who do not know Irish to begin learning it. A few weeks ago in the Gresham Hotel in Dublin, there assembled some of the men who had fought during the Rising of 1916 and in the fight for freedom up to 1921. It was an occasion for renewing old friendships and reviving the memories of old struggles in the cause of freedom. One speaker said that he hoped there would be unity soon between North and South. Great changes have come about in the state of affairs in Ireland since the days of Wolfe Tone, especially in the position of the Catholics, but we must admit that it is a sad thing to speak of the United Irishmen. They failed to win freedom for their country. Listen now to Wolfe Tone's account of events in Ireland; it has been translated into Irish by Padraig Ó Siochfhradha... .[12]

In this respect, Hartmann was doing as good a job as Conradh na Gaeilge could ever have hoped for. When living in Ireland he had purchased a copy of the Tone Diary translation for five shillings and took it with him when he returned to Berlin in 1939. It was a useful way of filling Irish language talks and was thoroughly in keeping with the Irland-Redaktion technique, devised by Mahr, of focusing on the past and, in particular, on Ireland's fight against the British. But not everyone at the Irish service took to Wolfe Tone's diary with the same enthusiasm as Mahr and Hartmann. When Hartmann asked John O'Reilly to broadcast 'lengthy extracts from the life of Wolfe Tone', the Clare man handed them back saying they would be of no interest to Irish listeners. But O'Reilly 'got rapped over the knuckles for doing this and was told to carry on'.[13]

While Hartmann and O'Reilly were relating segments of Wolfe Tone's diary to Irish audiences, fierce battles were continuing on the Eastern front. On 12 May 1942 the Russians began the Kharkov offensive, with the Germans counter-attacking five days later. By 28 May, the battle of Kharkov had ended in a Soviet defeat. On 31 May, Hartmann took Irish newspapers to task for repeating 'lies originating in English papers' regarding the military campaign in Russia. He described Russian losses in the battle of Kharkov: '250,000 Soviet soldiers taken prisoner, and the capture of 1,200 armoured cars, 2,000 large guns, aeroplanes and other war materials'. He continued:

This was the fiercest battle fought in this war so far on the Eastern front, and the Russian soldiers were better equipped with arms and war materials than the Germans at Kiev last year [the Germans took the city of Kiev on 17 August 1941]. The Soviets, and more particularly the British and Americans, were so scared as a result of this defeat that they had not the courage to admit the catastrophe. It would be difficult to surpass the nonsense that is at present being broadcast by the London and New York radios, and I wonder if there is any person in either country still ready to believe those lies. The British and their allies must be so ignorant concerning military affairs that they cannot distinguish between victory and defeat. There is a prevalent opinion that the German Radio and Press are strictly censored. All I can say is that if nonsense of a similar sort were being published by the German radio and press, the people would break their radios and have no other use for the newspapers than to bring them to a certain place. It is a great pity that so many of these lies originating in English papers should also appear in the Irish papers. But apparently that cannot be helped. Therefore listen to our English and Gaelic news. Believe me when I say that the Soviets have suffered a great defeat in this latest battle.

It was natural for Hartmann to try and win listeners over from the BBC and Radio Éireann on the basis that there was more truth in the Irland-Redaktion's news. What he declined to tell his Irish listeners, however, was that as head of the Irish service he was obliged to attend radio managers meetings at which the daily Sprachregelungen (broadcasting directives) were handed down from the Propaganda Ministry along with war communiqués from the German High Command (OKW). The radio managers' meetings were presided over by Dr Toni Winkelnkemper, who from 1941 to 1945 was head of the RRG's foreign services. Winkelnkemper dominated proceedings dressed in full SS uniform.[14] Had Hartmann's audience been privy to what was happening behind the scenes at the Rundfunkhaus they might have been less inclined to swallow his claim that German Radio was not 'strictly censored'. In common with other radio managers, Hartmann was clearly under great pressure to toe the propaganda line. His use of a lesser known language could, in theory, have enabled him to resist Dr Winkelnkemper's demands but, in fact, Hartmann's talks, when translated, appear as little more than standard Nazi propaganda tailored for an Irish listenership.

Footnotes

1.   Letter to author from Lorna Swire, Reading, 15 July 1991.

2.   'Special Easter Broadcast in Irish Gaelic and English for Ireland', 5 March 1942 (IWM, file E88). For whatever reason, Hartmann had

chosen, twice in the same broadcast, to overlook the fact that the 1916 Rising took place on Easter Monday.

3. Despite her Belfast Catholic upbringing, Charleton ignored the fact that the Volunteers only became known as the IRA after the formation of the First Dáil in 1919. See Coogan, 1970, p. 44.

4. German broadcast to Ireland (third transmission), 6 March 1942 (DFA, 205/108).

5. Letter to author from Francis Stuart, 14 July 1994. Notwithstanding Stuart's denial, the *Rambles in Eirinn* broadcast, if widely heard in Ireland, could have proved embarrassing for MacBride. It is tempting to conclude that the broadcast was a ploy to pre-empt any criticism by MacBride of Stuart's own broadcasts which were due to commence just eleven days later, on 17 March 1942. The ploy — if such it was — may not have been of Stuart's own making.

6. Author's interview with Éimear Ó Broin, Dublin, 10 June 1992. As a teenager, Éimear Ó Broin regularly listened to the Irland-Redaktion's programmes in Dublin with his father León Ó Broin, the man who had shared a holiday cottage with Ludwig Mühlhausen in Teelin, Co. Donegal in 1937. León Ó Broin went on to become a noted historian and a senior civil servant — he was Secretary of the Department of Posts and Telegraphs from 1946 to 1967. His son Éimear later became staff conductor of the RTÉ symphony and light orchestras, and RTE singers.

7. Ní Mheara-Vinard, 1992, p. 194. In addition to *The Frost is All Over*, the Irish Army's wartime monitoring reports identify the following songs as having been broadcast from Germany to Ireland: *The Hills of Donegal* (sung by G. Sanderson), *Mother Machree, Danny Boy, There's No Place Like Home, A Tiny Sprig of Shamrock, It was Springtime in County Clare, The Kerry Dances, Kitty of Coleraine, I Know Where I'm Going* (sung by Sally O'Brien), *Ireland Mother Ireland, The Irish Emigrant*, and *Come Back to Erin*. A speaker named Sheila McCarney was also monitored reciting a poem entitled 'Everlasting Voices'.

8. Stuart was born in Australia of Protestant parents from County Antrim. He returned to Antrim as a child and grew up there. In other radio talks he referred to his links with County Wicklow where he lived with Iseult in the 1920s and 1930s.

9. O'Reilly memoirs in *Sunday Dispatch*, London, 20 July 1952, p. 2, col. 6.

10. 'Irish Pianist's Message to "Dear Mummy"', Brase in English to Éire, 4 May 1942 (PRONI, CAB 9CD/207 BBC MR). In 1939 Mona Brase had been sent by her parents to attend summer school in Germany to improve her command of German. As well as being studied by MI5 in London, the transcript of her broadcast was relayed to the Cabinet Office in Northern Ireland. MI5's suspicions may have been aroused by the following remarks in Brase's talk: 'From the photos which a friendly stranger has passed, you have already seen that I am no more the small child of former days. From my voice and words you will recognise that I have made progress also in every other respect... Moreover, we are assured that separation will not last long and we may feel again the happiness of each other's presence.' After studying the BBC's transcript of her remarks, Brase told the author: 'I was not a pianist, only a schoolgirl who happened to have got stuck in Germany when the war broke out. I was there only for the summer school holidays, staying with friends of my mother in Berlin, and too young to be let try and return on my own back to Ireland. My parents never believed a war would come and were not worried, so they let me stay on until it was too late. As regards the broadcast... the talk I gave sounds just like the style my foster father [her father, Colonel Fritz Brase, died in 1940] used, so he must have set it out in German for me to translate into English.' Mona Brase cannot recall the identity of the 'friendly stranger' who delivered photographs to her mother in Dublin but she thinks it may have been someone travelling to Switzerland who sent the pictures back via Portugal (Brase interview, 8 October 1991).

11. Author's interview with Hartmann, 21 October 1990.

12. Hartmann, in Irish Gaelic for Ireland, 24 May 1942 (IWM, E88). Padraig Ó Siochfhradha, a noted Gaelic scholar who wrote under the pen name of An Seabhac (the hawk), was apparently unaware that his translation of Wolfe Tone's diary was being used for propaganda purposes on German Radio. According to his son, he never met either Hartmann or Mühlhausen (letter to author from Mr Ken Ó Siochfhradha, Sandycove, Co Dublin, 8 May 1993).

13. G2 report entitled 'Notes on John Francis O'Reilly's activities in the Channel Islands and Germany', 31 December 1943, p. 2 (NA, DFA A52 I, G2/3824).

14. Schwipps, 1971, pp. 22-3, 33.

13

The Coup d'État That Never Happened

In mid-1942 John O'Reilly became involved in a bizarre incident in the Berlin studios in which a dramatic announcement of a planned coup d'état in Dublin by British sympathisers was first scheduled for delivery on air but then dropped at the last moment on orders from the Foreign Office. In his memoirs, O'Reilly recalled Dr Hartmann handing him a script to be broadcast.

On reading this I was astounded to see the names of prominent Irish and Anglo-Irish personalities who, it was stated in the script, were engaged in a plot to overthrow the Irish government and form a provisional pro-English government until British occupation forces arrived. This report, or script, came from the German Foreign Office. It was divided into two sections. The first part was to be broadcast that night and the remaining portion on the following night. The first part was, in fact, broadcast to Ireland by me. It consisted of a warning to the Irish people to be ready for an important disclosure on the following night. As I sat before the microphone on the following night with this document before me, and ready to broadcast, I heard a tap at the window of my cubicle. It was Dr Hartmann. He opened the door of the cubicle and, without comment, picked up the document from the table before me. He then substituted for it an innocuous commentary whose contents I cannot now recall. After the transmission I went to Dr Hartmann's office to find out the reason for the withdrawal of the sensational announcement at the last moment. He told me that a few minutes before I was due to broadcast the second half of the document, he had received an urgent telephone call from the Foreign Office to stop the broadcast 'at all costs'. I never learned the reason for this surprising action, nor what happened to make the Foreign Office authorities change their decision so suddenly. I was astonished. But I felt that if there were any truth in the allegation contained in the document, the Irish people and the Irish government should be fully warned.

The cancelled coup d'état talk may have been originally designed to spread confusion in official circles in Dublin and, perhaps, to throw suspicion on politicians such as James Dillon who opposed neutrality and was in favour of Ireland supporting the Allies. For whatever reason, it seems that Adolf Mahr got cold feet at the last minute and ordered Hartmann to cancel the broadcast. Back in Dublin 18 months later (having been flown home to County Clare by the Luftwaffe, ostensibly for a spying mission) O'Reilly told G2 interrogators in Arbour Hill prison about the coup d'état episode, but 'they scoffed at my story'.[1]

Hartmann explained after the war that he had come under pressure to include anti-Jewish material in the Irland-Redaktion's programmes. As such material was seldom broadcast to Ireland, one must accept at face value Hartmann's explanation that he resisted the pressure as far as possible. There were exceptions to the rule, however, such as the anti-Semitic 'Patrick Cadogan' talks in 1943, which Hartmann blames on William Joyce. A notable exception to Hartmann's 'no anti-Jewish material' rule came on the night of 19 July 1942, when Irish Army monitors picked up a broadcast by Susan Hilton, which included the following.

> In America there were and are millions of Jews. In the US the Jewish population, which was only 937,800 in 1897, was estimated in 1927 to be 4,228,029 and this figure must have been doubled during the past 15 years. Suppose then that there are eight million Jews in the US, and that is only a minimum estimate, it means that the population of the 26 Counties is only one third of the Jews in the US. In New York alone there were 1,873,390 Jews in 1927, now a safe estimate would be three million, almost the entire population of Ireland.

Although there had been occasional anti-Jewish references on programmes to Ireland before this one, Hilton's talk was the most blatant to date. The technique of giving listeners Jewish population statistics — with the inference that the exploding numbers were out of control — was standard Nazi propaganda designed to provide a raison d'être for Hitler's so-called final solution, the extermination of the Jews, whom Nazi philosophy regarded as Untermensch or sub-human. Susan Hilton herself told British military investigators in 1945:

> All my talks were sheer propaganda directed against the war and the Irish coming into the war, saying that it would do Ireland no good. Hartmann wanted me to attack England, and I was furnished with items of German news and typed material from the Foreign Office and Propaganda Ministry setting out the tendency of the day's propaganda I was to follow.[2]

Given the nature of her 19 July talk, it is possible that Hilton did not write it herself but that it was part of the material handed out daily to the Irland-Redaktion. Hartmann, presumably, took the view that minimal use of anti-Jewish material would keep the SS radio bosses off his back.

In Susan Hilton, Hartmann had found a malleable soul to do his bidding. It is worth noting that Hilton was the only member of the Irland-Redaktion to have arrived in occupied Europe as a prisoner of war — the ship on which she had been travelling from Britain to Burma in 1940 was captured by a German warship in the Indian Ocean — and, having first refused to undertake a spying mission to Ireland, she escaped further incarceration by agreeing to write articles and later to broadcast for German Radio. Francis Stuart noticed Hilton's 'fondness for drink' and it is clear from a number of sources that she was heavily dependent on alcohol.

Hilton's predicament is reflected in her letters to Ireland which reveal a depressed psyche. On 26 March 1942 she used official German Radio notepaper to write a letter to her brother Edward, then living at the Moat House in Oldcastle, County Meath. The letter read:

> My Dear Edward, by now you will have heard that I am here working at the above address [77 Kaiserdamm, Berlin]. Maybe you sometimes hear me. I speak mostly at 8.15 [p.m.] over the station Rennes and some other shortwave, but I never can remember... I am well and fortunate to be alive after the fun and games I have had all over the world. Cheerio, your many times drowned sister, Susan.[3]

As well as being read by the Gestapo, the letter was intercepted by British Intelligence who tipped off their Irish counterparts in G2. It threw an unwelcome spotlight on Edward Sweney who never received his sister's letter but did become the subject of an official investigation. G2's contacts with MI5 were well developed at that stage of the war and so it was a British official, not an Irish one, who was despatched to check up on Edward Sweney at his poultry farm in Oldcastle. Almost 50 years after the event, the latter recalled it in detail. The official sent to the Moat House was John Betjeman, then attached to the British diplomatic representation in Dublin, officially as a 'press and cultural attaché', but actually involved in intelligence work. Sweney remembers that Betjeman 'called at my place in the 1940s in a car when no one had cars, and asked whether the local church had pews in it or not. I told him I didn't know but suggested he could get a chair to stand on and look through the church windows to see for himself'.[4] Betjeman's question was a pretext to engage Sweney in conversation but the wily farmer did not take the bait. At around the same time Sweney also received a phone call from the German Minister in Dublin, Eduard Hempel, but he can no longer recall what Hempel said. Hempel, presumably, heard Susan Hilton's broadcasts or was tipped off about them by the authorities in Berlin or Dublin and decided to do some checking for himself.

Meanwhile, in Berlin, Susan Hilton was having doubts about the war and, in particular, any negative consequences that might arise for her after the conflict. On 19 May 1942 she wrote from her flat at Klopstockstrasse to her friend Biddy O'Kelly who lived with her parents at Pine Hill on the Vico Road in Dalkey, County Dublin:

> ... it is our parents' fault that there is a war now. Each generation makes mistakes and God knows we are suffering now... I write transmissions, perhaps you hear them. Every day there's something or other. At the moment they are running two of my series called "Have you forgotten?" and "Places in the News". Then I speak my own commentaries. I feel such a fool, but then at other times I think I am perhaps speaking to you and to other people I know. Try and tune in and let me know what you think and what other people think. I want to know whether I can show my face in Ireland after the war or not.

Later, at the Rundfunkhaus, she continued the letter, telling her friend of drinking bouts and billiard sessions with her Russian colleague Sonja Kowanka.

> I am sitting in my office now. The radio is playing softly and a Sondermeldung [special announcement] is coming through. There is a green tree looking in at the window. The traffic is rolling along the street. Night is coming and I am smoking my little pipe. I like smoking a pipe, it soothes me. The only thing that disturbs me is that when I raise my eyes I see maps on the wall, map after map. They seem to be part of my life now. I think when I die, a map will be found wrapped round my heart.[5]

When the secretary of the Irish Legation in Berlin, Eileen Walsh, investigated Susan Hilton's circumstances at about this time she reported that the broadcaster had 'sunk to a low level', but also noted that Hilton was far from being 100 per cent pro-German, adding: 'While she was willing to say what she thought of the British, she did not hesitate to tell the Germans what she thought of them'.[6]

Almost a month later, on 10 June 1942, Hilton wrote to her friend Biddy O'Kelly again, this time displaying obvious signs of depression.

> Never have I felt so utterly homesick and shut away as I do now. Biddy, nothing can ever make up to me for these years of unbelievable, soul destroying loneliness. I try to shake these morbid thoughts off me. I go to the races and gamble as hard as I can. I work hard so as to forget.

Hilton's descent into alcoholism and depression — leaving her increasingly at the mercy of her Nazi hosts — may go some way towards explaining why, just over a month later, she agreed to broadcast the talk on Jewish population statistics.

Hilton was due to part company with Hartmann and Mahr before the year was out, as were two of her colleagues, John O'Reilly and James Blair. O'Reilly was the first to go, deciding that after a year in the Irland-Redaktion he 'had become a little tired of the routine work of broadcasting every night'. The Kilkee man was soon to offer his services for a spying mission to Ireland, but another factor that led him to quit the radio was resentment over 'the unwarranted interference of the English section in our Irish section broadcasting'. O'Reilly recalled that while William Joyce was 'supremely indifferent to all competition', another English service staffer whom O'Reilly identified only as

> X, an Anglo-German [probably the Glasgow-born Nazi, Eduard Dietze, or the English-educated Wolff Mittler], resented the presence of our Irish section. On more than one occasion he tried to curtail our broadcasting. Eventually he succeeded in persuading the authorities to have our scripts brought under the control of the English section.

Hans Hartmann confirmed that all scripts prepared by his Irland-Redaktion had to be submitted for approval to the England-Redaktion before being broadcast, and added: 'The Irish department was no more than an appendix to the English department, and the censorship was done by the English department'.[7]

At the radio centre, O'Reilly told Hartmann of his decision to leave. After the war he wrote:

> I knew I could trust Dr Hartmann. He appeared to have considerable influence in the Foreign Office. He was a member of the National Socialist party and he was obviously attached to Ireland.

Alarmed at losing a genuine Irish member of his team of announcers — the only other one was Francis Stuart — Hartmann contacted Helmut Clissmann who was then attached to the German Army's Brandenburg Regiment but Clissmann, who knew Hartmann from his time in Dublin, was not able to intervene. Hartmann finally agreed to O'Reilly's departure on condition that he found someone Irish to replace him. The substitute was O'Reilly's friend, Liam Mullally, an English-language teacher at the Berlitz school in Berlin. As Mullally began work at the radio centre, O'Reilly made his way to Bremen on 17 September 1942 to begin training as an espionage agent for German naval intelligence.

While Hartmann was reluctant to let O'Reilly leave, he later had no option but to get rid of Susan Hilton and James Blair following an embarrassing incident in the Berlin studios. Hilton herself said nothing of the incident after the war apart from stating that Blair had been sacked 'for being incompetent, although he was competent'. But the facts behind the sackings emerged later in the war when O'Reilly told G2 officers that:

Hilton proved unreliable and fond of drink, and Blair's services were not satisfactory as he was believed to be getting stale. Following a scene in which Susan Hilton used endearing terms to Blair while he was in the announcing box and still on the air, their services were dispensed with.[8]

Hilton may have been the worse for drink when she made the blunder on air, or it may have been a deliberate mistake to free her from the Rundfunkhaus she had grown to hate. For his part, James Blair later found another broadcasting job with the Nazis' Inter Radio company based in Graz, Austria. Hilton joined him there in 1943.

Footnotes

1.   O'Reilly memoirs in *Sunday Dispatch*, 27 July 1952, p. 2.

2.   Susan Hilton (née Sweney) statement to MI5 at Liebenau internment camp, Germany, 30 June 1945 (LCD CRIM 1/1745).

3.   The 'many times drowned' reference is to the fact that the vessel *Kemmendine* — aboard which Mrs Hilton was sailing from Britain to join her husband in Burma — was scuttled by the German raider *Atlantis* (after she and the other passengers and crew were taken prisoner) in the Indian Ocean on 13 July 1940. Hilton was later put aboard a German prison ship the *Tirranna* (another victim of the *Atlantis*) which, in turn, was sunk off the French port of Royan on 22 September 1940 by a British submarine, *HMS Tuna*. (Hilton/Sweney file, MA, G2/4102; and Hilton statements to MI5 in LCD file, CRIM 1/1745). Further details of Mrs Hilton's travels are contained in Mohr, 1955. Long after the war, Mrs Hilton joked to friends that when rescue boats arrived to take survivors ashore at Royan, she said: 'No thanks, it's safer to swim' (author's interview with Margaret Schaffhauser, 9 November 1992).

4.   Author's interview with Edward Sweney, Oldcastle, Co. Meath, 9 June 1991. In the 1960s John Betjeman was appointed as Britain's Poet Laureate.

5.   Hilton to O'Kelly, 19 May 1942 (MA, G2/4102). According to a local resident, Mrs Natasha Weyer-Brown, Biddy O'Kelly's father, Joe, was 'anti-British, pro-Nazi and a friend of the German ambassador [Dr Hempel]'. Alone among residents of the Vico Road, an exclusive

coastal strip nine miles south of Dublin, Joe O'Kelly deliberately kept his house lights on during the blackout to help guide German bombers to UK targets. Mrs Weyer-Brown says: 'People on the coast were pro-Allies. They had an unwritten law observing the blackout, thus not helping the Germans. They were annoyed to discover that Joe O'Kelly had all his lights blazing to guide German raiders' (author's interview with Mrs Weyer-Brown, Vico Road, Dalkey, County Dublin, 14 April 1995).

6.   Extract from report of undated interview with Miss Eileen Walsh, secretary to William Warnock (MA, G2/4535, 4102).

7.   Hartmann interview, 28 December 1990. The extent of the England-Redaktion's interference in Irland-Redaktion affairs is disputed by Hartmann's wartime assistant, Hilde Spickernagel, who notes that: 'The English section handed the translation of the daily Wehrmachtsbericht [Defence Forces' report] to the Irland-Redaktion but, to my knowledge, there was no other attempt by the English section to influence the programmes of the Irland-Redaktion'. Dr Spickernagel admits, however, that she 'never took part' in the radio managers' daily conferences, which Hartmann attended, and so she could 'only guess' at who handed down the broadcasting directives there, and 'whatever may have been discussed at those daily conferences' (Spickernagel letter, 9 February 1992).

8.   O'Reilly file (NA, DFA A52 I).

14

Through Irish Eyes: Francis Stuart's View from Berlin

As he pondered the year 1942, Francis Stuart may have welcomed the intellectual stimulation of preparing radio talks as a diversion from the boredom of teaching. On 11 July 1942 he wrote in his diary: 'My work at the university is often a nervous strain. The debate class means trying to get a few silent girl students [most male students had been drafted into the army] to open their mouths about some God forsaken subject and keeping this up for three quarters of an hour'. Over at the Rundfunkhaus, on 24 July 1942, he told his listeners that

> in the long run we [the Irish] shall only gain by our refusal to be interested by the whole conflict which is raging in the Anglo-Saxon countries. A little more patience and endurance, especially for those of you in the North, and our place in the world will be securer than ever before.

By mid-1942 Stuart had decided to accede to Hartmann's request to contribute a series of weekly talks to Ireland under the title 'Through Irish Eyes'. The writer's diary entry for 1 August 1942 noted:

> Wrote the first of weekly talks to broadcast to Ireland. Had lunch with Frank Ryan and discussed these with him. He agreed that they must not be propaganda in the sense that the flood of war journalism from all sides has become, and that of course they must support our neutrality. He suggested, and I fully agreed, that there must be no anti-Russian bias.

The lack of any anti-Russian bias would eventually lead — in January 1944 — to Stuart parting company with Hartmann. But for the moment Hartmann was content to accept Stuart's line, commenting after the war that the Irish writer 'was a sincere man and often didn't hold back with criticism but what I realised was that he particularly liked the Russians'. Ryan and Stuart were both taking a risk in not falling in with the general anti-Soviet propaganda line from Berlin at that time, but their decision was understandable. Frank Ryan belonged to the leftist Republican Congress wing of the IRA in the 1930s and his socialist tendencies led him to take up the fight against Franco in the Spanish civil war. Despite his left wing views, Ryan owed his life to the Nazis who had saved him from death row in Burgos prison. In the circumstances, there was little Ryan could do but play along with the Germans in the hope of returning home. As for Francis Stuart, although he did not tell his German hosts as much, he felt Russia's role in the conflict was an 'honourable' one since the Soviets had been attacked first by Hitler. While this view would not have gone down too well with Dr Winkelnkemper in the Rundfunkhaus, Stuart did stick to his beliefs in this respect by never using his talks to attack the Russians.

Launching his weekly talks on 5 August 1942, Stuart told listeners he had no 'desire to join the ranks of the propagandists' and went on to spell out why he had chosen to work in Berlin after the war had begun:

> I am heartily sick and disgusted with the old order under which we've been existing and which had come to be from the great financial powers in whose shadows we lived. If there had to be a war, then I wanted to be among these people who had also had enough of the old system and who, moreover, claimed that they had a new and better one... I had begun to see that no internal policy for Ireland could ever be completely successful unless joined to an external one that would not shed our ancient links with Europe and European culture... I not only want to bring something of Germany and German ideas to you but I also try, in Berlin University and elsewhere, to make people here, and especially young Germans, conscious of Ireland and interested in her problems and outlook.

Indulging in a bout of homesickness — it was over two and a half years since he had seen Ireland — Stuart spoke of 'the Antrim bog lands where I spent my boyhood, a small farmhouse and a row of trees around one side of it for shelter, and a bicycle leaning up against a whitewashed wall. I feel now that the very mud on the tyres of that bike is sacred...'. Then, speaking directly to his former IRA comrades, Stuart added:

> ... to those comparative few who not only love Ireland but who are ready to sacrifice all for the freedom of Irish soil, I do not flatter myself that I can teach you anything. I will only say this, that you may now feel isolated and alone, but have patience. The past has belonged to the politicians and the financiers, the future is going to be yours.

While a study of Stuart's talks in the 1942-44 period reveals that he stuck to his pledge not to include any anti-Russian bias, Hartmann and Mahr ensured there would be no pro-Russian bias either. At the same time as Stuart was beginning his weekly talks, the Nazis' Sicherheitsdienst or security service was reporting that in Ireland 'BBC propaganda has no influence. German broadcasts are preferred'.[1] In Dublin meanwhile, Eduard Hempel, the German Minister, was monitoring the broadcasts from Berlin and advising the Foreign Office on reception strength and suitable programme content. As early as Christmas 1939 Hempel had advised the English service of German Radio to play up the fact that people in Ireland were sending 'cigarettes and Christmas gifts to German POWs in England'. In mid-1940, when Hempel feared a British invasion of Ireland, he 'urged Berlin to cut down propaganda that played up the British threat and suggested German assistance in reunifying the island'. In fact, the idea that Ireland would be reunited following a German victory was a key theme in Mühlhausen's talks from 1939 to 1941.

Early on in the propaganda war, Hempel had complained that German propaganda techniques were at times flat-footed and he criticised the research and analysis that went into the broadcasts. He told Stuart to make a plea to the proper authorities in Berlin to show more sensitivity in their transmissions. Hempel had also advised against anti-English propaganda on the radio but this was disregarded by the Irland-Redaktion.[2]

On 30 August 1942, Stuart attacked the death sentences passed in Belfast on six IRA men found guilty of murdering an RUC constable, and appealed directly to Churchill to lift them.

For its size, Ireland has poured out more blood, tears and sweat than any other nation. We do not know whether, having asked your own people for such endurance, you believe you can give a final recompense. That is not our affair. What is our affair is that Irish blood, sweat and tears should not have been spilt in vain. And we tell you now that the blood of those six Irishmen will be about the last that you and your fellow statesmen will have the opportunity to spill within the seclusion of prison walls.

One of the six IRA men, 19 year old Thomas Williams, was executed in Belfast on 2 September 1942, prompting the following commentary from the Irish service the next day:

German public opinion has reacted very keenly to the tragic news of the Belfast execution yesterday, and the stirring reports of anti-British and anti-American demonstrations all over Ireland which came in today. Horror and indignation at this newest act of British terrorism have given room to a sincere feeling of admiration for the indomitable Irish spirit which revealed itself in these acts of protest and rebellion.

On 17 September 1942, Francis Stuart noted in his Berlin diary that 'a message came through from Hempel saying my radio comments on the Belfast death sentences had gute Wirkung (a good effect). If my talks have even a minute influence in helping to keep our neutrality they aren't just waste, as I often think'. Stuart's personal diary revealed what his broadcasts never did — that, after six months at the Rundfunkhaus, he was developing doubts about the value of his talks to Ireland. He would have been buoyed up, however, to know just how closely his words were being listened to by the authorities in Dublin. As 1942 drew to a close, Stuart's broadcasts were being monitored in Dublin, not so much by a loyal audience as by officials at the Department of External Affairs and G2. On 2 December Stuart commented on prison sentences passed on three IRA men, including the IRA's Northern commander, Hugh McAteer:

These three members of the IRA, sentenced for so-called high treason... belong to the same great tradition as the soldiers of the past who made it possible for a part of our country to stay out of this war... These men who have just been sentenced by a British court belong to the advance guard of our nation... The time is past when any of you can look on the men without sympathy or understanding... The time is past for these small internal hostilities.

We must stand firm in the face of all that threatens us as one people.

Stuart did not mince his words. The clear message was that Ireland was threatened by Britain, not by Germany. But unknown to him, for the first time since starting his weekly talks, Stuart had forced the Department of External Affairs to sit up and take notice. Four weeks after the broadcast, on 30 December 1942, the Assistant Secretary of External Affairs, Frederick Boland, met Dr Hempel to protest about Stuart's propaganda line. In his report of that meeting, Boland wrote:

> I told Herr Hempel that, while it was quite true to say that large sections of opinion in this country resented and protested against the imprisonment by the Six County authorities of men for activities arising out of the crime of partition, it might be regarded, even by the same sections of opinion, as quite a different thing for Germany to champion the cases of such men. Hugh McAteer was said to be a member of the IRA. In a recent IRA leaflet he was described as chief of staff of that organisation and his name was on the list of men wanted by the police here in connection with the murder of Detective Sergeant O'Brien. That being so, the holding up of McAteer on the German radio as a hero was likely to be resented by many people here and to furnish a concrete example for use by those who charged Germany with aiding and abetting the IRA against the Government.

According to Boland, Hempel 'quite saw the point and agreed with what I said. He thought it very probable that neither Francis Stuart nor anybody else in Germany knew who Hugh McAteer was. I gathered he would draw Berlin's attention to the point'.[3]

While diplomats in Dublin argued the toss over Francis Stuart's comments on the sentencing of three IRA men in Belfast, no one in the Irland-Redaktion seemed overly concerned about the main thrust of the war. For example, Rommel's retreat from El Alamein (2-3 November 1942) as well as the mammoth battles involving the German Sixth Army at Stalingrad went unreported by Hartmann's team. The Stalingrad commentaries for Ireland only began in 1943 once the Germans had lost the battle.

Stuart's diary for the period just before Christmas 1942 reveals that he was more concerned with press criticism of his broadcasts than anything else: 'Was shown an April number of the illustrated

English weekly *Picture Post,* in which it said the Irish were not impressed by my promises. What promises, for heaven's sake? But I shall have to get used to worse than that and from more serious critics'. His diary for 19 December 1942 shows that Hartmann was continuing to screen Stuart's talks carefully:

> I mentioned the refusal by Irish government to renew my passport in my weekly broadcast talk [script], and showed it to Hartmann who rang just now and said it would have to be taken out because the British must not get to know of it. For all I know it may have been done on the advice of the British.

The lack of a valid passport was the least of Stuart's problems as the war dragged on into its fourth year. It was now impossible for him to return home, and he resigned himself to seeing out the remainder of the war as a guest of the Third Reich.

Footnotes

1. Carter, 1977, p. 97.

2. Duggan, 1975, p. 209; Fisk, 1983, pp. 403-4.

3. Frederick Boland's minutes of meeting with Hempel, 30 December 1942 (DFA 205/108). Details of McAteer's status in Coogan, 1970, p. 231, and Fisk, 1983, p. 378.

15

The 'Triumph' of Stalingrad

By the time 1943 dawned, Hartmann had lost three of his old broadcasting team — O'Reilly, Hilton and Blair — but he had gained two others. On 4 January a secret memo about German Radio's Irish service, drawn up by William Warnock at the request of Frederick Boland, was passed to G2. As well as Francis Stuart, it named James Blair, Liam Mullally, Nora O'Mara, Hans Hartmann and Hilde Spickernagel. While Warnock made it his business to know what was going on in the Irland-Redaktion — there were, after all, few Irish people in wartime Berlin — he had, unwittingly or otherwise, helped the service to sound more authentic by allowing Stuart to listen to Radio Éireann programmes on the Legation's radio set. In addition, Warnock's secretary, Eileen Walsh, regularly delivered Irish newspapers to Francis Stuart so he could keep up to date on what was happening at home.[1] According to his memo, Warnock did not realise that Blair had been sacked, but he was right about O'Reilly's replacement, Liam Mullally, as well as the fact that Hartmann's assistant Hilde Spickernagel (née Poepping) occasionally read the news bulletins. Unknown to Warnock, Dr Spickernagel was about to leave Berlin to have a baby and she would not return to Hartmann's service.

The new and unknown quantity was 25 year old Nora O'Mara whom Stuart put up in his flat when she was pregnant and had been abandoned by her Ukrainian lover. O'Mara had worked as an actress in Vienna and was a member of Goebbels' Reich Theatre Chamber, a body that ensured only Nazi sympathisers got acting jobs. She had also worked as a secretary for Hermann Goertz before he flew to Ireland on a spying mission in 1940. During the war O'Mara remained something of a mystery, for example, giving her birthplace on official documentation variously as Philadelphia and London. Despite her claim to be 'involved in regular radio broadcasts to Ireland',[2] the only record of her work amounts to two broadcasts in mid-1943 made under her assumed name of Róisín. Susan Hilton later claimed that she had written radio scripts for O'Mara.

The Irland-Redaktion also gained a new listener in this period. On 9 January 1943 Maurice Irvine took over from BBC monitor Jane Charleton who returned to Belfast — homesick, according to Irvine. The new recruit met Charleton — a friend since childhood — in his native Belfast and, on hearing she was leaving the BBC monitoring service, applied for, and got, her job. Unlike either Angus Matheson or Jane Charleton, Maurice Irvine did not have a university background in Gaelic studies and had learned Irish from the Christian Brothers in Belfast. The 24 year old monitor was looking for adventure having recently left a 'boring' job in the Civil Service in Dublin. Irvine was to remain at the BBC until July 1944 when MI5 judged it was no longer fruitful to tune in to the Irland-Redaktion.

Meanwhile, Hartmann still had a loyal, if small, team around him and would need every member of it to tackle the turbulent waters that lay ahead as the tide of war turned against the Third Reich. With fewer military successes to announce, Berlin's Irish team was put in the unenviable position of having to make crushing defeats sound like glorious victories. Hitler had launched his invasion of Russia on 22 June 1941. Eighteen months later the fate of his Eastern campaign hinged on the fighting at Stalingrad, one of the epic battles of World War II. In mid-September 1942, German Army group B had entered the suburbs of Stalingrad but their advance was checked in mid-November when the Russians opened their counter offensive to defend the city. By 22 November, units of the Red Army had met up at Kalach, thus encircling the German Sixth Army in Stalingrad. In mid-December 1942 the German General, Erich von Manstein, opened a counter attack to relieve the Sixth Army. By February 1943, however, the battle was over with General von Paulus surrendering the remains of the Sixth Army to Soviet troops. The actual surrender, on 2 February, merely confirmed what had been known in Germany for some time — that the eastern campaign was foundering, along with Hitler's hopes of winning the wider war.

In common with German Radio's other European services, Hartmann and Stuart broadly followed Goebbels' directive to describe the defeat at Stalingrad in terms of German bravery and triumph. On 3 February 1943 the Propaganda Minister had instructed the German media to make sure that 'the heroic struggle of Stalingrad will become the greatest epic of German history'.[3]

Tuning into Berlin's programmes on 30 January 1943, an Irish Army monitor noted that 'Francis Stuart, with but scant apology, launched into a eulogy on the German Sixth Army in Stalingrad... thus more or less identifying himself with pro-German propaganda. From this date, although still maintaining that he is no propagandist, Stuart has been steadily and openly pro-German'. The army officer could hardly draw any other conclusion having heard Stuart say that: 'What the men, officers and generals of the German Sixth Army are doing at Stalingrad is altogether beyond the ordinary standards of bravery'. On 6 February, four days after von Paulus surrendered, Stuart was back on the air telling Irish listeners that:

> Last Wednesday the German people received news of the end at Stalingrad. If I were a German I would be proud to belong to a nation which could produce such men. As it is, I am glad to be among them. If Ireland is to come nearer Europe, two things are necessary, a better understanding in Ireland of Europe, especially of Germany, and a better understanding of Ireland on the Continent. Besides speaking to Ireland about Germany, I speak to Berlin University students every week about Ireland. Today I spoke of Liam Lynch and Cathal Brugha, of Yeats and Synge and Pearse, for a nation's soul is revealed in its soldiers and poets. I would refer again to Stalingrad. The Irish would understand what the German people felt. This has moved Germany more than any other event of the war, for while such victories as the fall of Paris might be attributed to the perfection of the German war machine, this is a triumph of flesh and blood.

Hartmann also weighed in with much the same propaganda, translated into Irish, saying that the bravery of German troops in holding down hundreds of thousands of Russian soldiers for two months 'would never be forgotten'. He praised 'the spirit of the Stalingrad defenders' adding, 'when nothing else was left these men defended themselves with knives against Soviet guns and aircraft. The bravery of these men was saving Europe from Bolshevism'. On 6 February, Hartmann gave Irish listeners a dose of the red scare tactics:

> Germany has suffered a severe blow. What is the opinion of Europe on the situation now? Some people are still blind to the danger confronting them. They imagine they could defend their own little countries if it were necessary. But other people are more sensible. It can be said that great uneasiness is spreading in Europe. And this uneasiness will certainly increase, although Mr Churchill is doing his best to weaken the minds of people who feel it.

On Wednesday, 24 February 1943 Irish Army monitors tuned into a comedy sketch on the Irland-Redaktion entitled 'The Lady Interviewer' in which it was noticed that 'the following passage was completely out of tune with the rest of the script':

Maid: I have a young man.

Lady: What is the name of this prince?

Maid: Jobson.

Lady: Not one of the Jobsons of North Dublin?

Maid: No, he comes from Arlen way.

Lady: Do you read much?

Maid: Not much. Mostly the *Irish Independent* and *Tit Bits*.

Despite spotting these references, the G2 officers did not bother to check that day's *Irish Independent* for clues as to the reason for the strange broadcast. Had they done so they would have found an unusual notice for the Red Bank Restaurant in Dublin — one of the favourite pre-war haunts of Nazi members of the German colony. It read: 'Red Bank Restaurant. Sunday 1–9. New Lounge'. Since the Red Bank hardly ever advertised in that newspaper, the advertisement could have been aimed at alerting German sympathisers to a meeting there four days later on Sunday, 28 February. At the time German Naval Intelligence was preparing to send John O'Reilly home to Ireland on a spying mission. Was the Red Bank meeting convened to prepare a secret welcoming party for the Kilkee man? In the event, O'Reilly's mission was postponed until December 1943.[4]

Meanwhile, anxious to find a diversion after the doom of Stalingrad, Stuart and Hartmann must have welcomed the approach of St. Patrick's Day 1943 with some relief. Stuart captured the tone by recalling the 'American occupation of the Six Counties' a year earlier, along with the hanging of Thomas Williams in Belfast.

> We have shared all these emotions with you... In all this we are one family. But even though we are far from home, we know there will be many of you who for a few hours will forget everything in the excitement of a game of hurley, the first flat racing of the season, or whatever other sport you may decide on to celebrate the holiday. And, my God, that is what we would like to be doing too — to forget this war and all the rest of it, at Croke Park, or Baldoyle, or wherever it might be. And one day we will. One day we will have a great hurley match, or a great race meeting to celebrate peace, and we will hold it outside Belfast, to celebrate the return of the Six Counties.[5]

That St Patrick's Day, the Irland-Redaktion tried more 'red scare' material and — flying in the face of what had befallen Belgium, Holland and Luxembourg — sought to assure listeners that Germany respected the rights of small neutral states.

> The fear of Bolshevism grows in proportion to its proximity. The new order is already established in the hearts of those determined to preserve their homes and culture. Some agitators have been referring to the position of neutral countries, especially Spain and Ireland, and saying that they would prove good jumping off grounds for an Allied expedition in Europe. Germany has always respected the rights of neutrals and will always do so in future. Britain and America do not hesitate to violate the rights of small nations in their endeavours to widen the sphere of the war. The position of Ireland on the outer rim of Europe is unique. The Irish resolve to keep out of the war has been categorically stated by de Valera. Everyone in Germany understands this viewpoint. The hardships imposed by the war on Ireland are serious. Our sympathies for Ireland are deep, for we realise that for centuries her people have been suffering from brutal British oppression. Today, on St

Patrick's Day, we can assure the sons and daughters of Éire that
they have a definite spot in every German heart.

Throughout April, Hartmann kept up a steady stream of talks in
Irish on a variety of subjects. On 13 April he scoffed at Allied attempts
to open up a second front, reminding Irish listeners that 'German
soldiers stand ready to repel any attack, and ready too, to attack
England'. In fact, the plan to invade England, codenamed Operation
Sea Lion, had finally been abandoned a year earlier on 13 February
1942.[6]

On 17 April, Hartmann accused 'the Jewish Bolsheviks and their
English friends' of remaining silent about the Katyn massacre of
Polish Army officers, adding:

> London and Moscow have put their heads together to concoct a
> plausible excuse, but the only thing they can think of is to blame
> it on the Germans, or to say that there were prehistoric graveyards
> in the vicinity, and that it is these which the Germans have found.
> No one has ever heard of prehistoric corpses shot through the
> neck or with Polish Army uniforms. Nothing more cynical has
> ever been uttered. It is a cynicism of which only Jewish Bolsheviks
> could be capable.

Hartmann was right in saying the Nazis did not carry out the Katyn
forest massacre, but it would take another 45 years for the truth finally
to emerge when the Soviet leader, Mikhail Gorbachev, formally
admitted Russia's wartime responsibility in the affair.

On 20 April 1943 Hartmann was praising Hitler:

> This is the Führer's 54th birthday, and this is an occasion for us to
> return him thanks for all he has done for us, and to pray to God to
> give him health and strength during the coming year to work for
> his people. With most great men, people see only their glory.
> They tend to forget all the hardship and suffering they may have
> endured. You in Ireland have had many great men, perhaps more
> than any other nation on earth. Therefore, I believe you will regard
> the struggle of the German nation and the work of the Führer with
> understanding... The whole German nation is engaged in a
> desperate struggle under the leadership of the Führer, but everyone
> in Germany has absolute trust in his power to clear away all
> difficulties in the way of Germany and of Europe.

Such material was standard fare on German Radio's foreign and
domestic services which always marked the birthdays of senior Nazi

figures such as Hitler, Goebbels and Goering. After the war, Hartmann described his role in the Nazi propaganda machine as 'accidental', and he may well have felt uneasy in being obliged to read out eulogies to Hitler — particularly as his friends in the Gaeltacht and in Dublin were listening. In reality, by mid-1943 few doubters, including Hartmann, would have had 'absolute trust' in Hitler's ability to win the war.

Footnotes

1.   Was the assistance given to Stuart by Warnock and Eileen Walsh as inadvertent as it appeared? At that stage of the war Stuart often played golf with the two Irish Legation officials. He told this author that Eileen Walsh 'always kept me informed about matters at the Legation and Irish affairs, as we shared the same pension [boarding house] for a time' (Stuart interview, 19 June 1992). But was there more to it than that? Did all three, consciously or subconsciously, share a certain pro-German bias? Dan Binchy had left Berlin in 1932 disgusted by what he saw as Hitler's 'opportunism' (Keogh, 1988, pp. 29-33). Binchy's successors at the Drakesstrasse Legation, however, do not appear to have shared his abhorrence of Nazism. Charles Bewley, as we have seen, was sacked by de Valera in 1939 for his pro-Nazi outlook. Even the Secretary of the Department of External Affairs in Dublin, Joe Walshe, 'was not renowned for any deep philosophical repugnance to national socialism', according to Lee (1989, p. 248) who adds that: '[Joe] Walshe's tenderness towards the new masters of the continent in 1940 also presumably found expression in the performance of the Chargé d'Affaires in Berlin, William Warnock, whose "unquestionable" hostility to Britain could easily be interpreted as sympathy for national socialism'. As for the Legation's secretary, Eileen Walsh from Youghal, she was struck by the power of the Jews in Germany when she arrived in Berlin in 1933, as she stated in an interview with the author (10 July 1992): 'There was a lot of poverty, you know, really. The people were very poor and the Jews really had control, had everything. There is no doubt about it, they had. The poor Germans coming out of university had no hope of a job.'

According to Eileen Walsh, Bewley 'was always very pro-German and anti-British... the Department [of External Affairs] wanted to get rid of him'. Although Bewley had been at Oxford with the then British

Chargé d'Affaires in Berlin, he [Bewley] was 'never very friendly with him'. Walsh described Bewley as 'quite eccentric' 'very brillant' and 'biased towards Germany'. In addition, Walsh said Bewley lived in great style in Berlin: 'He kept quite a big staff, including a butler' and 'he was an art collector'. Warnock, according to Walsh, 'was always neutral' and 'never met Ribbentrop'. Eileen Walsh left the Irish Legation in August 1943, after ten years service in Berlin, to return to Dublin.

2.   Ní Mheara-Vinard, 1992, p. 193. In her memoirs, published in 1992, O'Mara claimed her Irish father died fighting for the British Army in World War I (p. 117) and that she was later adopted by the British General, Sir Ian Hamilton (who commanded the ill-fated Gallipoli campaign in the First World War).

3.   Balfour, 1979, p. 309.

4.   Captain John Smyth, 'German Broadcasts to Ireland', memo dated 1 April 1943 (MA, G2/X/0127 FWB part 3). While Captain Smyth and his G2 colleagues spotted the unusual references, they do not appear to have followed them up. There is no evidence in files of the period of either G2 or the Special Branch having carried out surveillance at the Red Bank on Sunday, 28 February 1943. The broadcast reference to the *Irish Independent* and the Red Bank advertisement in the paper on the same day could hardly have been a coincidence since the restaurant was not a regular advertiser in the paper. The last time an advertisement for the Red Bank had appeared in the *Irish Independent* was on 2 December 1942, some three months previously. It is worth noting that another advertisement for the restaurant appeared in the *Irish Independent* a week later on Wednesday, 3 March 1943, with the same wording: 'Red Bank Restaurant. Sunday 1 — 9. New Lounge'. This could have referred to another meeting to advise of the cancellation of O'Reilly's landing by German naval intelligence due to a 20-hour Allied bombing raid on the naval base at Wilhelmshaven on 25 and 26 February (*Irish Times*, 27 February 1943, p. 3, col. 5). It appears that the Red Bank advertisement was not the only example of coded messages being used on the Irland-Redaktion. On 4 August 1943, while O'Reilly was being trained for his rescheduled mission to Ireland, the radio service put out a talk on Sir Roger Casement. The vital clue was that in 1916 O'Reilly's father, a retired RIC man, Bernard O'Reilly, had arrested Casement shortly after his arrival in Kerry from a U-boat. Was this a tip-off that an attempt would be made to land O'Reilly in

Clare? The answer would appear to be yes. The Casement broadcast was done by 'Patrick Cadogan' (see Chapter 18) a cover name used by William Joyce (Lord Haw Haw) when addressing what he termed his 'followers' in Ireland. In his own memoirs, O'Reilly recalled meeting Joyce in Berlin 'one sunny afternoon, late in August 1943... "I hear you are returning to Ireland", he [Joyce] remarked casually. It was now my turn to feel startled. How did Joyce get this secret information? It was shared by a select few' (*Sunday Dispatch*, 20 July 1952, p. 2). It is clear from this recollection — written just nine years after the event — that Joyce was one of the 'select few' privy to O'Reilly's mission. In addition, the Irland-Redaktion occasionally serenaded listeners with a song entitled 'It was Springtime in County Clare'. When the attempt to land O'Reilly from a U-boat was dropped, the plan later resurfaced in the form of a parachute drop. O'Reilly was eventually flown to Ireland, from Rennes in occupied Brittany, in a Luftwaffe bomber. The parachute jump landed him near his home town of Kilkee on 16 December 1943. His father, Bernard, handed him over to the police and collected a £500 reward. John O'Reilly spent that Christmas in Dublin's Arbour Hill prison (O'Reilly memoirs, *Sunday Dispatch,* June to December 1952).

5.   Stuart, in English for Ireland, 16 March 1943 (PRONI CAB 9CD/207 BBC MR). Curiously, Stuart's vision of peaceful people enjoying sporting pursuits was similar to de Valera's famous 'comely maidens' speech which was broadcast the following day to America. In that talk, the Irish leader spoke of 'a land whose countryside would be bright with cosy homesteads, whose fields and villages would be joyous with the sounds of industry, with the romping of sturdy children, the contests of athletic youths, the laughter of comely maidens... ' (Lee, 1989, p. 334). As regards Stuart's comments, in 1942 and 1943, on the execution of IRA man Thomas Williams, Fisk (1983, p. 397) makes the point that 'the Axis powers [through their radio stations] displayed no parallel sympathy for IRA men executed in Éire on the orders of de Valera's government'.

6.   For details of Operation Sea Lion, see Cooper, 1978, pp. 246-9, 254-6.

16

Berlin's Advice:
Don't Vote Fine Gael

When de Valera called a general election for 22 June 1943, Francis Stuart began a series of talks to coincide with the run up to polling day. Of the many talks he had broadcast in the previous 13 months, only his comments on the IRA leader Hugh McAteer had prompted a mild protest by External Affairs. But when the writer committed what the Irish government saw as 'an unwarrantable interference in our internal affairs', things took a more serious turn, culminating in a formal diplomatic protest to Berlin.

Stuart launched his election offensive on 10 April, telling his listeners:

> I have never in these talks taken any sides in party politics and I'm certainly not going to do so now. As a matter of fact until we are a free and united nation I don't see how we can have, anyway, these party politics in Ireland because there can only be one aim of any party and that is the return of the Six Counties and the independence of our whole island from foreign domination. If there is any party or any individual candidate whose aim is less than this or different to this then I hope and believe that you will show the true spirit of Ireland by rejecting these people. That must be, and I believe will be, the first consideration before you in the coming election. The second will, I think, be your desire to remain out of this war, and I share that desire with you... It is not my business to go into detail about who you will vote for but in general I will only say that those who during the last years have shown themselves most determined to keep the 26 Counties of Ireland

outside the influence of the great financial powers are those best fitted to guide you through the rest of this world crisis. We must not forget that an election confined to the 26 Counties cannot be the full and free expression of the people of Ireland. It's only a makeshift and not a very satisfactory one at that. And secondly I think that in voting you should also give special preferences to those men who have shown themselves sincerely concerned for the welfare of the whole people of Ireland, and reject those who seem to look on the question of unemployment as a decree of destiny which is outside their power to do anything about. But above all don't think I am taking it on myself to try to dictate to you how to vote. I have no such idea. It is simply that the very fact of my having been at what I may call the centre of Europe during most of this war has given me a kind of bird's eye view of Ireland and events at home that may have a certain interest and value for you. I am far from Ireland and beyond the reach of all the opposing camps, the party cries, and I see clearly that in reality we have only need of one party, a party that stands for a free and united Ireland.[1]

On 8 May, Stuart had more advice for voters.

It is no good believing that party [Fine Gael] protesting that they too have always advocated neutrality... the small section that believe in a close co-operation between us and the great Atlantic powers should give Fine Gael their one vote. And the handful of Dáil members with this outlook are or have been members of this party... I do not for a moment anticipate any such gains [for Fine Gael], but on the contrary I think that this party will dwindle into insignificance... the overwhelming majority of you are at one in your wish for a free and united country and as far as I know there isn't one who'd ever threaten this except a handful of so-called Irishmen either belonging to or in touch with the Fine Gael party.

As far as de Valera and his ministers — who were of course regularly circulated with transcripts of the talks from Berlin — were concerned, Stuart had gone too far. The government in Dublin decided to make a formal protest about the broadcasts. This time there would be no discreet talk with Hempel in Iveagh House — the protest note would be handed directly to the Foreign Office in Berlin, ironically the location where de Valera's own civil servant, Adolf Mahr, was now in charge of radio propaganda to Ireland.

On 27 May the terms of the protest were cabled by Frederick Boland to William Warnock at the Irish Legation in Berlin, as follows:

Francis Stuart has been making broadcasts to this country
discussing the forthcoming elections and advising people to vote
against Fine Gael. Such broadcasts are an unwarrantable
interference in our internal affairs and are apt to prove most
embarrassing and harmful to the government. Please act
immediately to ensure that nothing of the kind will be broadcast
in future.[2]

To the government's dismay Boland's cable was too late to stop
yet another election broadcast by Stuart on 29 May, just over three
weeks before polling. In this talk he kept up the pressure on Fine
Gael.

Even if these elections were to result in our most reactionary party
getting into power, which however will certainly not be the case,
it would not mean that Ireland as a nation would renounce her
struggle towards unity and independence. It would simply mean
that the struggle would become even more difficult and the ends
be delayed. Most of our politicians have made election speeches
in which one might think that our existence as a nation depended
on them remaining in power. That is certainly not so. The most
that any political party can do is to remain faithful in all their
legislative activities to the spirit of Irish nationalism, as expressed
both for and suffered for, through the centuries until today. They
are not inventors of this spirit, they are not even the custodians, so
to speak, of it, for you are that. The most that they can do is to see
that the official policy of the 26 Counties, internal and external,
does not contradict it.

Despite Dublin's order for him to act immediately, Warnock did
not get around to visiting the German Foreign Office until 31 May
when he personally handed the protest note to a senior official named
Hencke. The next day, 1 June, Warnock cabled Dublin, saying: 'Saw
new Under Secretary of State Hencke this morning. He stated matter
would be attended to. There could be no question of intentional
interference in Irish internal affairs'.[3]

Also on 1 June, Hencke reported to his superiors at the Foreign
Office that:

The Irish Chargé d'Affaires yesterday handed me this aide-
memoire in which objections are made that the Irish citizen Francis
Stuart has used the German radio to influence Irish choice in
choosing sides in the war. The Chargé d'Affaires added orally

that his government had no objections that the German radio talks about Ireland, e.g. even in an anti-English sense. However, when an opposition party in Ireland is attacked by the German radio his government suspects Germany is applying pressure on Ireland to take sides.[4]

Dublin's protest was, in fact, never made public, possibly because the government had no wish either to admit they had been upset by the talks or to boost Francis Stuart's audience through controversy.[5]

While the incident led to a cooling of relations between Germany and Ireland for a time, Francis Stuart considered the whole affair amusing although it backfired on him because, soon afterwards, Warnock refused to renew his passport. Stuart recalls that 'Warnock put on his top hat and morning suit [laughs] and went to the German Foreign Office and lodged a protest that the Germans were allowing me to interfere in a sovereign state which was neutral. Of course, the German Foreign Office couldn't care less'. Warnock's secretary, Eileen Walsh, says Stuart's suggestion that Warnock wore a top hat and morning suit is 'nonsense', although she confirms the rest.

In the wake of the election, Hempel advised the German radio and press to take the line that 'de Valera, by his clear, energetic and successful policy, had earned the trust of the people'.[6] The German envoy's advice was ignored by the Irland-Redaktion, but Warnock's diplomatic protest had the desired effect. From 31 May until polling day on 22 June, neither G2 nor the BBC heard any more Irish election talks from German Radio.

Dublin only protested twice in the entire war over the contents of Irland-Redaktion programmes, and on both occasions Francis Stuart was involved — first when he praised Hugh McAteer and, secondly, when he advised voters not to back Fine Gael. The common denominator in both cases was that Stuart had touched a raw nerve by drawing attention to two of de Valera's adversaries — the IRA and Fine Gael. In addition, the actual programme material complained about by Dublin may not have been what stung de Valera most. For example, External Affairs protested to Hempel that 'the holding up of McAteer on the German radio as a hero was likely to be resented by many people here and to furnish a concrete example for use by those who charged Germany with aiding and abetting the IRA against the Government'. But, quite apart from Stuart's praise for McAteer, it must have been particularly uncomfortable for de Valera to hear the Irish writer's earlier plea to Churchill to lift the death sentence on 19 year old Thomas Williams in Belfast when, at the same time, the Taoiseach was using military tribunals to execute IRA men in the 26 Counties (German Radio never commented on the latter executions). Similarly, in the case of Stuart's election talks, Éire's delicate neutral position was cited as the pretext for a diplomatic protest, yet the real reason was not too difficult to discern. As far as de Valera was concerned, German Radio's advice to vote against Fine Gael might well have had the opposite effect, spurring voters with pro-Allied — or simply anti-Nazi — sympathies to back Fianna Fáil's main rivals. In addition, de Valera may have been upset by Stuart's clear call for voters to back extreme republican candidates. In the end neither Stuart nor Dev need have worried too much because Fine Gael lost 13 seats in the election. And, despite losing his overall majority, the Taoiseach remained in power with the backing of a new farmers' party, Clann na Talmhan.

Stuart's election talks in April and May 1943 were not the only such commentaries put out by German Radio during the war. On 12 October 1942, their black propaganda unit Station Debunk appealed to listeners in the USA 'to avoid voting for Franklin's party at the coming [congressional] election'. On 14 January 1943, the Irland-Redaktion welcomed the defeat of the Unionist candidate Sir Knox Cunningham in the West Belfast by-election, saying 'while this one by-election won't bring about the liberation of the Six Counties from the Anglo-American yoke, it is undeniably a step in the right direction'. Even the BBC was handing out electoral advice in the war. In March 1943, its Danish service urged listeners to 'vote Danish... choose a Rigsdag [parliament] of men who will say no to any further concessions to the Germans'. By contrast, in June 1943, the BBC was barred from covering the Irish general election by Churchill's Tipperary-born Minister for Information, Brendan Bracken, who said:

> The public would be horrified if they heard anything from the BBC about de Valera and those lousy neutrals: people of Irish stock overseas are heartily ashamed of Éire's attitude.[7]

Footnotes

1. Stuart's advice to the Irish electorate to 'give special preferences to those men who have shown themselves sincerely concerned for the welfare of the whole people of Ireland' was a thinly disguised call to back extreme republicans. Since Sinn Féin was not fielding candidates in the 1943 election, the writer was urging support for independent republicans and extreme republican parties such as Ailtirí na hAiséirighe (Architects of the Resurrection) and Córas na Poblachta (System of the Republic). In the event, no candidates from either of these fringe parties, nor the three independent republican candidates, succeeded in winning seats in the Dáil (see Walker, 1992, pp. 154-61).

2. Boland to Warnock, 27 May 1943 (DFA, A72, Francis Stuart 'restricted file').

3. Stuart's 'most reactionary party' talk went out on Saturday, 29 May 1943. Boland had cabled Warnock two days earlier on Thursday, 27 May but, presumably, Monday, 31 May was the earliest appointment the Irish diplomat could get to see Hencke; Warnock to Boland, 1 June 1943 (DFA, 205/108 German broadcasts to Ireland).

4. Hencke memo, 1 June 1943 (DFA, A72). The tale seems to have changed in the telling because what Hencke reported Warnock as saying is somewhat different from Boland's blunt message of 27 May.

5. In any case, the Dáil had been dissolved on 26 May pending the 22 June election. The new Dáil did not sit until 1 July 1943.

6. Duggan, 1975, p. 219.

7. Cathcart, 1984, pp. 127-8.

17

Dicing With Death

Even in the midst of his electioneering broadcasts, Francis Stuart could find time to devote talks to other subjects. In mid-May he strayed onto very thin ice with a speech that could easily, on his own admission, have cost him his life after the war.

Prompted by fresh hints of conscription in Northern Ireland following the election of Sir Basil Brooke as Prime Minister there, Stuart took the dangerous step of advising British soldiers from Ulster to mutiny. On 15 May 1943, speaking directly to his fellow northerners — presumably, although he did not specify it, of the Catholic, nationalist variety — he offered them the following counsel.

> It is just possible, though unlikely, that they will force you into their army but it is quite impossible to make you fight their battles for them. They cannot make you fight for the continued occupation of your own corner of Ireland. For that is what, among other things, any military success for the British and American forces means. Therefore, if the worst should come to the worst and any of you be conscripted and be sent to one of the battlefields, you have only to wait for a suitable opportunity and go over to the Germans. That has been proved to be not a very difficult thing to do in the latest form of warfare where there are no very determined lines and where there is rapid movement. As I say, you have simply to submit to the training and all the rest and wait patiently until you are actually at the front and then — having arranged a suitable plan among your fellows, even if you happen to be only two or three who will probably be split up among different regiments —

you can go over to the Germans or to the Italians as the case may be, and I can promise you that you will be received as friends and well treated as soon as you've explained who you are. For the case of the Six Counties is well known here in Germany. It is true, of course, that you will be separated from your families and friends at home, but at least that is better than that you should get killed in fighting for the continuance of the enslavement of those families and friends under the government of Sir Basil Brooke. And I say you will be treated with every consideration, both during the war and as long after it as you would have to remain away from your home.'[1]

This talk displayed a naiveté which was uncharacteristic of Stuart's broadcasts either before or after. Did Mahr or Hartmann put him up to it, or was the writer being deliberately disingenuous? Whatever the motive, Stuart was wide of the mark in thinking that northerners embracing his own brand of republicanism would ever find themselves wearing British Army uniforms. And even if they did somehow find themselves fighting for the Union Jack somewhere in a foreign field, Stuart's advice to cross over to the German or Italian lines — essentially to desert — was fraught with danger and would have led anyone attempting it to their death or to a POW camp. In addition, at that stage of the war — May 1943 — there was no second front in Europe, only the Russian front, where British troops would not be deployed. More curious still is the fact that Stuart's advice to mutiny was based on the assumption that Germany and Italy would win the war — something that in the wake of Stalingrad seemed less and less likely.

If Stuart was even half serious about his suggestion to British troops from Northern Ireland to desert, his motives were sure to have more to do with harming the British war effort than with filling German and Italian POW camps with Irishmen from the north. Was Stuart aware that he was putting his head on the block by making such a broadcast, which a victorious British Army would see as treasonable? The answer would seem to be yes, but he did it anyway — a view that could also sum up his role in wartime Berlin. Asked if he thought the British might have tried to conjure up a Lord Haw Haw-style case against him after the war — had he fallen into their hands — Stuart replies 'Yes', but adds that his capture by French forces 'was not accidental, I arranged it so... When we saw the war ending we moved into the part of Germany which was obviously going to be where the French were fighting'.[2]

As the Allied armies swept eastwards through Europe after the June 1944 D-Day landings, MI5 officers went with them searching for traitors who had sided with the Nazis. That Stuart escaped British retribution was due as much to his 'engineered' capture by French forces as to the fact that the BBC's monitoring service failed to identify him as the speaker in the 'mutiny' broadcast, even though Irish Army monitors knew who the broadcaster was. Despite well developed co-operation between G2 and MI5 at that stage of the war, the Dublin authorities do not appear to have briefed their British counterparts about the author of this sensitive broadcast. The British, however, did seek Stuart out while in French custody but dropped their enquiries when they found they had the wrong man — they were actually looking for an England-Redaktion announcer named Norman Baillie-Stewart.

If his plan to evade the British had not worked, does Stuart think they would have executed him? He comments:

> It could have been possible but it would have been so unlikely really, looking back, for a neutral writer with quite a readership who had made certain broadcasts. There was no question of treason. As a neutral you can express opinions even on a combatant's radio service. I don't say there weren't travesties of justice — they were endless — but that would have been one. Needless to say, during the whole business, I didn't take it into account.

Footnotes

1.   Francis Stuart talk, 15 May 1943 (MA, G2/X/0127, FWB part 4). The same talk was recorded by the BBC whose monitors failed to identify Stuart as the speaker (see Fisk, 1983, pp. 400-1).

2.   Author's interview with Francis Stuart, 17 November 1989. Author's letter to Stuart, 6 July 1994, and Stuart's written reply of 7 July 1994.

18

The Cadogan Broadcasts

At the beginning of May 1943 monitors in Dublin's McKee Barracks reported the following announcement from German Radio: 'We will now present our listeners in Ireland, Mr Patrick Joseph Cadogan, who comes to us from New York where he has made his home for the last 20 years'. Although only on air for five months — from 2 May to 1 October — the Cadogan talks are notable for their extreme anti-Semitic content. But who was the new announcer? Fifty years after the war, none of the survivors of the Irland-Redaktion could remember anyone named Cadogan having worked with them, which suggests the name was a cover.

On 5 May 1943, Cadogan launched into an anti-Semitic tirade which had no equal on either the England- or Irland-Redaktion. He commented on 'the demand of the English Jews that Anglo-Saxon broadcasting corporations refrain from broadcasting any plays with a Christian theme or tendency, the reason being of course that the reawakening of Christianity in England might provoke anti-Jewish feeling'. Cadogan ended his talk 'with a fervent prayer that Saint Patrick may smile on Erin's green isle and keep her free from this Jew-instigated war. I say good night to you all my Irish and Catholic brothers and sisters'.

On 18 May Cadogan felt moved to lecture his Irish listeners again on the 'evils of Jewry and Bolshevism', commenting:

These two terrible evils, Judaism and Bolshevism, are so real that I must bring home to you my fellow Irishmen, the great danger to our country, to our holy faith, that lies in the Jewish plans... Be on your guard for the protection of our holy Catholic faith and for the salvation of Ireland.

On 20 May Cadogan said that while he had voted for Roosevelt in 1932, the US President had

surrounded himself with a Jewish brains trust from whom he took his orders... Since Roosevelt's first election, there has been a steady influx of Jewish influence into every stratum of life in America. Even in the city of New York, where once upon a time we Irish proudly and capably ruled in politics, the police force and the fire department, the Jews have gained complete control, and the good names of the Irish cops, such as Kelly, Murphy and McDermott, have been replaced by Cohen, Goldwyn and Sax.

On 23 May, Cadogan revealed more about himself, saying: 'Today I attended holy Mass in a beautiful church in the suburbs of Berlin. Somehow this little church reminded me of another little church in Bundoran, County Donegal where my family used to spend the summer vacation'. In later talks, Cadogan quoted lengthy extracts from the speeches of the Canadian Catholic priest, Father Charles Coughlin, who had been banned from major American radio networks for 'attracting an anti-Semitic following'.[1]

By the end of May, Cadogan's talks had attracted the attention of the Department of External Affairs in Dublin, which was supplied with transcripts of them by G2. The transcripts were passed to Government Ministers like Frank Aiken but no action was taken. On 1 June, after assuring Irish listeners about the 'wonderful conditions under which people live in German-controlled territory', Cadogan delivered yet another anti-Jewish outburst:

In all countries who have not effectively protected themselves and their national life from the menace of organised Jewry, the Jews have axed and elbowed their way to, first of all, places of influence and then, finally, to offices of paramount power. So safeguard your neutrality in Ireland by safeguarding Ireland from Jewry. Safeguard your holy Catholic faith by combating by all means the antichrist, and the antichrist today is Judo-Bolshevism.

Given the blatantly sectarian nature of these broadcasts, it is not hard to see why whoever made them chose to hide behind a cover name. So who was the broadcaster masquerading behind the name Patrick Joseph Cadogan? A number of people in the Irland-Redaktion used pseudonyms. For example, the sobriquet Pat O'Brien was used by Blair, O'Reilly and Mullally. Other assumed names such as Maureen Petrie, John Costello, Ella Kavanagh and Sheila Ní Kearney (all in the 1942-43 period) appear to have been used only once or twice. Among the female broadcasters at the Irland-Redaktion, Sonja Kowanka used the name Linda Walters on air. Kowanka was a fluent English speaker but had never been to Ireland and knew nothing about the country, so her talks were scripted by her friend and colleague Susan Hilton. As already mentioned, Mrs Hilton used the name Susan Sweney on the Irish service, and the name Ann Tower when broadcasting to Scotland.

Some Irland-Redaktion broadcasters used false names simply because their real names did not sound Irish enough. According to Hans Hartmann's assistant, Dr Hilde Spickernagel — who read Berlin's Irish news bulletins anonymously — some of the pseudonyms were 'rather too romantic to seem likely'. She notes that it wasn't only broadcasters' names that were made up: 'Life stories were also frequently invented or modified, some of them being quite incredible'. Patrick Joseph Cadogan's life story would, in part at least, fit that description.

Half a century after the war, mystery still surrounds the phantom broadcaster's true identity. Maurice Irvine, who monitored the Cadogan talks for the BBC, says the speaker was 'the nearest equivalent to Joyce' that he had come across on the Irish service, and adds: 'He didn't give the impression of being a man of any great culture or education'. Of Cadogan's accent, Irvine said: 'It seemed to vary a bit. Predominantly American in his vocalisation and his intonation, but maybe occasionally a certain more Irish element came across. The name Cadogan is not a particularly Irish one, but he may have been born in Ireland and spent some early years there, and was then taken to the States and brought up there'. According to his radio colleague Norman Baillie-Stewart, William Joyce was 'brilliant' at imitating an American accent.[2] On the possibility of a link between

Cadogan and William Joyce, Maurice Irvine says: 'I would be very doubtful about the identification of Cadogan with Joyce. Even given that Joyce could put on a convincing American accent, the quality of their voices was in my recollection quite different — Joyce's sharp, cutting, mocking, Cadogan's somewhat rough and earthy'.

When asked about Cadogan's real identity, Francis Stuart comments: 'The Irish service did not have any Cadogan in it. There were only three or four of us: myself, Susan Sweney [Hilton], Liam Mullally and Hartmann. Cadogan must have been a cover name for someone else, perhaps someone in the English service'. Dr Spickernagel knew of no one called Cadogan and, in any case, she left the Irish service at the end of 1942, over four months before the Cadogan broadcasts began. She added: 'Blair, as far as I can remember, did not have an American accent but then an American accent is very easy to imitate'.

When asked about Cadogan's identity, Nora O'Mara (Róisín Ní Mheara-Vinard) refused to furnish any reply, even though she was making broadcasts from the Rundfunkhaus in mid-1943. The head of the service at the time, Hans Hartmann, says: 'There was no person of that name broadcasting in the Irland-Redaktion and I cannot recall ever hearing of Mr Cadogan'. But Hartmann suspects that William Joyce may have been behind the Cadogan talks, and adds:

> Perhaps he [Cadogan] was a figure set up by quarters outside the Irland-Redaktion to convey propaganda to certain Irish listeners. I may call attention to the fact that I had refused, towards the end of the war, to allow William Joyce to speak to [what Joyce termed] his 'Irish followers' in the frame of the Irland-Redaktion as, to my mind, this field was adequately covered by the contributions of Francis Stuart, dealing mainly with cultural aspects.

So who was Cadogan in reality? Given his English public school background and his years in Ireland, Francis Stuart is unlikely to have been able to affect a convincing American accent and, in any case, he has denied any role in the Cadogan episode. James Blair is a possible candidate for the title. He had been sacked from the Irland-Redaktion in 1942 and later joined the Nazis' Inter-Radio service from where he could have done the broadcasts. According to Dr Spickernagel, Blair could have affected an American accent. However, while Blair had a knowledge of US affairs (having worked as a proof-reader on an American newspaper in Paris as well as being a stringer for papers in the United States), it is unlikely that he could have originated the Cadogan scripts, some of which displayed a detailed knowledge of Irish and American affairs.

Despite their ability with languages, both Hartmann and Mahr can be ruled out because of their heavy German accents when speaking English. As for Mullally, his participation is unlikely and, at the time, he was preparing to leave the Irland-Redaktion for Austria. According to Francis Stuart, he spent the remainder of the war working as valet for Norman Baillie-Stewart in Vienna.

Given that Maurice Irvine was somewhat removed from the Rundfunkhaus scene, the most likely explanation of Cadogan's real identity — which Stuart hints at and Dr Hartmann suggests — is that William Joyce himself did the Cadogan talks. Few other people in the English service would have had the capacity to script material with such a detailed Irish and Irish-American content, still less assume a convincing American accent which crucially, as Maurice Irvine notes, 'seemed to vary a bit'. In addition, Irvine noted that the person doing the Cadogan talks 'may have been born in Ireland and spent some early years there, and was then taken to the States and brought up there'. In fact, Joyce was born in Brooklyn, moved to Ballinrobe in County Mayo when he was three and to Galway when he was six (this could explain 'Cadogan's' recollection of childhood holidays in Bundoran, which is only 70 miles from Ballinrobe). Joyce left Galway for England when he was 15. Although this upbringing is somewhat the reverse of Irvine's guess, it might have given rise to a similar accent, albeit an assumed one.

Other evidence points to Joyce's involvement. In a broadcast on 18 July 1943, Cadogan said he had visited a POW camp in Germany. Joyce is on record as having visited a POW camp.[3] In addition, the final Cadogan talk was broadcast on 1 October 1943, some seven weeks after Hartmann and Stuart left Berlin for Luxembourg (to avoid increased Allied bombing that was threatening the Rundfunkhaus). Joyce was also in Luxembourg at the time.[4] Moreover, of all the broadcasters in the England- and Irland-Redaktions, William Joyce never made any effort to hide his anti-Semitism, and neither did the person delivering the Cadogan talks.[5]

How much did Hartmann know about the Cadogan episode? While claiming no direct knowledge, he suspected Joyce of involvement and it is reasonable to conclude that, having been rebuffed by Hartmann when he offered to broadcast on the Ireland-Redaktion to his 'Irish followers', Joyce may have wished to settle the score. Hartmann's opposite number in the England-Redaktion, Dr Fritz Hesse, was not beyond indulging in such ploys — he had already allowed John Amery to conduct fake broadcasts, pretending he was at the Russian front.[6] It is unlikely that Joyce could have got away with his Cadogan ruse without Dr Hesse's knowledge. In essence, whether Hartmann knew what was going on or not, there was little he could do about it. Had he objected to such material being broadcast by Joyce — who was considered the star performer by the radio's management — he would almost certainly have been overruled by Hesse and the all powerful head of foreign services, Dr Toni Winkelnkemper. Technically, the Cadogan talks could have been piggybacked onto the Irish service from the nearby England-Redaktion studios, even without Hartmann's knowledge, because both services sometimes used the same wavelengths. But whatever technique was used it seems that, in this case, Dr Hartmann was outwitted by Lord Haw Haw.

Footnotes

1.   Barnouw, 1968, pp. 47, 133-5, 221.

2.   Baillie-Stewart, 1967, p. 157.

3.   Cole, 1964, pp. 159-60.

4.   German broadcast by Mr. Cadogan, 6.15 p.m., 1 October 1943 (MA, G2/X/0127, FWB part 4). According to Cole (1964, p. 213) 'In October [1943, William] Joyce had another trip, this time to Luxembourg, where he stayed at the Hotel Alfa with his current girl friend. While there, he recorded his *Views on the News* as usual'. See also ref. no. 4 of Chapter 15.

5.   Cole, 1964, pp. 302, 311.

6.   Author's interview with Francis Stuart, 24 February 1990. See also, 'Amery Executed Against Advice', in *The Daily Telegraph*, 8 February 1995, p. 11.

19

All Aboard for Luxembourg

O n 22 June 1943 — polling day in the Irish general election and, coincidentally, the second anniversary of Hitler's invasion of Russia — Hartmann was still predicting a Soviet defeat.

> Today, after two years of war [in Russia] we can say that we are far stronger in men and material than when war broke out... the Soviet Union has lost up to the present about 20 million men, killed, wounded, and taken prisoner; almost 50,000 big guns, over 40,000 planes and at least 26,000 tanks... the supply position of both soldiers and civilians in the Soviet Union is very bad and gets worse daily. Severe famine seems likely from the end of this summer.

There was more than a little inconsistency in the fact that while he was forecasting a defeat for Russia, the very next day, 23 June, Hartmann was admitting that:

> Very heavy damage has been caused to the beautiful [German] city of Krefeld. Whole districts have been destroyed. When workers returned from one of the factories outside the city they could not find their houses. Many of them lost their wives and children in a single night but one of the workers said that in future they would live by their machines.

On 25 June Hartmann spelled out Germany's preparedness to repel any Allied invasion.

> England has been talking and threatening invasion of Europe so much that everyone thinks it is time she did something to show

she is in earnest. It is a matter of indifference to us in Germany. We know England has enough ships and men to make landings at different places. We are waiting for them. Our defences are completed and we have hosts of experienced soldiers to man them, and to drive back into the seas any of the enemy who do succeed in landing.

The D-Day landings were still a year off, but Hartmann's acknowledgement of Britain's naval power could be interpreted as an admission of weakness.

On 29 June, Hartmann was trying to turn an RAF attack on Cologne's Catholic cathedral to propaganda advantage.

Today will be remembered as a black day in the history of mankind. An English air raid has destroyed the great and beautiful cathedral church of Cologne. I need not say that it is a terrible loss, not only for Germany but for the whole of Europe. Few people have not heard of this lovely and marvellous church; people from many lands, including Ireland, have visited and heard Mass in it. It will be difficult for anyone, and especially for any Catholic, to restrain his tears on hearing that the greater part of the aisles no longer exist. It is for England a lasting shame. Hundreds of years will not suffice to efface the crimes they are committing over Germany. Berlin political circles say that the cruelty being displayed by England is one of her most deeply ingrained qualities. It is true and, to anyone who doubts it, one need only point to the terrible things done by the same gentlemen in Ireland — the Penal Laws, the churches destroyed or burnt, the lonely rocks where Mass was celebrated by hunted priests, the thousands of gravestones and cairns throughout the land where someone was done to death by the English. But it is becoming evident that all the English have not easy consciences. Some of them are becoming anxious. They fear that some day they will have to pay a terrible price for what they have done.

This was Hartmann on his best form — turning Germany's misfortune to propaganda advantage and introducing current and historic Irish angles for his target audience.

On 1 July, Hartmann returned to the same topic, telling his listeners:

The anger of Europe at the bombing of Cologne cathedral increases day by day. This evil deed has aroused in the heart of everyone in Germany a cold hatred for England. The cathedral is a national monument, quite apart from its importance as a shrine of the

Catholic faith... the English knew it was a national monument, and they bombed it in an attempt to weaken the morale of the German people. We hear, however, that many people have asked the bishop not to clear away the ruins but to leave them as an eternal monument to the cruelty of the English air raids.

On the ground in Berlin the situation was as bad if not worse than Dr Hartmann was painting it, for, as well as commenting on the increasing Allied air attacks, members of the Irland-Redaktion were falling victim to them. Because of the bombing, a decision was taken to move the Irish service out of Berlin to the relative safety of Luxembourg, 400 miles to the south west. Hartmann delivered one of his last talks from Berlin on 7 July 1943, in which he said he would be off the air but did not mention his planned departure from the Rundfunkhaus.

And now friends, here is a note about my daily talks in Gaelic. I shall not be able to give these talks for some time to come but I hope that we shall have Gaelic on our programme again before the day of the Gaelic League commemoration [of its 50th anniversary on 31 July 1943]. Until then my best wishes to you all.

Francis Stuart delivered his final broadcast from Berlin on 24 July, still emphasising the neutrality angle.

By our passive opposition to American policy in this war we may sacrifice a certain immediate popularity in that country. We may not be included amongst those small nations to be saved by Mr Roosevelt and his gang, but one thing is certain — in a few years there is going to come a reaction, both in England and America, to this war, to the whole policy behind it and to the whole hypocritical spirit in which it was waged. It will be a reaction even more violent than the one after the last war that produced, amongst other things, a flood of pacifist literature. Roosevelt and his gang of warmongers are going to be swept into obscurity and discredited a good deal more thoroughly than even Wilson was. People in America, and especially our own people in America, are going to see very clearly that there was, after all, a great deal to be said for our neutrality.

Hartmann was optimistic in thinking he would be back on air by the end of July. In fact, the Irland-Redaktion was off the air for nearly two months until mid-September. Just how bad the situation had become for the broadcasters in Berlin was described by Stuart's lover, Madeleine Meissner, who wrote of buildings in the capital crumbling 'like sandcastles'.[1] Stuart himself wrote in his diary of 'Blazing houses all around and a strong wind, probably caused by the suction of the flames... An eeriness living amid burnt-out houses, especially at night. The ruins in the darkness and the waiting'.[2] It was time to leave for calmer pastures without alerting listeners to the worsening conditions. On 12 August 1943 Hartmann, along with his wife and son, as well as Stuart, Meissner and Helen Hartmann's sister, Gertrud Neugebauer, boarded a train for Luxembourg. For the next year the Grand Duchy would be their home. The evacuation of the radio staff was only partial, however, and some of the radio's other European services — including the England-Redaktion — remained in Berlin. Those who stayed behind took a great risk. As Hartmann had feared, the Rundfunkhaus was badly damaged by bombs during an air raid on 22 November.

The Radio Luxembourg studios, situated in the Villa Louvigny, had been incorporated into the Reichsrundfunk network four weeks after the German invasion of the Grand Duchy on 10 May 1940. The first sign that the Irish service had resumed broadcasting came on 18 September 1943 when Francis Stuart announced he would be giving his talks twice a week from then on. Hartmann had persuaded the writer to double his output, having by then lost the services of most of his team, including John O'Reilly, Susan Hilton, James Blair, Liam Mullally, Sonja Kowanka and Hilde Spickernagel. But a new broadcaster, named Johann Mikele, made regular talks on the Irish service.

A month later, on 16 October, Francis Stuart was back on the air, anxious to convince listeners he was still living in Berlin.[3] He referred to Germany no less than four times in the following short contribution.

> I came here to Germany in 1940 because I saw it was essential that at least one or two Irishmen should be here in Germany while there were thousands in England and America. But I am certainly not sorry that I came. But here from Germany I can say what no Irishman would be allowed to say anywhere else, neither in England, America, nor in Ireland itself. I can speak to you here from Germany and tell you the truth about this war, and I shall go on doing so as long as the hospitality of the German Wireless is given me, even although there may be a group at home who would

do whatever they can to stop me speaking to you and to impute to me motives of personal gain or ambition.

Stuart's sideswipe at the 'group at home' was aimed at de Valera's government which had succeeded in silencing his series of election broadcasts three weeks before the June election. And just in case the Dublin authorities did not get the message, Stuart added:

> I have the greatest suspicion and dislike for all politicians and, so far as I come under their notice at all, they have the same suspicion and dislike for me.

Hartmann's resumption of talks in Irish was noticed by the BBC — on 514.6 metres, the Calais transmitter, on 25 October 1943 — when he commented on the 'war in the Pacific and Far East, and Mountbatten's visit to see Chiang Kai-Shek'. In the closing months of 1943, Hartmann's talks were being picked up, on average, every two days by the BBC. The general tenor of his talks in November and December 1943 was overwhelmingly anti-Soviet, displaying German disquiet that pending the opening up of a second front, the main threat would come from the east. From the Luxembourg studios on 23 November, Hartmann told his listeners: 'The Anglo-Saxon intention of abandoning Europe to Bolshevism if they should succeed in winning the war, is becoming more and more apparent'. Given the sweeping territorial gains made by the Red Army up to May 1945, it can be seen with hindsight that Hartmann's prediction was partly correct.

This brand of propaganda, designed to make listeners fear the advance of communism, actually mirrored many anti-Soviet speeches by Irish Catholic bishops at the time. And it was a line that also found a ready sounding board in non-ecclesiastical circles in Dublin. For example, at around the same time, an American legation official in Dublin, Daniel Terrell, reported to Washington:

> More and more, as the war goes on, there is talk in Ireland of the horrible things Russia will do to all of us after Germany's downfall. Dr [Richard] Hayes [director of the National Library, seconded to G2], for instance, all but made a flat statement that Ireland had less to fear from a German victory than a Russian triumph.[4]

On 24 November Hartmann was in an emotional mood, reminding his listeners that while in Dublin, Carna and Gweedore in the late

1930s he 'had come to love the Irish people and to have a deep admiration for their ancient Gaelic culture. Ireland has given much to Europe in the past and could give a great deal in the future'. Hartmann thought it unlikely that Irish culture would die out but there was one danger against which he would warn the Irish people:

> Bolshevik ideas were very prevalent in England and they might find a fertile breeding ground among the Irish workers now in England whose poor living conditions rendered them very susceptible. Such people could do grave harm to the native culture on their return.

On 26 November, Hartmann applied the same theme to Moslems in the Middle East. The Soviets, he said, were trying 'to spread Bolshevik ideas' in Arab cities and ports where the inhabitants 'are susceptible to foreign ideas'. On 20 December, the Irish service was telling its listeners that 'Germany was strong enough not only to defend Europe from North, South, East and West but also to adopt the offensive. Whatever happened, England would be an unimportant country after the war'.

On Christmas Eve, Hartmann stressed the neutrality line, recalling times past in Dublin. The BBC monitor's report read:

> He was thinking today of the time he had spent in Ireland and especially his last Christmas there in 1938. He described a party for Irish and German children in the Gresham Hotel, Dublin, at which he played the part of Father Christmas. After the distribution of presents a concert was held and it would be difficult to find anywhere a merrier or more peaceful scene. But then came the war, first starting in a corner of Europe and then spreading till now it enveloped almost the whole world. He was very glad however that the Irish government had been able to preserve the peace in Ireland, or at least in the greater part of the country. Men were not forced to shed their blood for the British empire. The English and their allies had caused immense sufferings to the people of Germany so that Christmas this year could not be as peaceful and happy as it was before the war but it would be a Christian Christmas. Germans at home and at the front could celebrate it and all would, at least, have some hours of pleasure and would derive from them solace and strength and renewed vigour to continue the war more determinedly than ever. In conclusion he again congratulated Ireland on her escape from the horrors of war

and hoped she would continue in her present course until all danger
was past.[5]

Footnotes

1.   Madeleine Stuart, 1984, p. 33.

2.   Francis Stuart, 1984, p. 39. Stuart vividly recalls working in the
      Rundfunkhaus during bombing raids: 'Actually broadcasting, you don't
      have time to think of your safety. We had rubber masks or mouthpieces.
      You weren't speaking directly into a microphone; you were speaking
      directly into this rubber thing — like when you are under anaesthetic
      — so that the noise of bombs is presumably excluded. But I think the
      vibration still interfered with the acoustics' (author's interview with
      Stuart, 17 November 1989).

3.   No broadcasts by the Irland-Redaktion from Luxembourg ever alluded
      to their place of origin. The impression was thus created that, apart
      from a 54-day break in transmissions (from 25 July to 17 September
      1943, inclusive), the team had never left Berlin and nothing was amiss.

4.   Terrell to Kuhn, 16 September 1943 (USNA, CL-1566-BG).

5.   By the end of 1943, programme output to Ireland had been reduced
      from a maximum of one hour a night in the first half of the year, while
      based in Berlin, to a simpler format of only one nightly talk, at 7.15
      p.m., after the move to Luxembourg. During 1944 the output was
      increased to three bulletins per night. From Berlin, Hartmann's service
      had been able to use a number of transmitters to broadcast to Ireland.
      These ranged from the powerful shortwave ones at Zeesen (on 28.45,
      31.35 and 41.44 metres) — also used by the England-Redaktion — to
      alternative transmitters in Rennes (431.7 m) and Calais (514.6 m).
      The Oslo transmitter (1154 m) was used from the end of 1941 until
      mid-1943. Some Irland-Redaktion programmes were also beamed to
      North America using Zeesen's shortwave facilities. These comprised
      a few anonymous talks, in English, on Irish neutrality, and three talks
      by Hartmann, in Irish, on 17, 20 and 31 May 1942. The first two
      criticised the arrival of American troops in Northern Ireland, while
      the third gave details of German successes in the battle of Kharkov on
      the Russian front. Translations of all three talks were provided by the
      BBC, via British Military Intelligence, to the Cabinet Office in Northern

Ireland (PRONI, CAB 9CD/207 BBC MR). Meanwhile, Hartmann and his shrunken team were not that disadvantaged in Radio Luxembourg which, with a transmission strength of 120 kW, was one of the most powerful transmitters in Europe at the time. However, it was generally used for German domestic audiences. For better reception in Ireland, German radio engineers opted mostly for the Calais and Rennes transmitters.

20

Francis Stuart Draws the Line

I solated in Luxembourg and with a skeleton staff to put out the nightly programmes to Ireland, Hans Hartmann found himself attempting an unenviable balancing act as 1944 began. The biggest blow of his two year tenure as head of the Irish service came in January when he lost his key speaker, Francis Stuart, in a row over anti-Soviet broadcasts. Since the reasons why Stuart chose to travel to wartime Berlin in January 1940 — and to begin broadcasting two years later — have been the subject of debate ever since, it is only fair to look in some detail at his reasons for quitting the radio service.

Stuart describes his decision to stop broadcasting for the Nazis, as follows:

> I was pressurised. What I did say on one broadcast, perhaps more than one, was that if I suddenly stop broadcasting it would be because I refused to say certain things, and that's why up to the present I'd never been asked to say things which I wouldn't agree to. But then they began to suggest to me that the Bolsheviks, as they called them, must be extremely unpopular in Catholic Ireland, and wouldn't it be good if I cashed in on this and began talking about the Russian atrocities and the atheistic world view. I immediately refused because of all countries waging war... the only one which was waging what one might call a really honourable war were the Russians. They had been attacked in an extremely vicious and underhand way. They were protecting their country. They weren't carrying out devastating bombing on civilians such as the Germans and the Allies were. Whether, if they'd had the bombers, they would have, that's another matter. But they weren't

doing it and, therefore, I refused to make anti-Russian or anti-Bolshevik propaganda. Then my broadcasts were terminated. I didn't get into a camp but I was threatened with all sorts of things, and certain facilities I'd had were withdrawn from me. That was the end of my broadcasts.[1]

For almost two years, Hartmann had allowed Stuart a free hand to talk on Irish affairs and had turned a blind eye to the fact that the Irish writer was not willing to swing in behind the general anti-Bolshevik line following Germany's invasion of Russia — Operation Barbarossa — on 22 June 1941. According to Hartmann, Stuart

was a sincere man and often didn't hold back with criticism but what I realised was that he particularly liked the Russians. As far as I knew, or remember, he didn't speak about Stalin or anything else. He just spoke about the Russians which was not objectionable because there must be a major difference between Stalin and the Russian people.[2]

In fact, Hartmann was mistaken in presuming that Stuart did not admire Stalin. After the war Stuart told one interviewer: 'Stalin attracted me very much at one time'.[3] Hartmann was also unaware that, prior to Barbarossa, Stuart had made enquiries about taking up a teaching job in Moscow. The Irishman asked two of his Russian students at Berlin's technical college (where he taught in addition to Berlin University),

'Would it be possible for me to lecture in a school or in a university in Russia?' They said, 'By all means', and they gave me an introduction to somebody at their embassy on Unter den Linden. I went round and was asked, naturally, quite a few questions. I think the sponsorship of this young man [Stuart's student] was a help to me. I left them details. They phoned me a few weeks later to say the application was in Moscow and it was being processed. Then the attack on Russia came and that was that. Later, some White Russians, whom I'd got to know quite well in Berlin, told me 'you were lucky. You wouldn't have lasted any time in Moscow'. I don't know about that. These were White Russians and they had to put another aspect on it.

One of Stuart's final talks, on 8 January 1944, included the following references.

It is of no importance at all that the Tricolour should fly from the City Hall in Belfast instead of the Union Jack, if Belfast workers are to find it as hard to live and support their families as before. Such freedom is merely illusion and such nationalism a farce and a danger... the first thing to do is to face the truth. Until Dublin becomes a much better place for the average working family to live in than Belfast, we lose more than half the force of our claim to Belfast. This may not be a very palatable statement, but I think that to most of you it is quite obvious.

This broadcast, in effect, signalled Stuart's departure from the standard republican ethos on reunification. Perhaps the war had made him rethink everything and, hence, his decision to leave the Irish service.

But by the beginning of 1944 Hartmann was less interested in Stuart's ideas about ending partition than in getting him to broadcast anti-Soviet material which by then had become the central element of Nazi propaganda. It is unlikely, however, that Hartmann would have gone as far as to sack his only remaining Irish broadcaster, given the shortage of radio staff available in Luxembourg. While no one now recalls who tried to pressurise Francis Stuart into making anti-Bolshevik comments on air, the two people most likely to have forced him to break with the Irish service were Hartmann's boss, the ex-Foreign Office official and then head of foreign radio services, Erich Hetzler, and Adolf Mahr, then still with the Foreign Office's political broadcasting division and a regular visitor to Luxembourg where he kept an eye on the Irish radio propaganda effort he had set up just over two years earlier.

When Stuart refused to do any more broadcasting, he was allowed to return to Berlin on condition that he report to the Rundfunkhaus there. Stuart and Madeleine Meissner left Luxembourg together in February 1944 but never went near the Berlin radio centre. It soon became clear that the radio authorities were not prepared to take Stuart's decision sitting down. On 23 March he noted in his diary: '... just lately, some threats on the telephone, presumably because I would not give more radio talks'. The phone calls came in the middle of the night, warning him that if he did not resume broadcasting to Ireland he would be arrested and thrown into a camp. After a trip to Silesia with Madeleine, Stuart returned to Berlin where, on 2 May, he noted in his diary:

More attempts to coerce me back to broadcasting... they have confiscated my passport and I also receive threats over the phone. They won't arrest me as long as they think there is some chance of my resuming the broadcasts to Ireland, perhaps even agreeing to denounce the 'Asian hordes'. Luckily, I have some fairly well placed protectors.

With the help of his friends in the Foreign Office — notably, the influential Under Secretary of State, Ernst von Weizsäcker — Stuart got his passport back within a few days, and commented: 'A relief! Not that, I think, I was in any great danger'. But he was wrong to dismiss the potential danger so lightly. A few Irland-Redaktion broadcasters suffered at the hands of the Nazis. For example, Sonja Kowanka was obliged to do forced labour in a factory after the Gestapo intercepted her letters and objected to what she had written in one of them. She was only saved by the intervention of Susan Hilton. Hilton herself was incarcerated in a camp at Liebenau, south west Germany, in August 1944 — suspected by the Gestapo of spying for the Allies. An England-Redaktion member, James Gilbert, was sent to a concentration camp for several months in 1943 after refusing to broadcast for Hetzler.[4]

Whether he wanted to leave Luxembourg because he could not bring himself to preach anti-Soviet propaganda, or simply because he saw that the war was entering its final stages, Stuart could consider himself lucky to have got away with crossing Hartmann, Mahr and Hetzler. But there may have been another altogether more personal reason for Stuart's decision to quit. According to Helmut and Elizabeth Clissmann, 'Stuart could not succeed in having his German girlfriend [Madeleine Meissner] hired to work in the Irland-Redaktion' even though she had gone to Luxembourg with him the previous August to introduce his talks. As well as this, the Clissmanns say that Stuart 'had vowed to leave if they [the radio's management] changed his scripts again. That had already happened once when the words "due to the interference of the Red Army" had been inserted into a script at short notice and he had inadvertently read it out on air. Stuart was vehemently opposed to being forced to take a political position in his weekly talks'.[5]

In 1940, Dr. Edmund Veesenmayer tried to engineer a coup d'état against de Valera's Government with the help of senior IRA figures. In 1944 he sought Frank Ryan's help to beam anti-Roosevelt propaganda from a bogus Irish radio station.

Dr. Toni Winkelnkemper was head of German Radio's foreign services from 1941 to 1945. He presided over radio managers' meetings dressed in full SS uniform

GÁRDA SÍOCHÁNA

£500 REWARD

The above sum will be paid to any person giving information resulting in the arrest of JOHN FRANCIS O'REILLY, internee, who escaped from custody at Arbour Hill Detention Prison, Dublin, on the night of 5th-6th July, 1944

Landed by Parachute in Clare, 16th December, 1943, and had been in custody since that date.

DESCRIPTION :—Born Kilkee, Co. Clare, 7th August, 1916; height 5' 11½"; weight 152 lbs.; fair hair; blue eyes; fresh complexion; slim build; wore dark brown suit with red stripes; black shoes; rubber soles and heels, believed size 10; bare head; sports shirt. May be wearing a light grey showerproof overcoat.

Information may be given to any Gárda Station.

Proportionate rewards will be paid for information concerning this man which will assist the Gárda in locating him.

'Wanted' poster for John O'Reilly, after his escape from Arbour Hill Prison, Dublin, in July 1944. O'Reilly worked for German Radio from 1941 to 1942. The Germans sent him home on a spying mission in December 1943.

British Army engineers examine Lord Haw Haw's (William Joyce) last tapes.
Joyce's final broadcast went out from the Hamburg studios on 30 April 1945, the day
Hitler committed suicide in his Berlin bunker.

Adolf and Maria Mahr in wartime Berlin, with Hans Boden (left, who formerly worked at the German Legation in Dublin) and Heinrich Greiner (right, who worked at the Solus lightbulb factory in Bray).

Heinrich Greiner (left) and Charles Budina in wartime Berlin.
Before the war, Greiner worked at the Solus lightbulb factory in Bray.
Budina ran the Kilmacurragh Park Hotel in County Wicklow.

Hans Hartmann in
Luxembourg,
March 1944.
Left to right:
Gertrude Neugebauer,
Elizabeth Clissmann,
Helene Hartmann (née
Neugebauer),
Hans Hartmann and
(foreground)
his son, Detlef.

Wolfgang Dignowity
was picked by Goebbels to
run a new nightly radio
service to Ireland.
But he only lasted five
months in the job — from
June to October 1941.
He was replaced by
Hans Hartmann.

Adolf Mahr
pictured in 1948.

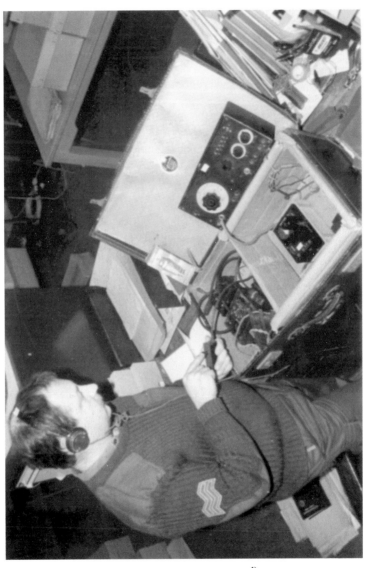

Irish Army Private Bertie Egerton tests John O'Reilly's spy transmitter at the military archives in Dublin.

O'Reilly parachuted into his native County Clare from a Luftwaffe bomber in December 1943. He worked for German Radio from 1941 to 1942.

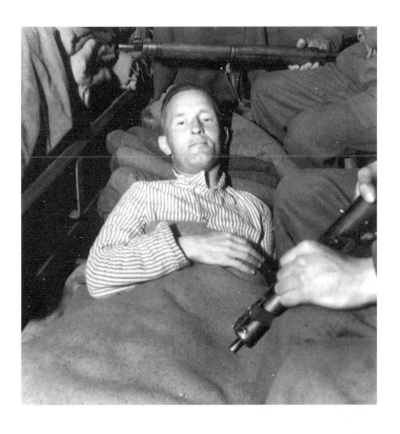

William Joyce (Lord Haw Haw) at the point of a sten gun
after his arrest near the Danish border at
Flensburg, Germany, on 28 May 1945.
He was hanged at Wandsworth Prison, London,
on 3 January 1946.

Bremers Hotel in Apen, Northern Germany. Hartmann's Irish
Radio Service put out its final programmes from this building
from 26 September 1944 until 2 May 1945.

Adolf Mahr in 1948.

German soldiers guard the Radio Luxembourg studios,
where Hartmann's Irish Service was based
from September 1943 to August 1944.

Francis Stuart pictured at his home in Dundrum, Dublin.
Stuart worked for German Radio's Irish Service
from 1942 to 1944.

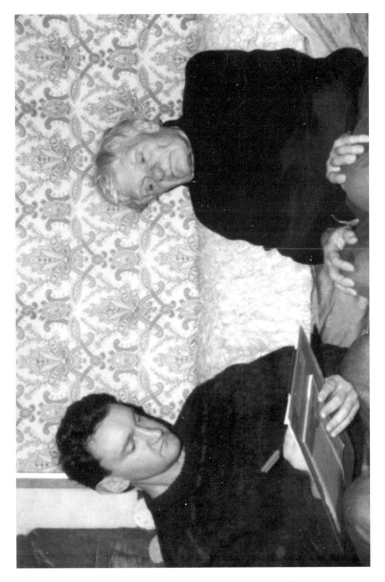

The author
interviewing
Francis Stuart
in Dublin

Susan Hilton
in England, 1960.

Mahr pictured
shortly before
his death in 1951

Dr. Hans Hartmann in retirement
in Cologne, Germany, 1990, aged 81.

Hugh Byrne of Teelin,
County Donegal.
Professor Mühlhausen spent six
weeks in Byrne's cottage in
1937 learning Donegal Irish.
The German took hundreds of
photographs in the area.

Edward Sweney,
Oldcastle, County Meath.
His sister, Susan Hilton,
broadcast to neutral Ireland in
1942. He claims she was
mistreated by the Nazis, the
French Army and MI5.

Irish language and
folklore expert,
Séan Ó Heochaidh,
taught Irish to
Ludwig Mühlhausen and
Hans Hartmann in
Donegal in 1937

Maurice Irvine
from Belfast — the BBC's
last Gaelic monitor.

For a variety of reasons then, Stuart had made the final break with the Irland-Redaktion. His university lecturing job would only last another six months as all third level institutions in the Third Reich were closed down for the 'total war' effort following the attempt to assassinate Hitler on 20 July 1944. Increasingly uncertain times lay ahead.

Footnotes

1. Author's interview with Stuart, 17 November 1989; Elborn, 1990, p. 165.

2. Author's interview with Hartmann, 21 October 1990.

3. In 1994 Stuart told one interviewer: 'I saw him [Hitler] and other dictators like Stalin, however much I disagreed with them on other matters, as blind Samsons pulling down the pillars of society — war lords. The system had to be destroyed by someone and after it was destroyed, I hoped, a whole new society would emerge' (Stuart interviewed by Ulick O'Connor, *Sunday Independent*, 13 November 1994, p. 11). Stuart had been thinking seriously of leaving Berlin for Moscow but Hitler's invasion of Russia in June 1941 put paid to any such plans. He commented: 'I would have got out but there was no getting out after that' (author's interview with Stuart, 17 November 1989). Trapped in Berlin, he decided to make the most of it, living the good life with the help of extra ration cards from Frank Ryan who, according to Stuart, 'was treated like a diplomat by the Germans'. On one occasion, Stuart recalls, he shared a night-club table with Ryan, Helmut Clissmann and a founder member of the Nazi party (see Chapter 10, pp. 57-8). Asked by this author if he ever felt he had been taking the side of evil against good in wartime Berlin, Stuart replied: 'No, I didn't. I felt I was too closely involved with a brutal and barbarian regime for my own good or for my own liking. That I was opposed to good, I never felt for a moment, because I never felt that the Allied nations were anything but probably equally evil. Although, equally or not, it's a very fine point, but at least probably even more corrupt and more hypocritical. I was oblivious to the fact that I was involved. As long as they looked like — although to me they didn't — being victorious, I specially felt that. When it was obvious they were going to lose the war, to be on the side of the losers at the end of such a huge war was to me as a writer a very valuable experience. I went to Germany

under a misapprehension of course... I thought Hitler would have been some sort of international revolutionary destroying the whole system, which I soon found he was far from' (author's interview with Stuart, 17 November 1989).

4. Details of Kowanka's and Hilton's treatment are contained in LCD file CRIM 1/1745. In British military custody in 1945, James Gilbert told MI5 officers what happened to him after leaving the Grossbeeren and Wuhlheide concentration camps: 'A Gestapo man came and took me down to the Gestapo headquarters in Prinz Albrecht Strasse. There I was told that I would be released on one condition — that I would continue working for Hetzler. I had to sign a paper to the effect that I would carry out Hetzler's orders obediently, and that were Hetzler ever to make any complaint about me in the future I must expect still severer measures. Then I was released. My memory had been slightly affected, and I could not remember where my wife [a fellow Rundfunkhaus employee named Christel Artus] lived. I knew she had moved from Stralauerallee, but I could not remember where. I wandered round for a while until I found I was near the office of a Professor Mahr whom I knew slightly. He was a very nice old man who had at one time been keeper of the Royal Treasurers or something in Dublin. He was shocked at seeing me but was very kind and helpful, and was able to tell me my wife's new address, and at last I found my way back to her' (LCD, CRIM 1/1783). James Gilbert remained with Hetzler's European broadcasting service until nearly the end of the war. Gilbert was finally arrested by US military police on 9 March 1945. After the war he moved to live in Dublin (as did his radio colleague, Norman Baillie-Stewart) where he worked for the *Irish Farmers Journal* and the *Irish Times* as agricultural correspondent. Contemporaries of Gilbert's at the *Irish Times* recall that he was refused permission to travel to Canada because of his war record (author's interview with Mr Donal O'Donovan, Bray, 31 January 1997). James Gilbert was born in Mahableshwar, India, on 13 March 1917.

5. Author's interview with Mr and Mrs Helmut Clissmann, Dublin, 11 September 1990.

21

Using the Irish to Topple Roosevelt

Despite the growing threat from the east, in early 1944 Nazi Germany's propagandists were still trying to prevent Franklin D. Roosevelt's fourth bid for the White House that November. Presumably, Berlin was gambling that a less hawkish, Republican candidate in the White House would seek an early end to the war and so help Germany to sue for peace and retain her pre-war borders. The Nazis were prepared to use fair means and foul to halt Roosevelt. During the war they ran a total of 19 so-called black propaganda stations, all pretending to broadcast from their target areas but emanating from Germany or her occupied territories. These stations were run under the umbrella of the highly secret Büro Concordia, whose day-to-day running was in the hands of Erich Hetzler. For 13 years Hetzler had lived in England where he studied at the London School of Economics. Later he was recruited as Ribbentrop's England specialist and remained as a personal assistant to the Foreign Minister until the start of 1940 when he moved to the Rundfunkhaus.[1] Adolf Mahr, as we have seen, was a daily visitor to Concordia's offices at Berlin's Sportsfeld where he represented the Foreign Office and was in touch with Walther Kamm, variously in charge of overseas short-wave services and the European service's medium and long wave sectors.[2] When Mahr first drew up his Irish radio propaganda blueprint for Ribbentrop in March 1941, he proposed that as well as broadcasting directly to Ireland, a secret transmitter or G-sender should be established to reach Irish-American audiences in the United States. Given Mahr's regular contact with Büro Concordia, it is not difficult to see how he came by the idea. Mahr originally wanted the secret station to 'express the views of the American Irish' and use that lobby to swing public opinion in America against US entry into the war.[3] After Pearl Harbour, however, the plan was modified, first to hinder the Democratic Party's chances in the 1942 congressional elections and, later, to block Roosevelt's fourth bid for the White House.

But was it worth Mahr's while to target Irish Americans in this way and for these ends? The available figures suggest it was. In the early months of the war an estimated half a million Americans were said to be interested in listening to German short-wave radio programmes. In January 1941 a Princeton University study put the total American audience for European short-wave broadcasts somewhere between 3 and 7 million listeners. According to the researchers, German Radio's American audience on any given day was 150,000.[4] But Mahr had more ambitious plans; he wanted a sizeable slice of the Irish-American population which he estimated at 5 to 6 million. There was a catch, however. The Irish-Americans' traditional support for the Democratic party would, in practice, make more difficult Mahr's task of swinging that lobby against Roosevelt, a Democratic President. But Goebbels' and Ribbentrop's men were undaunted by such considerations.[5]

On a visit to Berlin in 1942 from his chosen exile in Italy, Charles Bewley was asked by Hans Dieckhoff (the former German ambassador to Washington who was then head of the department for Anglo-American affairs in the German Foreign Office) 'whether there is any propaganda which might help us to detach the Irish vote from Roosevelt in the coming election. It is of the greatest importance that Roosevelt should be defeated'. Bewley suggested the Germans 'could secure at least a portion of the Irish vote for an anti-Roosevelt candidate if you promised that, in the event of a German victory, Germany would create an Irish Republic for the whole island, including Ulster'. But Dieckhoff shook his head saying, 'It is contrary to the policy of the German government to make any declaration during the progress of the war on its intentions after the victory'.[6]

In the summer of 1943, the Foreign Office again sought advice on propaganda tactics to prevent Roosevelt's re-election, this time from the senior IRA figure Frank Ryan who was still living in Berlin. Unlike Bewley, Ryan was against the idea from the start and wrote a top secret memorandum strongly disagreeing with the plan. Ryan reasoned that since Ireland was not at war with the United States such a scheme could provoke a 'violent American response'.[7] On 26 August 1943 a meeting of the German Foreign Office's North America committee was held to discuss the status of various black propaganda radio stations. Dr Kurt Georg Kiesinger reported that

> a Polish secret station was already in its early stages of existence, to address mainly Polish officers... the Croatian station was disrupted by sabotage. Finns and Hungarians were not reachable by any programmes at the moment... a suitable person for the Irish station was now available. Irish people in the USA could be addressed twice weekly through this station.[8]

The identity of the so-called suitable person was not revealed to the meeting, but the Foreign Office may have been under the mistaken impression that Frank Ryan (after he was asked his opinion but before he wrote his refusal) might agree to broadcast — he had done so on Radio Madrid during the Spanish civil war — or, at least, write scripts for someone else to broadcast to the target Irish-American audience.

As a Foreign Office employee with direct responsibility for Irish affairs, Adolf Mahr seems likely to have known of the North America committee's plan. At an earlier stage Mahr had advised the Foreign Office 'to recruit suitable speakers, even collaborators amongst the Irish inmates of prisoner of war camps', although he insisted that 'the newscaster must speak with an American accent'.[9] Hans Hartmann, on the other hand, was kept in the dark about the project, and the Foreign Office clearly did not intend using anyone from his Irland-Redaktion for the anti-Roosevelt broadcasts. In any case, Hartmann had already left Berlin for Luxembourg two weeks before the North America committee's meeting.[10]

At the beginning of 1944, Helmut and Elizabeth Clissmann were also asked for their views on the propaganda plan. Helmut Clissmann was then serving as an army cadet in Hanover while his wife was living in Copenhagen. According to the Clissmanns:

The German political machine, and especially Ribbentrop the Foreign Minister, wished at all costs to stop Roosevelt getting elected for a fourth term. Posters had appeared in Berlin describing the American President as 'Public Enemy Number One'. The order came down from Ribbentrop to launch an anti-Roosevelt campaign on radio. Veesenmayer at the Foreign Office was given the job of carrying the order through. It was decided that the message would be to try and persuade the Irish, Polish and Italian minorities in America that the US should get out of the war in Europe.

But the Clissmanns had already made up their minds the idea was a bad one and 'saw at once that this would not work with the American Irish'.[11] According to Mrs Clissmann:

It was decided to divide the ethnic groups — Polish, Italian and Irish — people who, for one reason or another, might possibly be against America's war effort. The Irish were the most likely since they were looked upon as having a traditional conflict with England. But it is inconceivable that it would have made the slightest difference to the war effort. Vis-à-vis the Irish in America, the concept was that an Irish radio station should be set up in Germany, or within the German orbit, purporting to come from Ireland, which would carry propaganda supposedly from Ireland against Roosevelt.

Mrs Clissmann adds:

The Propaganda Ministry had nobody capable of advising them as to whether such a project was feasible. They searched around for people who knew Ireland and came, among others, on my husband Helmut... it was suggested that I should be fetched from Copenhagen, should be warned as to what was afoot so that I would inevitably take the proper negative attitude and go through the motions. Part of the motions included going to Luxembourg to see how the Irish service worked.

Mrs Clissmann was instructed to find out from Hartmann's team 'what they knew and where they got their Irish news from'.[12]

So it was that in March 1944, just over a month after Francis Stuart had left Hartmann's team, Elizabeth Clissmann — the Sligo-born wife of a German soldier — set out from Copenhagen to Luxembourg on a secret mission she knew was doomed to failure.

Footnotes

1. Howe, 1982, p. 69; Balfour, 1979, p. 134. The black propaganda stations included: La Voix de la Paix (the Voice of Peace, for France); the New British Broadcasting Station (for Britain. William Joyce wrote many of the scripts); Radio Caledonia (for Scotland, where Susan Hilton worked before joining the Irland-Redaktion); Workers' Challenge (for London's East End); Lenin's Old Guard (for Russia); the Christian Peace Movement Station (for Britain. Hilton also worked there); the Nut Cracker (for Holland); Radio Humanité (for France); Radio Free America; Radio Free India; the Voice of Free Arabia; and a Welsh Freedom Station (Balfour, 1979, p. 139).

2. Mahr memo, 'English language programmes to Ireland', 9 September 1941 (AA, 62407); Cole, 1964, p. 111; Balfour, 1979, p. 471.

3. Mahr report, 'Radio Propaganda to Ireland', 18 March 1941, p. 9 (AA, R67483).

4. Rolo, 1943, pp. 96-7. By February 1941 just over 8 hours of German shortwave programmes were being beamed to North America every 24 hours. This phenomenal output was maintained until the end of 1943 (Schwipps, 1971, pp. 45, 70, 73-4).

5. Mahr had possibly underestimated the size of the target audience. Dr T. Ryle Dwyer puts the Irish-Americans at 'about 15% of the population of the United States' in the 1939-45 period. With a total US population of 132,457,000 in 1940 (US Department of Commerce's *Statistical Abstract of the United States 1991*, p. 7, table 2), Dr Dwyer's estimate means that the Irish-American population, at the time Mahr was writing, was almost 20 million. Dr Dwyer notes that the Irish-Americans' 'political importance far outweighed their numerical strength. For one thing, their concentration in the most populous states and their tendency to support Democratic candidates made them a very potent force within the Democratic Party' (Dwyer, 1977, p. 24).

6. Bewley, 1989, pp. 197-8. Bewley claims (p. 189) that he turned down an offer from Ribbentrop of a job at the German Foreign Office in wartime Berlin.

7. Cronin, 1980, p. 228.

8. Schnabel, 1967, pp. 470-1. It is clear that by August 1943 Mahr's plan to beam propaganda to Irish-Australians had been scrapped.

9. Mahr report, 18 March 1941, p. 9 (AA, R67483).

10. Letter to author from Hans Hartmann, Cologne, 12 July 1993. Hartmann was unaware of the North America committee's meeting on 26 August 1943, but when he got wind of it early in January 1944 (having seen Frank Ryan's report) he immediately tried to recruit Ryan to the Irland-Redaktion, fearing 'a rival station' (Cronin, 1980, p. 229).

11. Author's interview with Helmut and Elizabeth Clissmann, Dublin, 11 September 1990.

12. Author's interview with Mrs Elizabeth Clissmann, Dublin, 19 October 1990.

22

Secret Mission to Luxembourg

B ecause of the importance attached by the rival Foreign and Propaganda Ministries to her mission to Luxembourg in March 1944, Elizabeth Clissmann was granted a travel permit, rare for civilians, to leave Copenhagen for Hanover where her husband Helmut was in barracks. Arriving by boat and train in Hanover she found 'the house of a friend bombed, the moon shining through where the roof should be and dozens of cats wandering around mewing. It was very strange. Another friend's house was unoccupied with two milk bottles and a newspaper outside the door'. Mrs Clissmann took refuge in an air raid shelter and was later briefed on the radio project by her husband who had been granted special leave to meet her. Next stop was the Grand Duchy of Luxembourg, occupied since May 1940 by the German Army. There she was scheduled to spend one week.

The studios housing Hartmann's team were situated at Villa Louvigny in a Luxembourg city park. Mrs Clissmann describes her trip as

> a very funny week because the purpose of my visit was strictly secret — strenggeheim as the Germans call it — so there was to be no explanation as to what I was doing there. I was to just appear, be given a desk and a chair in an office and find my way round; try to find out tactfully what was happening. Of course, I immediately became the centre of suspicion. Everybody saw his job being at risk. At that late stage in the war the loss of a job could be fatal because you'd be drafted. Therefore, it wasn't just a question of

losing your job, it might be a question of losing your life. So, there was intense interest in my presence there, and resentment. But, on the whole, I managed to get over that and made some nice friends, and began to find out what they knew.

The displaced Irland-Redaktion Mrs Clissmann saw in Luxembourg was chaotic,

> Hartmann was working in difficult conditions. He was doing a nightly broadcast in Irish at six or seven each evening but had no direct Irish news of any kind. I discovered that, in fact, they had very little information. They listened to Radio Éireann when they could. Mostly the reception was defective. They got synopses of news from foreign newspapers delivered to them, having been translated into German in order to be censored, from the central Propaganda Ministry. It was then busily retranslated back into English which kept everybody happily occupied for hours and hours every day. Out of these synopses of newspaper reports they could deduce a certain amount of what was happening in Ireland but, as most Irish people themselves realised at the time, very little was happening. There was a fuel scarcity, black bread and the death of a parish priest in Ballina. Since the news was also censored from Dublin there was practically nothing else, which wasn't much help for a German station that was going to try to pretend that it was an Irish station. Where would you get any information? It was quite clear that there was no information in Luxembourg.

At the studios Mrs Clissmann met Adolf Mahr whom she had known in Dublin before the war. Having been privy to the proceedings of the North America committee six months earlier at the Wilhelmstrasse in Berlin, the Austrian was well aware of what Mrs Clissmann was doing in Luxembourg.[1] But even in the midst of war Mahr, ever the archaeologist, could not resist the temptation of making a field trip, as Mrs Clissmann recalls:

> He brought us all from the Irish transmitter on a Sunday to Trier to see a memorial monument erected in the fourth century by the Romans who had a large woollen industry on the banks of the river there. They recorded all the activities of their families on the different sides. It's about the height of four or five men, a very imposing thing to look at. I had never heard of it. He brought us all there in the very cold, bitter weather and gave us a lecture on it.[2]

At Luxembourg, Mrs Clissmann continued to have misgivings about the anti-Roosevelt transmitter plan and, as she explains, so did Mahr:

If, on such a transmitter, there should be great rejoicing about Japanese victories over Americans, it was perfectly obvious that was going to be very counter productive in Ireland. But, it was part of the policy of the Propaganda Ministry and more than likely was agreed at the highest levels in the anti-Comintern pact. Therefore, it was a matter of policy that it had to be pushed through. It was very difficult for Dr Mahr in these circumstances as the representative of the Foreign Office. He tried, without conflict or loud noise but very quietly, to see that certain fixed doctrines would not be pushed through on the Irish transmitter... he lived in Ireland for many years and reared his children here. He would, of course, know that no Irishman was going to rejoice about Japanese victories over Americans.

Mahr was in a quandary. Three years earlier he had been responsible for suggesting secret transmissions for Irish-American audiences designed to prevent America from entering the war. But with America now firmly entrenched in the conflict, Mahr was being obliged to carry out a Foreign Office plan — but one he had not originated — to target the same Irish-American sector with a view to hindering Roosevelt's re-election ambitions. Whatever about Mahr, the Clissmanns were determined that Veesenmayer, Ribbentrop's right-hand man, would receive a report knocking the G-sender plan on the head.

The war had been going on for four and a half years at that stage. Mrs Clissmann found Dr Hartmann's radio team

pleased to be in Luxembourg because it was relatively quiet. There were no big air raids and the food was much the same as in Germany itself. One of the advantages was that there was still some wine, whereas in Germany there was practically no wine left at all. I think they felt they were in a good place and it was very important to try and stay there. Everybody was very worried about how the war was going, naturally, so there wasn't any sense of complete relaxation, but in a bad world they were not in the worst place.

While living conditions were better than those in Germany, some of the poor working conditions appeared to be self inflicted, as Mrs Clissmann remembers: 'I met a German girl responsible for recording Radio Éireann, who went off duty ten minutes before the news programme came through and, therefore, constantly marked the book "impossible reception", and went home'. The girl said that when she had monitored the Radio Éireann news and typed it up 'no one had paid any attention to it'.

At the start of her fact-finding mission, Mrs Clissmann discovered to her amazement that the Irland-Redaktion did not have a single map of Ireland.

> I wanted to trace where the Bishop of Kilmore sat because I couldn't remember. In that connection I haphazardly said, 'Can you show me the map and I might be able to find it?' They said, 'There isn't any map'. So they had no news and no geographical information or reference books. It was very difficult. The Bishop of Kilmore cropped up in connection with Monte Cassino [the famous monastery had been destroyed by American bombers on 15 February 1944]. He had made a statement that the Allies should be ashamed of themselves for destroying this invaluable historic and cultural centre. This, of course, was a comment at which the Germans rejoiced and, knowing how susceptible the Irish were to the utterances of bishops, they wanted to give this full value. As it turned out, the Bishop sat in Cavan.

As well as Adolf Mahr there were two other pre-war friends of Elizabeth Clissmann's in Luxembourg: 'I had known Dr Hartmann and his wife in Ireland and felt very at home with them. They were very hospitable and I had my evening meal with them most days, otherwise I stayed in an hotel'.[3] Hartmann, in fact, knew of Elizabeth Clissmann's planned visit to Luxembourg, and the reason for it, a full two months beforehand. He had also discovered Frank Ryan's memorandum — disagreeing with the plan for a secret Irish-American station — which carried the initials F.R. (while living in Germany, Ryan used the cover name Frank Richard). On discovering who 'F.R.' was, Hartmann sought him out to work as a translator/adviser for the Irland-Redaktion. With Francis Stuart gone, Hartmann was naturally anxious to find another Irish person to replace him. At first, Ryan was annoyed that Hartmann had discovered him; he was, after all, supposed to be living incognito in Berlin. But Ryan saw a ray of light in the offer and, in a letter to Clissmann on 8 January 1944, wrote:

> Hartmann was afraid of a rival station and asked Stuart would I come to Luxembourg as an adviser there. I told Stuart to tell him that he [Stuart] had heard from Haller (or someone in Berlin) that the whole scheme of a Geheimsender [secret radio station] is dropped. I thought then that the matter ended there. Now Stuart tells me that Hartmann is most anxious to meet me and is going to apply for permission to that effect. I see just one possible good point in the affair. If Hartmann can give me translation work in

Luxembourg I've no objection to giving him my opinion whenever he wants it. So far as I can see, he is the last hope for me to find something to do. I'm doing nothing about the matter yet. I'd like to talk it out with you first and get your advice.

Five days later, on 13 January 1944, Ryan wrote to Clissmann again:

In a recent letter I mentioned to you about Hartmann. The matter has now gone further — more so than I like. The following I have from Haller: Hartmann rang him. Hartmann also rang Vau [Veesenmayer]. Vau and Haller are enthusiastic about the proposal and say it would be very nice for me there in Luxembourg. (When I hear that I begin to have doubts naturally. However, Vau will throw light on it when he comes back). I didn't ask Haller how Hartmann knew Vau was at the Führer Hauptquartier [Hitler's field headquarters in east Prussia], nor how he could ring him there. I believe there's a 'slight' inaccuracy in Haller's statement to me.[4]

This letter lends some credence to the notion that Frank Ryan was, indeed, the 'suitable person' available to work on the secret station mentioned at the Foreign Office's North America committee meeting in Berlin just over four months earlier. Veesenmayer had been chosen to see the plan to fruition and was now urging Ryan to relocate to Luxembourg where he could work with Hartmann and Mahr, the Foreign Office's link man.[5] But the plan to get Frank Ryan to the Luxembourg studios hit a major snag during February and March when the IRA man's health deteriorated and he underwent treatment for pneumonia in a Dresden sanatorium.

Meanwhile, following her week-long visit to the Irland-Redaktion, Elizabeth Clissmann was on her way to Hilversum in the Netherlands to investigate the operation of Büro Concordia's Free India Radio service.

There were about 23 Indians there transmitting on shortwave. The transmissions were being received in India while purporting to come from Burma. The British never found out where they came from. It was a most successful operation. The success of that operation was what inspired this concept Goebbels had that one could fool the Americans as to where the [Irish] transmissions were coming from. But the Indian operation was an entirely different one to anything that Goebbels had in mind. The most important factor was that when the Indians made their agreement with the Germans to set it up, it was a strict condition that the

Indians would run it 100 per cent as they chose and nobody was to interfere.

On 2 April 1944 Frank Ryan again wrote to Clissmann saying he was 'wondering about Luxembourg' and since he 'knew fewer people than ever in Germany it was ridiculous to decline to meet Hartmann. He has books, especially in my own language'. Ryan speculated that he could get news and a room in the Grand Duchy and 'could kill three or four weeks in Luxembourg waiting for summer'. As long as it was 'clearly understood' he was going there for a holiday, Ryan added, 'there'd be no cause for misunderstandings on business or political matters'. He presumably did not want to get too deeply involved in the Luxembourg radio project until he had a chance to check it out personally. Despite these misgivings, by the beginning of May 1944, Ryan had made up his mind to go and see Hartmann in Luxembourg. On 2 May he wrote to Clissmann: 'By the way, it might be good if you dropped a line to Hartmann and told him I'll visit him early June'. At the end of May, Ryan left the Dresden sanatorium and returned to Berlin to get a passport. He wanted to visit Elizabeth Clissmann in Copenhagen before seeing Hartmann in Luxembourg. Ryan arranged to have his photograph taken but it was to be his last and showed the pale, drawn face of a seriously ill man. Within days of the picture being taken, Ryan's health failed and he died in Dresden on 10 June 1944. Francis Stuart and Elizabeth Clissmann attended the funeral.

But what happened to the G-sender project, the feasibility of which Mrs Clissmann had been sent to Luxembourg and Hilversum to investigate? She recalls:

> I was sent there by my friends to make sure that this thing died as fast as possible. It wasn't difficult, therefore, to find reasons why it should; they were ready made. Those few people who knew about Ireland — who had been asked about it [the Irish-American radio project] and were so convinced from the first moment that it could only be a mess — were only delighted that it didn't start.

Did Mrs Clissmann report back to Berlin? 'Yes. I wrote out a thing to say how hopeless this all was. There was no basic information available, there were no people who had the necessary knowledge, nothing'. Whom did she have to report to, Mahr? 'No. I think it was possibly to Dr Veesenmayer. He was the man at the Foreign Office who was in charge of most Irish things but I'm not sure that he was still there because afterwards he went to Budapest. So I wouldn't have the slightest idea, in fact, who was there [in the Foreign Office] at the time. Dr Veesenmayer had been the man I knew best'. As Mrs Clissmann rightly says, Veesenmayer would hardly have been in a position to consider her negative report on the G-sender since, in March 1944, he was named Reich Minister in Budapest — a title which, in effect, put him in overall control of German-occupied Hungary. In June, however, she visited Veesenmayer in Budapest to tell him of Ryan's death and to suggest that news of the IRA man's passing should be made public. But Ireland was no longer on Veesenmayer's priority list; his mind was on other matters. By the time the Red Army captured Budapest on 13 February 1945, some 570,000 of Hungary's 825,000 Jews had perished on Veesenmayer's orders.[6]

Footnotes

1.   According to his curriculum vitae (supplied by the German Foreign Office in Bonn) in 1942 Mahr was in charge of radio programming to Ireland. By 1944, however, he was head of Ru II (covering England, Ireland and English-language programmes for the British Empire) and Ru XI (dealing with special information matters). The latter section, created in 1942, is thought to have dealt with the Foreign Office's secret transmitters (letter to author from Dr Ansgar Diller, German Broadcasting Archive, Frankfurt-am-Main, 16 May 1993).

2.   The Igel column — situated 5 miles upriver from Trier — is a burial monument of the cloth merchant family of the Secundinii, dating from around 250 AD. The square sandstone object is 76 ft. (23 m) high and is the tallest Roman burial column north of the Alps.

3.   These quotations, and her subsequent ones in this chapter, are taken from the author's interview with Mrs Clissmann on 19 October 1990.

4.   Extracts from Ryan's letters are from Cronin, 1980, pp. 229-31; Haller had either embellished his statement to Ryan, as Ryan suspected, or Hartmann did indeed have a hot line to Veesenmayer at Hitler's field headquarters, perhaps via Mahr. According to Mahr's daughter, Ingrid Reusswig, her father visited the Wolfsschanze (Wolf's Lair, the codename for Hitler's field headquarters at Rastenburg, East Prussia) in 1944, although she does not know why (author's interview with

Mrs Ingrid Reusswig, 28 July 1994). Another explanation for Haller's comments to Ryan is that Haller — realising which way the war was going — wanted Ryan to reach the relative safety of Luxembourg. Cronin (1980, p. 275) speculates that Frank Ryan may have 'thought that he could get to Ireland more easily from Luxembourg than from Berlin'.

5.   What remains a mystery is why Hartmann was left out of the plan for the new Irish-American station. Perhaps Veesenmayer felt that Hartmann, as only a 'paper member' (Mrs. Clissmann's phrase) of the Nazi party, could not be fully trusted and was not as committed to the cause as someone like Adolf Mahr.

6.   Carter, 1977, p. 123; Cronin, 1980, pp. 252-3. Veesenmayer first went to Budapest in the autumn of 1943 to try and topple Hungary's leader, Admiral Horthy, and succeeded in bring about a coup d'état the following spring. Veesenmayer's wartime activities in Croatia, Serbia, Slovakia and Hungary are detailed in Rich, 1974. Stephan (1963, p. 261) notes that Kurt Haller accompanied Veesenmayer to Budapest in the spring of 1944. Stephan told this author that, after the war, Haller verified the contents of the manuscript for *Spies in Ireland* (based on Abwehr II's war diary) while on his deathbed (Stephan interview, Cologne, 28 December 1990). According to Francis Stuart, Veesenmayer was a 'Jew exterminator' (Stuart interview, 17 November 1989). Lt. Col. John Duggan notes that Veesenmayer 'had proved his ruthless efficiency in liquidating Jews in Hungary and Czechoslovakia, for which he was sentenced to seven years' imprisonment by the Nuremberg tribunal (Duggan, 1989, preface *xv*). Whatever Elizabeth Clissmann's thoughts about Veesenmayer were, she chose to keep them to herself. But her discretion was not reciprocated by the German SS Colonel who, 30 years after the war, appeared to regret he had not chosen the Sligo woman for his Irish coup d'état plan in 1940. In July 1977, in a rare interview at his heavily fortified home in Darmstadt, Germany, Veesenmayer told Duggan of his 'vast admiration' for Mrs Clissmann, adding: 'She was a great Irish woman; such fire, such zest and a mother to boot. If only Ryan and Russell had her head or her zeal and initiative, things could have been far different in Ireland with a better prospect of bringing about a coincidence of Irish and German interests' (Duggan, 1979, appendix XXIV, p. 423).

23

End Game

With Francis Stuart gone and Frank Ryan dead, Hartmann was finding it hard to put an authentic Irish gloss on his programmes from Luxembourg. The nearest he got to a real Irishman was William Murphy from Bessbrook in County Armagh. Murphy, a Berlitz teacher, visited Hartmann at the beginning of 1944 but failed to impress the German in translation and announcing tests. He was thrown out after only a few weeks, having earlier been rejected too by William Joyce. As well as the difficulty of finding Irish news, the Irland-Redaktion was no longer using the Rennes and Calais transmitters — which were already overloaded with civilian and military traffic — and was obliged instead to use the Luxembourg station (on 1293 metres) as well as Hilversum (on 301.5 and 415.5 m). Both these transmitters were less suitable than Rennes which had a strong signal across the sea to Ireland, uninterrupted by any land mass. To make his task easier, Hartmann exchanged news items with other language services. Thus, on 22 February 1944, the Dutch home service carried Cardinal MacRory's 'pastoral letter to young Irishmen not to become infected with communist ideologies in the United Kingdom' which closely paralleled Hartmann's theme broadcast three months earlier, on 25 November 1943. Ireland's Catholic hierarchy was unwittingly providing useful propaganda material for German Radio's European services at this stage of the war. In addition to Cardinal MacRory, other Irish bishops figured in the European output. For example, on

12 March, the England-Redaktion reported that 'the Roman Catholic Bishop of Cavan approved de Valera's reply to the US demand to break off diplomatic relations with the Axis powers. Bishop O'Callaghan stated that de Valera had made a sensible, cautious and statesmanlike speech, which had met with the approval of the entire population of Éire'. On 17 March, Cardinal MacRory was back again, this time on the German home service, 'condemning the Anglo-US campaign against Irish neutrality', and accusing the British of having 'always treated Éire in a cruel and unjust manner. The Irish people will maintain their right to independence and freedom, and will have nothing to do with England'.

Irish stories also featured on one of Büro Concordia's clandestine stations, Radio National, which pretended to broadcast from Britain. On 7 April 1944 a Radio National announcer told listeners:

> We are inclined to despise the neutrals out of jealousy that they are out of it. I know Ireland is despised more than any other neutral, but we must remember her struggle to maintain her newly found freedom and independence, and that she is a very poor country whose ambition is to put herself on a level with the richer countries of Europe... Most of us are inclined to think a country remains neutral in order to make money, but this is not so in Ireland's case. There are a few countries left who can see a little farther than the ends of their noses and so they are wisely staying out of this nightmare. Although they are suffering at the moment and we are looking down on them, there will come a day when we shall see who were the bloody fools to go to war and risk everything for the sake of the Lion of Judah.

Time was now beginning to run out for Hartmann and his team. Following the D-Day landings in Normandy on 6 June 1944, events followed in quick succession with the Red Army opening its summer offensive on 23 June and German Army officers attempting to assassinate Hitler on 20 July. But the immediate concern for the propagandists was how to make D-Day look like anything other than the beginning of the end. As the days following the invasion turned into weeks, Germany's propaganda services had to put a brave face on an event they had earlier predicted could either never happen or be easily repulsed. In his diary entry for 8 June, Goebbels wrote:

> The scene we are all obsessed with now is invasion. I am drawing up guidelines on how to handle this matter as far as domestic and

foreign propaganda are concerned. With foreign propaganda it is important that we present the news as quickly as possible... It must be made clear to the enemy just how great are the losses they are incurring. That will work best in England and the USA.[1]

Little is known about the detailed contents of Hartmann's talks for the remainder of the war. This is principally because the BBC's Maurice Irvine was invalided out of the monitoring service with tuberculosis on 25 July 1944 and a decision was taken not to replace him with another Gaelic monitor. Irvine himself thought MI5 saw no further value in translating German Radio's Irish language talks because the course of the war had irreversibly changed in favour of the Allies. Added to this was the fact that, according to Irvine and his fellow monitor Lorna Swire, Hartmann's talks had become repetitive and added nothing new in terms of military intelligence. Hartmann was 'a crashing bore' according to Swire, who adds: 'I remember looking at specimens of Dr Hans Hartmann's broadcasts and every one dealt with the same topic, viz. the evils of Bolshevism. I don't think he ever talked about anything else'.[2] All Irvine remembers from the first half of 1944 were talks in Irish by Hartmann and anonymous talks in English on Irish topics. Unlike the BBC, Irish Army monitors continued to tune in to Hartmann until the end of the war, though detailed transcripts were rarely typed up.

On 25 August 1944 Paris was liberated and by the beginning of September American troops were closing in on Luxembourg. One step ahead of the posse, the remaining Irish team — by then reduced to Hartmann, a secretary and a translator — moved northwards along with the other European services to the village of Apen, near Oldenburg, where they set up studios in Bremers Hotel. The crucial Calais transmitter had been lost to the Allies in August, so German radio engineers now worked furiously to get two new transmitters up and running — one for civilian audiences, the other for military use. Hans Hartmann recalls leaving Luxembourg 'in a hurry, and I think all the material which was there was captured by the Americans'. Before leaving the Grand Duchy, German troops tried to dynamite the studios but a local Radio Luxembourg engineer persuaded them to shoot holes in the transmitter tubes instead. When the Americans arrived at the station on 11 September, the engineer had the last laugh — recovering a complete set of tubes he had buried in the Villa Louvigny's garden four years earlier.[3]

At McKee Barracks in Dublin, G2 officers noticed something was amiss with the upheaval in the Irland-Redaktion's broadcasting hours and wavelengths.[4] A talk by Hartmann on Anglo-American supply problems was picked up in Dublin on 23 August 1944 but there followed a gap of over a month before Hartmann was heard again on 26 September. This suggests that the broadcasters fled Luxembourg on 23 or 24 August, just over two weeks before the Americans arrived. On 17 November 1944, Dublin picked up one of the last Hartmann talks reproduced in detail by G2 entitled 'Views on Neutrality'.

> Go mbeannaí Dia dhaoibh a chairde. When the convention was held in Dumbarton Oaks[5] the new machinery was outlined by means of which the world of smaller nations is to come under the dictation of the three great powers, Russia, England and America. Whatever organisation is devised to deal with the affairs of the world after the war, it is clear that the smaller nations are to have no voice, even in those matters affecting their own destinies. Full power is to be reserved to the three great powers mentioned. In their colossal vanity and insolence they see no need to consult the right of any state but their own, and for other countries there is to be a slavish acceptance of the decisions of these self-appointed arbiters of the world's destiny. If they think that peace can be established on injustice they are grievously mistaken. There is no chance for any country in Europe to save its own culture and religion except through Germany who has been, and is still, fighting to establish a complete and just peace.

As well as Hartmann, the radio team in Apen comprised the acting head of foreign radio services, Erich Hetzler, William Joyce and his wife Margaret, along with other members of the English service, in addition to Poles, Arabs and Indians working with Büro Concordia. Adolf Mahr was also there, as his son Gustav recalls: 'Father had remained with Büro Concordia all through the endless bombing of 1943-45, finishing up somewhere in the bogs of Oldenburg, west of Bremen, where they disbanded'. Against all odds the Apen team continued to put out propaganda programmes, thanks mainly to Hetzler's organisational abilities and Rundfunk engineers who provided the necessary technical back-up. No Irland-Redaktion programmes were picked up in Dublin from 14 to 25 December

1944, inclusive, but Hartmann was heard on 26 December giving a commentary on 'Hunger and Communism'. On 11 February 1945 a German broadcast to Ireland announced that the Fehmegerichte (courts with powers of summary execution) 'had been revived and had already taken action against collaborationists in Anglo-Irish War style'.[6] On 17 March — just seven weeks before the end of the war — the Irland-Redaktion managed to put out its last St Patrick's Day programme. Monitors in Dublin noted the broadcast began with a song, 'The Hills of Donegal', followed by a special commentary on St Patrick by Hartmann. Another song, 'The Emigrant', followed and the programme ended with the Irish national anthem. For the rest of March the format beamed to Ireland comprised war communiqués, news in English, news in Irish read by Hartmann, and music. At the beginning of April the programmes to Ireland were still on air. They included Hartmann's news in Irish at 8.45 p.m. followed by a commentary in Irish by Hartmann at 10.45 p.m. plus a summary of military news, music and political news from various countries.

But the overall situation had become so desperate that the German News Agency was reporting transmissions by a secret radio station in 'enemy-occupied Germany' controlled by the German Freedom Movement or so-called Werewolves.[7] Goebbels had authorised the use of an old long-wave transmitter at Nauen — 20 miles west of Berlin — for the Werewolves, a Nazi group set up to carry out an underground war of sabotage against the invading Allied armies and Germans who collaborated with them. This secret transmitter was on the air from 1 to 24 April 1945.[8] On 3 April Goebbels issued fresh guidelines for press and radio to devote themselves 'exclusively to re-establishing and increasing the power of resistance, the war effort and fighting morale both at the front and at home'. The Propaganda Minister wrote: 'The main task of the press and radio is to make clear to the German people that our Western enemies are pursuing the same infamous purposes and the same devilish annihilation plans against the German people as are our Eastern enemies'.[9] On 5 April, the Irish service was yet again quoting a member of the Irish Catholic hierarchy to support Goebbels' line: 'The Bishop of Clonfert in Ireland declared recently there will be a wider struggle in future than at present for the human souls — a struggle of the powers of light and darkness. Atheism is coming forward once again'.

With the military situation becoming hopeless for the Germans, a plan was hatched to get William Joyce to Ireland aboard a U-boat, but the order was never carried out as it was considered too risky. Instead, Goebbels issued a top priority order on 7 April which read: 'The Joyces are at all costs to be kept out of Allied hands'. Within days Joyce was moved from Apen to Hamburg where he pre-recorded his final broadcasts, the last one being transmitted on 30 April 1945. Despite the fact that Allied soldiers were closing in on all sides, Hartmann was still putting out a relatively normal service to Ireland. Just two weeks from the end of the war, and less than a week after the Red Army began its final Berlin offensive, the Irland-Redaktion programmes continued to go out on air with a mix of war communiqués, music and news. But there was more than a hint of despair in an anonymous commentary to Ireland on 22 April:

> Public utterances of British and American statesmen and propagandists have made it abundantly clear that one of the very first things the western powers, if victorious, want to abolish is the German conception of autarchy, meaning economic self-sufficiency. They say that in the interest of world peace, Germany must be denied the means of an independent livelihood. The primary function, of course, is that Britain and the USA enjoy the sacred prerogative to rule the world by economic power and, if necessary, by hunger and bombs. Ireland was depopulated and turned into a cattle ranch not because she wanted to be free but because it was in the best interest of the Irish themselves. The farms of the Poles were destroyed; their women and children perished by the thousands in the concentration camps. We heard from General Eisenhower that the Germans will be allowed to grow solely potatoes as the only means of subsistence; that Germany is to be transformed into what Ireland was a hundred years ago, a country hopelessly overpopulated, not because she could not support her people but because the established economic order condemned half of them to famine and starvation... So this is what the so-called Allied nations hold out as the future of the European continent. In the centre a German potato yard turned soon into a graveyard, and surrounding it an enormous Kügel [sphere] under the sway of Moscow, from Lisbon to Istanbul and from Narvik to Sicily.[10]

As the Irland-Redaktion put out its final programmes, the Second World War in Europe was entering its closing weeks; but the fighting continued. US and Soviet forces met near Torgau on 25 April, effectively dividing Germany in two. On 30 April, Hitler committed suicide in his Berlin bunker. Later the same day, G2 monitors in Dublin noted something was amiss with the evening's broadcasts from Germany and reported: 'Broadcast still announced as coming from Bremen. Usual announcer not on tonight'. On 1 May, Goebbels committed suicide in Berlin and that night Irish listeners were asked to stand by for a special announcement, in German, that Hitler had died. On 2 May, just five days before the German surrender, Hartmann took the microphone in Apen for the last time. G2 monitors heard him read a ten minute news bulletin in Irish followed by John McCormack singing 'Come Back to Erin'. It was a poignant swan song for the Irland-Redaktion.

At Bremers Hotel, Erich Hetzler was busy organising fake Dutch identity cards for his foreign staff. He advised everyone to leave quickly and 'do the best they could for themselves'. With American troops already in the area, Hetzler hurriedly burned all the records, tapes and radio scripts in the hotel yard before fleeing on a bicycle.[11] Hartmann was also on his way, heading for the nearby town of Westerstede where he could seek shelter with relatives. He recalls: 'When the radio service closed down, the last thing I heard from Ireland was that de Valera had declared he was sorry Hitler was dead, and he conveyed his condolences'.[12] But de Valera's controversial visit to Hempel came too late to be used as Nazi propaganda. The Irland-Redaktion had faded into the ether and would not be heard of again.

Footnotes

1.   'Goebbels — The Missing Diaries', *Irish Independent*, 13 July 1992, p. 8.

On 2 February 1945, while incarcerated in Brixton Prison, London, Hartmann's last Irishman, William Murphy, told MI5 interrogators that in July 1944 he had met Francis Stuart in Berlin: 'Stuart suggested that I should take up a job with the people with whom he was working, which turned out to be a secret radio station under the control of the

German Foreign Office... This station was named Buro Concordia' (PRO HO 45/25839, p. 11, pars. 72-5). Stuart denies ever having worked for Buro Concordia. When questioned about Murphy's statement, Stuart wrote: 'As far as I know and from what I heard from a German Abwehr officer, Kurt Haller, at the time, the William Murphy you mention was, or became, a minor British Intelligence agent. He gave all sorts of testimony to help his own ambiguous position' (Stuart to author, 15 January 1992). See also Bergmeier and Lotz, 1997, pp. 208 and 220.

2.   Letters to author from Lorna Swire, 17 October 1990 and 19 November 1990.

3.   On 11 September 1944 American troops took control of Radio Luxembourg after more than four years of Nazi occupation. The studios were used in turn by SHAEF (Supreme Headquarters of the Allied Expeditionary Force) and the US Office of War Information (for propaganda broadcasts), until being handed back to the Luxembourg authorities on 11 November 1945. The following day, the Luxembourg national anthem heralded the restart of the first programmes to be broadcast free of foreign interference for over six years (Graas, 1961, pp. 41-2; Barnouw, 1968, pp. 201-3).

4.   On 1 August 1944 the Irland-Redaktion was still based in Luxembourg and putting out three bulletins a night at 5.15 p.m., 6.15 p.m. and 7.45 p.m. Irish time on 41.44 metres. By the end of September (having fled Luxembourg for Apen) the Irish service was down to two nightly broadcasts — at 6.45 p.m. and again at 8 p.m. via the Bremen transmitter on 396 metres and Hilversum on 301.6 metres. During December 1944 and January 1945 the Irland-Redaktion's output was further reduced to only one occasional evening broadcast at 8 p.m. Irish time. The slot was changed to 8.45 p.m. from the end of January 1945.

5.   The Dumbarton Oaks (an estate in Washington, D.C.) conference — attended by diplomatic experts from the USA, the United Kingdom, the Soviet Union and China — was the first major step towards creating the United Nations. It was held from 21 August to 7 October 1944.

6.   The Fehme or Fehmic courts were used by the Nazis in the closing months of World War II to stop Germans collaborating with the arriving Allied forces. They were modelled on 'medieval Fehmegerichte, courts that dispensed a brutal form of justice' (Snyder, 1976, pp. 91-2).

7.   'German Freedom Movement: proclamation by secret radio station', *Weekly Review of the German News Agency*, no. 13, 9 April 1945, p. 2 (NA, D/JUS C 766).

8.   Balfour, 1979, pp. 408-10.

9.   Trevor-Roper, 1978, pp. 306-7.

10. Of those still remaining with the radio service only Mahr or Hartmann, with their knowledge of Irish history, could have written the 'Autarchy' commentary. It gives a clear indication that by 22 April 1945 the propagandists were thoroughly resigned to Nazi Germany's defeat. Yet, they continued to obey Goebbels' directives emanating from the ruins of Berlin.

11. Cole, 1964, pp. 234-5.

12. Author's interview with Hans Hartmann, 21 October 1990. On 2 May 1945 de Valera and the Secretary of the Department of External Affairs, Joe Walshe, visited Hempel at the German Legation on Northumberland Road where the swastika flag was flying at half mast. But the Taoiseach had not paid a similar visit to the American ambassador, David Gray, when President Roosevelt died on 12 April 1945 (18 days before Hitler's suicide). Contemporary newspaper reports note that the Dáil rose early on Friday, 13 April 1945 as a mark of respect to Roosevelt. During a sitting which lasted only 20 minutes, de Valera said: 'Personally, I regard his [Roosevelt's] death as a loss to the world' (*Irish Times*, 14 April 1945, p. 1; See also Dermot Keogh, 'The day Dev offered condolences to Nazi Germany', *Irish Times*, 11 January 1990, p. 15; Coogan, 1993, p. 610).

24

Aftermath

A bitter harvest awaited those who had thrown in their lot with German Radio's propaganda services. The post-war world made little distinction between those who had broadcast to neutral states and others more directly involved in the war effort. Some former Irland-Redaktion members were able to return to their pre-war occupations. They included Francis Stuart who, after being interned by the French Army for nine months, eventually returned to write in Ireland — where he still lives — in 1958 after first staying in Paris and later in London. On his release from Arbour Hill prison, John O'Reilly — the parachutist from Kilkee — bought a Dublin pub with the aid of his espionage money and a £500 reward collected by his father who had turned him in. Those directly or indirectly involved with the radio service, who chose to live in Ireland after the war, also included Liam Mullally, Madeleine Meissner (who became Stuart's second wife after Iseult's death in 1954), Charles Budina, Mona Brase, and Helmut and Elizabeth Clissmann. Nora O'Mara remained in Germany where she still lives, and Sonja Kowanka returned to her family in France, where she lived until her death in 1993. Dr Hilde Spickernagel pursued a teaching career in Germany where she was appointed as a secondary school principal.

Others were less fortunate. Susan Hilton was discovered by MI5 in the Nazi camp at Liebenau, south west Germany where she had spent the final nine months of the war. She was brought back to

London to face trial for 'assisting the enemy' and, on 18 February 1946, was sentenced to 18 months' imprisonment in Holloway.[1] A sad victim of alcoholism and confused loyalties, Hilton was the only member of the Irland-Redaktion ever to face trial and imprisonment, although others — like Meissner, O'Reilly, Stuart, Mahr and Mühlhausen — were interned without trial.

Members of the England-Redaktion faced far tougher sanctions from the authorities in London. Norman Baillie-Stewart, for example, was sentenced to five years imprisonment. But some paid with their lives, like John Amery who was hanged at Wandsworth prison on 29 December 1945. As well as facing charges arising from his broadcasting work, Amery was on trial because he had tried to recruit an SS unit from among British prisoners of war in Germany. On 3 January 1946, five days after Amery's execution, William Joyce, the England-Redaktion's chief announcer, was also hanged at Wandsworth.[2]

The defeat of Germany broke the Irland-Redaktion's most committed Nazi Party members, Mahr and Mühlhausen. Both men were ill-treated in Allied internment camps and never managed to put their lives back together again after being released in 1946 and 1948 respectively. Adolf Mahr — the man who created the daily Irish service of German Radio — was never to return to Ireland despite the fact that he was, technically, still a senior member of the Irish Civil Service on leave of absence from his post as director of the National Museum in Dublin. At first, Mahr escaped notice while living in the Oldenburg area. He even managed to get a message to Dublin asking an old friend at the National Museum to convey news of his whereabouts to his family, including his son Gustav who was then a prisoner of war in Canada. But Mahr's luck ran out when he was arrested near Oldenburg by British troops in late January 1946. He spent two and a half months in Falling Bürstal internment camp and, according to his family, was so badly treated that he almost died there. Gustav Mahr says his father was released from internment by the British military authorities 'for reasons of severe bad health'. A photograph of Mahr, taken on his release on 10 April 1946, shows an emaciated man in poor health. His daughter Ingrid says her father 'was so thin and sensitive that he could not even bear to be touched.

In the camp he had to sleep while lying on a paved stone floor. He was badly treated but said: "I am not giving them [the British] the fun of seeing me die here".[3]

Mahr tried to get back to his old museum job in Dublin but his path was blocked for a number of reasons: the first, a very public — and, for the Irish government, embarrassing — row in the Dáil in December 1945; the second, a damning report on Mahr drawn up by G2 for the attention of senior ministers. The row in the Dáil[4] erupted on 6 December 1945 when the former deputy-leader of Fine Gael, James Dillon, raised the Mahr issue directly with the Minister for Education, Thomas Derrig. The issue was a potentially explosive one for the government. In July 1934 Derrig secured the approval of de Valera's cabinet to promote Mahr — who by that stage had been a Nazi Party member for over a year — to the top museum job. During the war Dillon wanted Ireland to aid the Allies and, in February 1942, was expelled from Fine Gael for saying so. He now moved tactically to block Mahr's return to Dublin by asking the Minister for Education:

> How long the Director of the National Museum of Ireland has been absent from his position... for how long his absence from duty will be excused and when and by what method a successor will be appointed in the event of these positions being declared vacant?

Derrig replied that Mahr

> has been absent from his position since July 1939... I am not in a position to make any statement regarding the duration of Dr Mahr's absence and, as the positions [director and keeper of antiquities] which he held in the museum have not been declared vacant, the question of appointing a successor has not yet been considered.

Having lured his quarry into a vulnerable spot, Dillon now sprang the trap:

> Am I to understand that this gentleman returned to Nazi Germany in time to take part in the nefarious activities of the Nazis in that country and now, having backed the wrong horse, he is sitting there waiting to come back and land here as soon as the opportunity offers? Does the Minister think that such a person is a suitable person to reinstate as director of Ireland's museum, and, if he does not, will he terminate his employment with equitable compensation and get some respectable citizen of this country to

discharge the important duties of the two offices mentioned in my question?

In response, Derrig lamely fell back on a briefing note drawn up by his civil servants:

> Dr Mahr was appointed the official Irish representative to the Sixth International Congress of Archaeology to be held in Berlin in August 1939, and he left Ireland in the preceding month to attend that congress, bringing his family with him to spend a holiday in his native home in Austria. When war became imminent, he tried to return to Dublin but was unable to do so, owing to the delay in bringing his family from Austria. He then reported to the Irish Chargé d'Affaires [Warnock], with a view to getting a 'safe conduct' to return to Ireland, but it was not possible to have this done and he was granted leave of absence without pay until circumstances permitted him to resume his position. I am not in a position to say anything further at the moment, nor can I say when Dr Mahr will be in a position to resume.

Derrig's reply was factually correct but omitted crucial information available to G2 at the time — namely, that Mahr had planned to attend the Nazi Party rally in Nuremberg in September 1939 and that he had spent the war years working for the German Foreign Office. In addition, de Valera himself had known, at least since February 1939, of Mahr's Nazi activities in pre-war Dublin. Contrary to the impression given in Derrig's reply, the fact that Mahr became trapped in Berlin at the outbreak of war had nothing to do with his attendance at the archaeological congress, which was held there from 21 to 26 August.[5] Having fulfilled his duties as Ireland's delegate to the congress, Mahr and his family had a full seven days to depart for Ireland before war was declared on 3 September. It is clear, however, that Mahr was 'trapped' in Germany because of his wish to attend the Nuremberg rally.

Turning the screw in the Dáil, Dillon then asked:

> If this gentleman turns up tomorrow with the battle-stained flag of Nazi Germany wrapped around him, will he be reinstalled in this position? Will we go on retaining a gentleman seated in Germany for the last six years so long as the going was good?

Derrig, who must have been highly embarrassed by the questions, could only manage an off the cuff response:

The matter is being considered. No definite decision has been come to, pending a clarification of the position as to whether Dr Mahr will be in a position to return to his post... I think the Deputy has rather exceeded the privileges which apply to him as a member of the House in the statement he has made regarding a person who is still, technically at any rate, an officer of the Irish Civil Service.

The bruising Dáil exchange signalled publicly for the first time that someone who had served the Nazi cause during the war continued to hold a senior post with the Irish Civil Service. Having been caught off guard by Dillon, the government urgently demanded a profile of Mahr from Colonel Dan Bryan, the head of Army Intelligence. Bryan's report was sent to the government on 19 December 1945 and told de Valera and Derrig all they needed to know — and in the Taoiseach's case, some things he already knew[6] — about the Austrian archaeologist they had promoted eleven years earlier. It read:

Mahr was born in 1887 and would, therefore, be 60 and will attain the minimum limit for retiring in 1947. He was the group leader of the Nazi organisation in Dublin and as such was closely in touch with the German Legation and the Nazi organisation in London, and also with the German press agency in Dublin. He appears to have co-operated with, or possibly directed, Helmut Clissmann in at least cultural and propaganda activities. Just before the war, Mahr was succeeded as group leader by Mecking. Evidence at my disposal from two sources indicates that Mahr, in the later years of the war, directed or controlled the radio section which was sending German propaganda to Ireland. This section was evidently at this period under the control of the Foreign Office and not the Ministry of Propaganda. There are also some indications that Mahr was in charge of what was called the Irish Section in the Foreign Office. His name has also been mentioned in connection with his radio activities at one of the treason trials. Mahr, while resident in Ireland, was an open and blatant Nazi and made many efforts to convert Irish graduates and other persons with whom he had associations, to Nazi doctrines and beliefs. Apart from his pre-war and war activities, which brand him as a Nazi of some importance in relation to Ireland and make, in my opinion, any question of his immediate return unwise, there is no guarantee that further discoveries may not establish that his activities in connection with Ireland went further than propaganda. In the circumstances I recommend that no consideration be given to his return until the situation in regard to Germany and German nationals is much clearer.[7]

Luckily for de Valera and Derrig, Dillon did not attempt to raise the matter again soon. But the government was in something of a quandary over Mahr because, as the G2 report made clear, it would be impossible for them to grant him a full pension until 7 May 1947. Added to the embarrassing revelations of Mahr's wartime role for the Nazis was the fact that, from January to April 1946, the museum director was a prisoner in a British internment camp in Germany. Bryan's report effectively blocked whatever chance Mahr had of resuming his post in Dublin. Gustav Mahr sums it up as follows:

> As a result of a campaign launched by certain colleagues of happier days, claiming that he [Adolf Mahr] had been a Nazi spy in Dublin and, therefore, entirely unsuitable for resuming his post there, the Irish government pensioned him off at short notice with only twelve years of active service to his credit.[8]

James Dillon raised the spectre of Adolf Mahr one last time in the Dáil almost a year later, on 13 November 1946, when the Minister for Finance, Frank Aiken asked TDs to approve a supplementary estimate of £1,000 for 'temporary professorships in the Royal Irish Academy intended for certain distinguished foreign scholars who, for reasons arising out of the altered conditions on the continent of Europe, are unable for the time being to resume their careers in their home countries'.[9] Suspecting that the extra money for professorships was a ploy to get Mahr back into the country, Dillon went on the offensive again:

> I remember at one time there was a 'wangle' to restore to public employment in this country a gentleman who was at one time leader of the Hitler Youth in this country and a colleague of the head of the Gestapo in this city. I am happy to think that some references which I made here helped to scotch that plan and to ensure that the gentleman in question, having gone back to Hamburg has been left in Hamburg... Is Dr Mahr going to represent to us that he is a great authority on Celtic remains in and around Hamburg, and to sit down again in the Royal Irish Academy? If he got wind of the word, he would be coming like a tornado. He has been trying it for the last twelve months. I have no grudge against him but he took his hook out of this country on the eve of the war and thought that he would come back with a brown shirt and a swastika... will the Minister give us a guarantee that Dr Mahr, who is at present holding office on leave of absence without pay

as director of our museum, is not coming back under this scheme? Is he or any of his ilk going to come here under this scheme?

Aiken's reply appeared to take Mahr's side:

I take it that if the gentleman who was in charge of the National Museum were to come back to Ireland to work, it would be in the Museum and not in the Academy that he would work. I have no brief for him. I do not know whether he will ever come back to this country or not. Deputy Dillon wants to take advantage of this Dáil to abuse everybody, right, left and centre, to kick people who are down, but I say this for that gentleman, that he went towards the fighting, unlike Deputy Dillon.

Dillon: That is an offensive and impudent observation for you to make.

Aiken: No more offensive than the Deputy's.

Dillon: And the Minister is an impudent and offensive man.

Aiken: The Deputy thinks he has the sole licence to be offensive in this House. On every occasion on which he can throw dirt on the government and on his country, which he hopes will be used to get him patted on the back by the enemies of this country abroad, he comes in here and throws the dirt.

On the basis of these Dáil exchanges and the relevant G2 files, it seems the government decided to block Mahr's return some time after considering Colonel Bryan's memo of December 1945 — probably following Mahr's release from internment in April 1946. The Dáil debate of 13 November 1946 makes clear, however, that as of that date no public announcement readvertising the post of Director of the National Museum had been made.

Gustav Mahr concludes the story of his father's post-war years:

He had moved to Bonn where he had friends and the chance to carry on with his work as a prehistorian, making a scant living on lecture fees and research funds, and trying to launch out on a new career as director of an institute for mining history which had been his special field of interest ever since his early career in Austria. He succeeded in getting "denazified", so that he could have taken up the job with official approval. As his son, I was to be his assistant and librarian. He was to be returned his magnificent library stored at the National Museum. This happy development in his early sixties was too much for his ailing heart. He died in May 1951 at Bonn.

Heinz Mecking, the man who in July 1939 took over from Mahr as leader of the Nazi Auslandsorganisation in Dublin, had been an adviser to the Turf Development Board. Like other members of the German colony he left Ireland for Berlin on the outbreak of war. According to Klasmann, the company who supplied him to the TDB, Mecking then enlisted as an officer in the German Army. In 1941, after the invasion of Russia, he was sent to take charge of turf production there. He was later taken prisoner by the Red Army and died in detention at Tiraspol in Soviet Moldova on 18 December 1945.

After leaving the Irland-Redaktion in 1941, Ludwig Mühlhausen worked for the SS in occupied Brittany, liaising with pro-Nazi Breton nationalists whose native tongue he spoke fluently. On 11 May 1945 he was taken prisoner by the Americans at St Jacub in Austria. The first that Irish Military Intelligence knew of his capture was from a memo written by the former G2 officer Joe Healy — an acquaintance of Mühlhausen's from his student days in Hamburg almost 20 years earlier — to Army Headquarters in Dublin on 27 September 1945. By that time Healy had resumed duties as a lecturer at University College Cork, and told G2 he had received a letter from Mühlhausen written in July 1945 stating he was a prisoner of war in Naples. Healy noted that Mühlhausen held the rank of an Untersturmführer (Second Lieutenant) in the SS. In fact, Mühlhausen was destined to remain in detention as a prisoner of war for almost three years, being moved from one camp to another, from May 1945 until March 1948. On his release, one of his daughters described Mühlhausen as being 'physically and spiritually destroyed'. Subsequently, the professor who had travelled the Gaeltacht areas from the Blaskets to Donegal, had only a 'limited capacity' for academic work. His name appeared only once on a scholarly work as editor of a collection of fairy tales. Paralysed by a stroke, Mühlhausen died of a heart attack on 15 April 1956.

After broadcasting his final message to Ireland on 2 April 1945, Hans Hartmann fled Apen just ahead of American troops. The war years had been difficult ones for the German language scholar and his family but by carving a niche for himself in the propaganda service — he was, after all, one of the few people in Germany capable of doing Irish language radio talks — Hartmann had avoided military service and thus survived the war. Hartmann himself takes up the story of what happened next:

> I spent the period from 1945 to 1948 in a village near Apen, called Westerstede, where I had some relations. In 1945, I was visited there by two British secret service officers who interrogated me on the subject of British members of the staff of the Irland-Redaktion. At the beginning of the interrogation they pointed out to me that they were not interested in me personally nor the work I had done during the war.

Luckily for Hartmann, MI5 was only looking for British subjects who had worked for the Nazis and who could be brought to trial in London on treason charges.

While Mühlhausen was shunned by his former Celtic Studies colleagues after the war, Hartmann's friends rallied round him. Seán Ó Heochaidh, who had worked on Irish dialects with Mühlhausen in Teelin — and later with Hartmann in the north west Donegal areas of Gweedore and Cloughaneely — recalls that 'Mühlhausen was a real Nazi but to my mind Dr Hartmann was the opposite, which I think helped to save him in the end... poor Mühlhausen was thrown into a camp'. Seán Ó Súilleabháin, who had studied with Hartmann at the Folklore Commission from 1937 to 1939, received a letter from Hartmann explaining the dire straits he was in. He sent money to the German's family via the Red Cross, fearing his friend had been interned. Ó Súilleabháin — who died in December 1996 — recalled that some years later Hartmann

> came specially to Ireland to thank me and he said that I had saved their lives. Things were very bad in Germany at that time. I was fond of Hartmann, I knew him, and when you hear of somebody in trouble you try to help. We escaped the war here. I don't know what he said on the radio but... I did that because it was the only way I could get through to help him.

Contrary to the impression formed by Ó Súilleabháin and other friends of Hartmann's in Ireland, the German was never interned by the Allies, as he explains:

> I was never arrested, taken prisoner or put into a detention camp. I lived from the outset as a free man in the British zone where the living conditions at the beginning were hard in the extreme, causing

many anxieties and fears which I communicated to my friends abroad. But I managed, with the aid of my wife, to make a living by doing translations, working in a nearby bog to obtain fuel for heating and cooking, and by securing most valuable help from friends in Ireland.

In 1948 Hartmann joined the staff of Göttingen University where he lectured in Celtic Philology. In 1953 he obtained the Chair of Comparative Philology at Hamburg University where Ludwig Mühlhausen had also worked from 1928 to 1937. The new post gave Hartmann a free hand to continue his research on Celtic Studies. In the 1960s he returned to Ireland to record Gaeltacht dialects on audio tape and, as Seán Ó Heochaidh recalls, 'went back to Germany with a vast amount of wonderful material from some of the best speakers in North West Donegal'. Hartmann was also assisted in this research work by UCD's Professor of Irish, Tomás de Bháldraithe. Many language students have since made the trip to Hamburg to analyse and help catalogue Hartmann's huge collection of sound recordings in Irish.

Most members of the small Celtic Studies fraternity were content to welcome Hartmann back into the fold but not everyone was willing to forgive and forget his wartime role as a broadcaster for the Nazis. At a social function in Dublin in the 1960s, someone introduced the German scholar to Professor Dan Binchy with the words, 'Have you met Dr Hartmann?' Turning on his heel, Binchy replied: 'No, but I heard his voice.'[10] Binchy's attitude was exceptional, however, and must have been coloured by his experience as Ireland's Minister to Berlin from 1929 to 1932 where he witnessed Hitler's rise to power. Hartmann's post-war rehabilitation, both in Germany and Ireland, was in marked contrast to that of the SS officer Ludwig Mühlhausen. According to Éimear Ó Broin,

> Professor Mühlhausen's broadcasts were a particular embarrassment to Celtic Studies academic circles in Dublin because his work with the Irish language was highly regarded and was in such contrast to his activities as a blatant Nazi propagandist.

Reflecting on his role with the Nazi radio service 45 years on, Hartmann said:

I had no intention to make propaganda and made no preparations to do so. I even lacked the vocabulary I had to use for that. I remember that once, when I had to write my first talks, I went to the Irish Legation to see Mr Warnock with whom I was on very good terms, and I asked him to give me some Irish newspapers. From these I got the vocabulary needed to translate Wehrmachtberichte [German armed forces reports] et cetera. That was all I had, all that I could do. It was purely accidental that I went into the propaganda business. I don't consider it to my credit that I did it, at all.

Hans Hartmann lives in retirement in Cologne, Germany.

Footnotes

1.   Susan Hilton file (PRO, CRIM 4/1730). Mrs Hilton's brother, Edward Sweney, describes his sister's imprisonment as 'an injustice' and believes that she was 'very badly treated by the British, considering she had played a non-combatant role through radio programmes aimed at women civilians'. He also told the author that his sister 'may have been dragooned into doing it', adding, 'She is innocent of any blameworthy act. Her name should be cleared because what she did was inoffensive and caused no one any trouble. All her sentiments were pacific, in pursuit of peace, humane, and of extreme national value — because it was in the name of peace — at a time of terrible conflict. She was the victim of very cruel circumstances. I do not like to see anyone being exploited and cruelly treated. Susan was, in point of fact, incarcerated by the Germans and this fact should have been emphasised at her trial instead of which, apparently, it was ignored at great prejudice to a fair trial' (author's interviews with Edward Sweney, 9 June 1991, 14 September 1992 and 18 November 1992).

2.   One of Joyce's biographers makes the point that while 'it seemed necessary that a few should be hanged... with the deaths of Joyce and Amery, the Labour government felt that it had let enough blood to satisfy what the press represented as public anger at wartime treason' (Selwyn, 1987, pp. 216-8). Mrs Iris Cawley (née Marsden), an MI5 officer who escorted Susan Hilton from Germany to face trial in London, comments that Britons who worked for German Radio 'were all weak characters, except William Joyce who was the one who — quite wrongly, I believe — got hanged. Mrs Hilton was lucky we caught her rather late on when the Great British public had had their

scapegoat' (Cawley to author, 12 November 1994). After his execution at Wandsworth on 3 January 1946, William Joyce was buried in the prison cemetery. This, however, was not the end of the Lord Haw Haw story. Some 30 years later, on 20 August 1976, William Joyce's remains were reinterred at Galway's New Cemetery. The reinterment followed a ten year campaign by Joyce's daughter, Mrs Heather Iandolo, who commented at the ceremony: 'It had been my father's wish to return to Galway some day, and I am glad I was able to do this much for him' ('Former Nazi Broadcaster Reburied in Galway', *Galway Advertiser*, 26 August 1976, p. 1).

3.   Author's interview with Mrs Ingrid Reusswig, Dublin, 28 July 1994.

4.   Official Report, Dáil Éireann parliamentary debates, 6 December 1945, vol. 98, cols. 1549-51.

5.   The author is grateful to Dr Antje Krug of the German Archaeological Institute, Berlin, for information on the Sixth International Congress of Archaeology (Dr Krug's letter of 21 January 1997).

6.   G2 report on Adolf Mahr, unsigned, 19 December 1945 (MA, G2/130 Adolf Mahr file). The section of this report relating to Mahr's Nazi activities in Ireland would not have been news to de Valera since the Taoiseach had been informed of Mahr's fascist links almost seven years earlier. Neither would it have been news to de Valera's Minister for Education, Tom Derrig, whom Mahr had informed in 1938 that he (Mahr) 'was resigning from his leadership of the [Nazi] cell' (Walshe to de Valera, 22 February 1939, FLK, de Valera papers, file 953). In addition, G2 and the Department of External Affairs (of which de Valera, as Minister, was the political head) had known of Mahr's involvement in the German Foreign Office's radio propaganda operation for two years (Bryan memo — based on debriefing of John O'Reilly at Arbour Hill prison, Dublin — 31 December 1943, NA, DFA A/52 I, G2/3824).

7.   Unsigned G2 report on Adolf Mahr, 19 December 1945 (MA, G2/130).

8.   Letter to author from Gustav Mahr, Berlin, 28 November 1990. Adolf Mahr's daughter, Mrs Ingrid Reusswig, claims that some of her father's colleagues at the National Museum conspired to prevent his return to Ireland after the war in order to further their own promotion prospects (Reusswig interview, 28 July 1994). Her claim is not, however, supported by subsequent events since the only contemporary of Mahr's

to be appointed as director of the museum was Dr Joseph Raftery who did not get the job until 1976, some 30 years later. In the intervening period the museum was run by the following: Paddy O'Connor, acting director, 1940-45; Dr Michael Quane, seconded from the Department of Education to the museum as administrator, 1945-54; and Dr Anthony T. Lucas, director, 1954-76 (information supplied to author by Dr Pat Wallace, Director, National Museum, Dublin). In 1948 Adolf Mahr wrote to Dr Quane describing claims that he (Mahr) had been a Nazi spy as 'the most preposterous slander' (Mahr to Quane, 26 January 1948, NM, director's file no. 490).

9. Official Report, Dáil Éireann parliamentary debates, 13 November 1946, vol. 103, cols. 792-7. The Irish government's refusal to allow Mahr to resume his duties as director of the National Museum in 1946 was in marked contrast to its treatment of another Nazi member of the pre-war German colony in Dublin, Friedrich Herkner, who was also on the State's payroll. Herkner was appointed as professor of sculpture at the National College of Art on 18 March 1938. With other Germans he left Dún Laoghaire aboard the *Cambria* on 11 September 1939. A Sudeten German from Czechoslovakia, he saw action with the German Army at Stalingrad and Novogrod before ending up as a prisoner of war in Berlin. 'After the war, Herkner worked in Heidelberg and Vienna on restoring war-damaged monuments. Eventually, the Department [of Education] invited him back to Dublin, and he returned in 1947. The delay was occasioned by restrictions on travel imposed by the Allied authorities just after the war' (Turpin, 1995, p. 352).

10. Author's interview with Tomás Ó Cathásaigh, Department of Early Irish, UCD, 11 December 1991. According to Keogh (1988, pp. 29-33), Binchy 'had nothing but contempt for the opportunism of Adolf Hitler'.

Epilogue

One Man's Final Journey to a Concentration Camp

Arthur Kohn was an acquaintance of Adolf Mahr's in Vienna in the 1920s. The Jewish doctor had no way of knowing that, after Mahr's departure from Vienna to Dublin in 1927, Mahr would become the head of the Nazi Party in Ireland in the 1930s. Had he known that, Kohn may not have wasted the ink in writing to Mahr from Nazi-controlled Austria in 1939 seeking his help to escape to America.

The correspondence to Mahr concerning Kohn, monitored by G2 in mid-1939, paints a sad picture of the general air of inability or unwillingness to deal with the question of Jewish refugees seeking shelter in Ireland and elsewhere from the Nazis. The first letter[1] to come to light on the Kohn affair was dated 20 May 1939, from Frederick May - the noted composer - of 38 Marlboro Road, Donnybrook in Dublin, to Dr Adolf Mahr of 37 Waterloo Place, Dublin. May wrote:

> Dear Mahr, I should like to thank you for your letter. I thought that Dr Kohn had written to you quite lately, or I would have explained things to you more thoroughly. The truth is the Irish Government wouldn't allow him, or anyone else, to take up a musical or business position, even supposing he could obtain one. He has a visa for America which won't come into operation for some time, and the only conditions of his residence here are that it must be temporary, that he must do no work here, and that somebody must guarantee his maintenance. I don't know of anybody in a position to do this. I personally couldn't, though I'm sorry for him. I just had an idea

179

that you might have known of some rich philanthropist who specialises in such work; though if such a person existed in Ireland I should be as astonished as I should be pleased. Thank you again. Yours truly, Frederick May.

The next letter[2] to reach Mahr concerning Kohn was dated 22 May 1939 and came from Erich Stadlen, Guarantee Department, German Emergency Committee, Society of Friends (Quakers), Bloomsbury House, Bloomsbury Street, London WC1. Stadlen wrote:

Dear Dr Mahr, I am dealing with the case of Dr Arthur Kohn of Vienna, and my friend Frederick May has sent me your letter to him and his reply. The only comment I have to make on this is that Dr Kohn has naturally not a visa to America, but an affidavit, and that he is most likely to get his visa within the next two years. I need not tell you, of course, how desperate his position is. If there is anything you could do to help in finding a guarantor for the above-mentioned period it would be much appreciated.

Finally, Arthur Kohn himself wrote to Mahr on 14 June 1939. The letter,[3] from Dr Kohn's home at 40, Salesianerg, 4-79 Vienna, went as follows:

Dear Friend, Today I will merely take time to report that the miracle has happened, and that a Reverend in a little English locality has undertaken to harbour myself and my wife until my departure for America. I have heard from Herr May meanwhile that you also were making other efforts on my behalf and I thank you very sincerely accordingly. We will in this way hardly see each other again, but I hope that you will write to me once more. I will hardly get away from here before two or three months. Hearty greetings, Arthur Kohn.

In his position as the leading Nazi Party member in Ireland, Mahr must have found the representations on behalf of Dr Arthur Kohn difficult if not impossible to deal with. Any overt gestures of help on his part would have damaged his standing in the Nazi Party. There is no direct evidence that Mahr was anti-Jewish, although he would presumably have been obliged to follow the official Nazi line on the Jewish question. Mahr's postbag in 1939 contained some copies of an anti-Jewish newsletter entitled *Welt-Dienst*[4] (World Service) but these could have been unsolicited. When Mahr was effectively controlling the Irish section of German Radio from 1941 to 1945, anti-Jewish material was broadcast occasionally, but no more so than by other sections of the Nazi radio service.

What is certain is that in Dublin from 1933 onwards, Jewish people were considered *persona non grata* at the German Legation.[5] Adolf Mahr would have been in a position to influence this policy since his role as Ortsgruppenleiter (local Nazi group leader) made him more powerful than the German Minister, Dr Hempel. Mahr's influence was demonstrated in part by the fact that the Legation kept him informed of German nationals coming into and leaving Ireland. In addition he was notified of any German's change of address within the country.

Mahr had already left Dublin for Berlin when he received in his post the last such notification from the German Legation, dated 16 August 1939. It listed those Germans who had recently changed address and Jews had the word 'Jude' inserted in brackets after their names. In addition, all Jewish males had the word 'Israel' inserted in their names in accordance with Nazi practice. The change of address list ran as follows: Herrn und Frau Fritz J. Marckwald, c/o Mr Concannon, Eyre St., Galway (Juden); Herrn Karl Lanzendoerfer, 111 Tritonville Road, Sandymount, Dublin; Herrn H. Israel Heymann, c/o Mr J. Neville, 22 Leeson Park, Dublin (Jude). The list continued with recent departures: Herr und Frau Karl Meixner: Frl. Dorothea Krans; Herr Dr J. Hoven; Herr und Frau Broehl; Herr Krull; Frl. Resi Dorn; Pater Wilhelm Schulze; and Pater Friedrich W. Weber. The new arrivals, mostly Jews, were listed as: Herrn und Frau Gerhard Israel Rosenberg, 19 Fergus Road, Terenure (Juden); Herr Philipp Israel Moddel, 89 Grove Park, Rathmines (Jude): Herr Gerhard M.G. Israel Schloss, c/o Irish Steel Ltd., Haulbowline, Cobh (Jude): Herr und Frau Wilhelm Luz, 71 Clonmacnoise Road, Crumlin; Herr Dr Stefan Israel Lendt, 3 Mountjoy Square (Jude); Herr Siegmund Israel Liffmann, c/o Mr Mewey, 18 Belgrave Square, Dublin (Jude).

Dr Arthur Kohn, however, was never destined to appear on the German Legation's list of Jews entering Ireland as the war drew nearer. The Quakers' German Emergency Committee, which had first been set up when the Nazis came to power in 1933, continued to do its best to help Jews and others to escape from the Nazis. In fact, Dr Kohn was only one among thousands whom that committee tried to help and whose names today fill scores of dusty boxes in strong-room No. 5 at the Friends' House in London's Euston Road.[7] Despite the moves to help him flee Vienna, Kohn remained just a name on a card file. The optimism of his letter to Adolf Mahr in June 1939 proved to be badly misplaced. The 'two or three months' he said he needed to 'get away from here' proved all too inadequate as the Second World War intervened to seal Europe's borders and the Jewish doctor's fate.

Dr Arthur Kohn died on 5 April 1944 at Theresienstadt concentration camp.[8]

Footnotes

1.   May to Mahr, 20 May 1939 (MA, G2/130, letter no. 10/10/39).

2.   Stadlen to Mahr, 22 May 1939 (MA, G2/130, letter no. 10/12/39).

3.   Kohn to Mahr, 14 June 1939 (MA, G2/130, letter no. 10/164/39).

4.   *Welt-Dienst* circular to Mahr, postmarked 16 May 1939 (MA G2/130, letter no. 3/39).

5.   According to Duggan (1979, p. 64) 'German Jews in Dublin were never invited to any function in the Legation'.

6.   German Legation to Mahr, 16 August 1939 (MA, G2/130, letter no. 10/311/39).

7.   Letter to author from Josef Keith, Library of the Society of Friends, London, 23 March 1993.

8.   Letter to author from Hadassah Modlinger, The Holocaust Martyrs' and Heroes' Remembrance Authority, Jerusalem, 18 February 1993.

Appendix I
Mahr's Irland-Redaktion Blueprint

Foreign Office — Cultural Section
18.3.41
Professor Mahr
Report re. Radio propaganda to Ireland

I. Listenership

A. Ireland as a country

1) Circumstances of the population

Here it is essential to distinguish carefully between (neutral) Eire and British Northern Ireland. However, the border does not coincide with political differences.

The population of Ireland is slightly more than 4 million people. Approximately 3 million live in Eire and slightly less than 1.25 million in Northern Ireland.

The majority of inhabitants of Eire are Catholics and have a vivid national identity. Democratic ideologies are strong, as well as respect for America. There is little understanding of and absolutely no sympathy for National Socialism, mainly for reasons related to the Church. However, our fight against England gains great respect for us in strongly nationalist sections of the population; as the old saying goes, 'England's difficulty is Ireland's opportunity'.

Memories from times of the World War and Germany's achievements in the field of Celtic research are both contributing factors to the fact that enmity for the German people does not exist, even though the majority of Irish people would not wish a devastating defeat of England.

In today's difficult situation, most circles agree with de Valera's policy of neutrality, even those more sympathetic to England.

In Northern Ireland, two thirds of the population are more English minded than the English themselves. A third, ie. approximately 350,000 people, are Catholics, mainly nationalists and ill disposed towards England.

In both parts of the country (and beyond), Irish nationalists set their hopes on the reunification of Ireland as a whole along with full internationally recognised sovereignty as the outcome of the present war. De Valera shares these hopes, and last but not least, has founded his policy of neutrality on them.

2) Radio Reception

The number of wireless receivers in Eire probably amounts to 250,000 (as regards radio, Ireland was backward for a long time). Approximately half might be suited for receiving continental broadcasts. Up until the outbreak of the war, the listenership was more or less restricted to urban and rural intelligentsia. Farmers in the West, insofar as they were listening at all, only listened to the local Athlone station, which is nearly always audible.

Apart from this, only BBC programmes were suitable for the whole country, not only for language reasons but also because of their very good reception. For Irish listeners, they also provide a desired connection to the outside world because the programmes are obviously far superior to the broadcasts from Athlone.

In Northern Ireland, unionists only listened to BBC programmes, partly broadcast from the Northern Ireland station. This station has been closed down since the outbreak of the war. Since then, unionists only listen to BBC programmes from England. The interest in English language broadcasts from Germany should be smaller than amongst the audience in England. Before the war, nationalists in the North also had to rely on the BBC, but nonetheless quite liked listening to Athlone too. Since most were not well off, they spent relatively little time listening to radio.

This was the situation before the war. Naturally, since then a lot of changes have taken place. Particularly in nationalist circles (less so the unionists), an interest seems to have developed for English language broadcasts from Germany. Regarding the Gaelic broadcasts from Germany see the following paragraph.

3) The Language Question

Approximately 5% of the population of Eire speaks Irish (Gaelic) as their native tongue. They like to listen to the Gaelic language programmes from Germany (it flatters their linguistic identity), but as an important language in the political sense Gaelic is not relevant. The only Irish native speakers live in the West and are mostly small farmers. Gaelic broadcasts from the Continent can hardly be received by them. Therefore, they mainly listen to Athlone (Gaelic and English), and besides that perhaps the BBC.

However, not only native speakers listen to Gaelic broadcasts, but also a politically much more important element, namely language enthusiasts amongst the educated sections of society throughout the whole country, who initially had to learn the Gaelic language. In Gaelic language policy, which they defend with all their might, they see a nationalist political factor of the first order, and the Gaelic broadcasts from Germany naturally have a very positive effect on them. These must therefore be maintained. The only question remains the reception quality.

B. Additional Irish Listeners

The full extent of the Irish listenership cannot be recognized however, when considering Ireland by itself. Apart from the three and one-third million Irish with nationalist sentiments on the island itself, there are the emigrants, or the descendants of emigrants.

Thus at least one and a half million people living in Great Britain (London, Glasgow, Liverpool and in many other centres, as well as being spread throughout the whole country) would be conscious of their Irish extraction. In Australia, there are approximately 250,000, in Canada approximately 150,000, in the United States 5 to 6 million (all this without consideration of half-breeds totally absorbed in Anglo-Saxon culture).

Approximately two-thirds of Irish descendants living in Great Britain might be caught up in Anglo-Saxon political ideology, but at least a third would have nationalist sympathies. In Canada and Australia the situation could hardly be less favourable than this. In the United States, the percentage of consciously pro-Irish people is rather higher. The American-Irish are de Valera's prestige trump card, nationally and politically.

Yet all these elements, even if they are anti-Nazi and friendly towards England, are highly sensitive to any insults or moves against Irish interests and the Irish nation. Together, they represent a potential listenership with the possiblity of indoctrinitation against England, which is of no less quantity and importance than the listenership in the motherland.

II. Present Broadcasting to Ireland

A. Gaelic Programmes

After the outbreak of war, there was initially one programme in Gaelic per week broadcast to Ireland. Since the beginning of the offensive the amount of programmes has been doubled. They are on air now on Wednesdays and Sundays from 22.30 to 22.45 hrs (short wave DZD). Since those extended programmes only run in Gaelic, they practically only address the nationalists in Eire. They do not reach the older generation of nationalists (who were unable to learn Gaelic) and they do not reach the nationalists in Northern Ireland at all.

An investigation into the purely technical problem of radio reception is urgently required by the experts. It is suspected that the programmes often do not get through to the target audience. A while ago, a telegram was received by the Foreign Office from the German ambassador in

Dublin, in which he asked whether Germany was still broadcasting in Gaelic. He mentioned the correct wavelength, therefore he obviously had no reception on this wavelength (which was in fact being used).

The changeover of Irish programmes from the Hamburg-Bremen transmitter to short wave stations has undoubtedly impaired the reception in Ireland.

The Gaelic broadcasts have so far mainly consisted of news and commentaries, as well as the occasional talk.

B. The Lack of Programmes in English

English language programmes do not place from our side to Ireland. The Gaelic nationalists on the entire island and the emigrants who are unable to speak Gaelic are not addressed at all by their Irish identity, because our programmes in the English language are not aimed in their direction. In those English language programmes, Irish questions have so far been avoided intentionally.

The latter programmes are broadcast within the European service from the following German radio transmitters: Deutschlandsender, Breslau, Bremen, Friesland, Hilversum, Calais, Luxembourg and Rennes.

Rome broadcasts 20 times a day in English (on the Continent only Germany puts Gaelic programmes together). In addition, Rome has avoided, to date, broadcasting programmes in English specifically aimed at Irish listeners. There are, however, according to the grapevine, preparations for an expansion in this direction.

In summary, one can therefore say that the possibility of anti-English radio propaganda by means of the old-Irish culture has not been made use of at all. The Axis states mainly address Anglo-Saxons themselves with their English language programmes, and have not yet addressed those elements originally of other extraction but now totally integrated i.e. approximately 10 million people with an Irish ethnic identity, of whom 99 percent speak English as their mother tongue and who play an important, often highly important, part in all Anglo-Saxon countries.

C. Reasons for Caution to Date

They are clear. De Valera's adherence to Irish neutrality, which is of advantage to us, would have been impeded by strong propaganda. It would also have detrimentally influenced the English attitude towards Eire. Reasons against this caution might have been that a strong Ireland propaganda drive serves the cause of the anti-interventionists in the USA. The Irish-Americans are an important element from the point of view of U.S. domestic politics and the interventionists have made great efforts to win them over in favour of the war, so far without much success. De

Valera's biggest asset is the glorification of his support among Irish-Americans. There are moves to undermine this. They could then hope to have an easy game with Irish neutrality too. Therefore it is a disadvantage of our caution on Irish propaganda that we do not give the Irish-Americans active support in their fight for neutrality.

D. Cancellation of the Reasons for Caution

The time has come to increase propaganda in the direction of Ireland. The Iraq war represents a type of Dunkirk for English prestige. It also affects other satellite states. This upsurge can already be felt by the anti-interventionists in the USA since the Balkan campaign. Thus a large-scale psychological attack would also be called for in the Irish sector.

The Irish themselves feel that important decisions are in the air at the moment which could determine their fate too. Indeed, things have calmed down around the military bases but the bombings of Belfast have brought the war closer to home. They emphasise a new aspect of the Ulster problem and hit a sore spot of the first degree. Through Ulster, one part of the island is involved in the war either actively or passively. With England's destiny the Ulster question will be decided as well. In addition to that there are increased difficulties in shipping blockades and the war of nerves. In short, the Irish feel the question of reunification, and with that the final and total breaking free of the whole of Ireland from the British system, is entering a last, decisive phase.

We should now take this into account in our propaganda.

III. Possibilities for Expansion of Propaganda Directed to Ireland

For increased radio propaganda of this kind the following is the best structure:

A. Official German Broadcasting

1. To Ireland

a) In the Gaelic Language

The present extent of the Gaelic programmes must absolutely be maintained. However, their extension would be pointless.

b) In the English Language

The entire expansion would have to take place in English. Approximately 15% of the total quantity of English language services is not too much for Irish problems. Two-thirds of this would have to be provided for by the current English programmes; one-third would have to be newly created.

(These estimates also take into consideration the proposals for extended services listed below sub 2 and C.)

c) Stations
Here three demands are to be taken into consideration:
aa. The major part of the programmes must be transmitted over medium wave; short wave stations alone are not sufficient.
bb. The medium wave station must be a <u>major station</u>, preferably <u>Bremen</u>, <u>Freisland</u>.
cc. Besides that a <u>channel station</u> would be desirable (best would be Rennes, not just because of pan-celtic considerations which would be favourable for this Breton station, but also for simply technical reasons (good reception).

d) Transmission Times
Between 17.30 and 18.00 hours and then again between 21.00 and 22.00 hours (the reception improves with dusk in the long Irish summer evenings).
The programmes should not overlap with those of original propaganda to England.
It would also be inappropriate to attempt to block the news bulletins from the BBC. In that case, the Irish listeners most probably would prefer London.

2. To America

Broadcasting to the Irish-Americans by means of directional beams would <u>urgently</u> be desirable, preferably via the Rennes station. Three times per week would not be too often. The amount of programmes would be included in the total amount under para. 1 b.

B. Foreign Station

An expansion of programmes in the English language from Rome, which would address the Irish, would be very welcome. However, one condition for this would be strong German influence on the programme format (see para. IV) and good cooperation. The reason for this is the fact that reporting on Irish matters to the Italian public is intensely coloured by ecclesiastical information channels. We should do without this sometimes cloudy source.
On the other hand, the name Rome (the Papal city) will always find a certain receptive spiritual atmosphere in Ireland. This can be beneficial

for talks on Catholic religious tendencies, which have little conviction from our point of view.

C. G-Stations (Shortwave)*

(The extent of these programmes would be included in the total under para. 1 b above).

1) A G-station should express the views of the American Irish. One requirement would be cooperation with the America services. The newscaster must speak with an American accent. Such programmes would certainly be followed with great interest in Ireland.

2) A JapaneseG-station could in certain circumstances be deployed for the Irish in Australia.

Note: For all programmes under A and C it should be endeavoured to recruit suitable speakers, i.e. even collaborators amongst the Irish inmates of prisoner of war camps.

IV. Structure of the Programmes

The following main streams are under consideration:

A. Regular News Service: Under III A 1 b, III A 2, III B and III C 1.

B. News Commentaries: in all services listed in paragraph III

C. Talks: The choice of topics has to be determined according to the type of station.

The programmes are supposed to appeal to the independent national identity of the Irish around the world, to strengthen the neutral position of the country spiritually and to encourage reform into a non-belligerent stance, while the line can be maintained that upkeep of this neutrality is not only in their own interest but also in the interest of world reconstruction after the war. Elimination of the Ulster injustice is a basic demand of all Irishmen; it serves the economic future of the country, as well as the satisfaction against England and support for a new, better world order.

Topics:

1. Historical (including horror propaganda of historical content)

Author's note: G = geheim (secret)

a) The infringements of law by the English and their cruelties when conquering and oppressing the country. A nearly inexhaustable topic (Cromwell's scandalous deeds etc.). Also see IV 4 a.

b) The social destruction of the Irish people by means of confiscation of land, hunger, expulsion of countless people, abduction into slavery etc.

c) Persecution of Catholics. A nearly inexhaustable topic. Particularly suitable for Rome. Also see IV 4 a and IV 4 b.

d) Absolute bankruptcy of England's policy of colonialism in this, its oldest colony.

e) The epic struggles for Irish freedom since the conquest. Examples of heroic self-sacrifice of the Irish and the awful treatment of the conquered by England. Also see IV 5 a.

2. Ireland as a Contributor of Blood and Culture

a) The significance of Ireland as an object of exploitation by the Empire. Its formation without military and colonising achievements by the Celts unimaginable ('England's vampirism of Ireland').

b) The significance of the Irish for America. Emigrated to the land of freedom from England. Should they bleed under the American flag for England? (Germany no threat to America). That would mean denial of the American ideal and even if there were Americans prepared to do this, the American-Irish are not. Also see IV 6 d.

c) Ireland's spiritual achievements in missionary work past and present.

d) Ireland's contribution to modern English literature (which would be non-existent without the Irish) and in many other areas.

e) Irish awareness of the exiles and their descendants around the world, particularly in the USA.

Note to 1 and 2:
In European history there is no equivalent to England's treatment of the Irish. It was a crime against an equal, often even superior, neighbouring people lasting 700 years.

3. Social Matters

The Irish ideal of the Christian-Social state. The plutocratic philosophy as opponent of farmers and exploiter of urban workers (the latter important because of the large numbers of Irish workers in Glasgow, Liverpool, London etc.).

4. Religious Issues

a) The courageous adherence to the Catholic religion by the Irish despite all the suppression. Ancient friendly relations with Rome, Spain, Belgium, etc. Ireland one of Europe's oldest Christian countries. Also see IV 1a, IV 1 c.

b) Intolerance by Ulster Protestants past and present. Also see IV 1 c, IV 5 b, IV 8 e.

c) Maintenance of Irish neutrality as an act of convinced Christianity against the destructive forces of plutocracy, pretending to be Christian, yet representing the materialism and egotism of a bankrupt world order. He who stays neutral serves the truly Christian spirit of national reunification best.

5. The Irish State

a) Its resurgence against England's resistance. Also see IV 1 a, IV 1 e.

b) Its social and religious ideals. Also see IV 3, IV 4 a-c.

c) The segregation of the country according to English interests. Also see IV 4 b, IV 8 a-e.

6. Irish Neutrality

a) Eire merely makes use of its constitutional right (guaranteed by the Westminster statute) if it remains neutral. This war serves the interests of English money bags. No Irish interest is at stake. On the contrary, Ireland could only profit from an English defeat, yet not from a German one. Nevertheless, Eire remains neutral.

b) The Dominions should learn their lesson to guard their own rights too. Should they want to save England, then they should force it to the cause of peace, before it is too late, by retreating from the war.

c) The Irish are well acquainted with English political methods. Their neutrality can also be considered as the sharpest condemnation of the English-Jewish war. All the Irish in the whole world should follow this attitude of their motherland. English politics' self-righteousness, hypocrisy and cruelty are shared by the malicious agitators in the USA. This was already the situation in the World War. What did those elements do with the ideal of the People's Federation? Further:

d) Of the entire diaspora, the American-Irish have the greatest vocation to fight for Irish neutrality. With that they also protect their own neutrality. America 'threatened by Germany' ridiculous. Also see IV 2 b and the previous point.

e) Eire will neither sell off its freedom and neutrality for flour, ships, money or military bases, nor give it up for vague promises with regard to Northern Ireland. The Home Rule swindle during Redmond's and Carson's time can not be repeated. Eire will never allow English soldiers or those of another warfaring power willingly into the country, or Americans, even if there are Irish among them. This is in keeping with the national dignity of Eire. If English soldiers alone were stationed in Eire, then England would yet again begin its old game of violence.

f) Neutrality thus serves the understandable aim of keeping the terror of a new English war, which is of no concern to the Irish, away from Eire.

To keep it away from the entire island has unfortunately been impossible for Eire. This poor country has become victim to military actions by the English power in Northern Ireland. If many of the inhabitants had their say, particularly the nationalists, the country would be part of neutral Eire. The separatists in Belfast must take the greatest blame for things getting out of hand. The nationalists now have to suffer with them the bombardments in this English-Jewish war, which continues despite repeated peace offers on the part of Germany.

Nevertheless, Eire is sympathetic with her suffering neighbours in the North, Catholics <u>and</u> Protestants, and will help within her powers to ease their fate.

Indeed, this is highly necessary in view of the failure to deal with the refugee problem, resulting from bombings, by the English authorities in Belfast.

g) Eire's neutrality is therefore not pro-German or pro-Italian. Neither is it anti-British. It is simply pro-Irish. It is genuine neutrality and strives to shorten all the suffering. With that Eire also helps to alleviate the suffering of her Northern Irish brothers.

h) A united and free country amongst the states of the world desires to maintain permanent neutrality established under international law. Compare IV 8 f.

7.TheWar of Blockades and Nerves Against Irish Neutrality

Basic tendency:

The Irish recognize that the suffocating English blockade supported by the USA, aims to make Eire 'ready for war' against her will. But Eire will resist this blockade, just like the Irish have up to now victoriously overcome all other English attempts of rape. The Irish do not think materialistically and they were taught starvation by England herself. Compare also IV 6 e.

Description of Eire's artificially tightened blockade difficulties:

a) food shortages: bread, tea, coffee.
b) shortage of coal, fuel, timber etc.
c) shortage in industrial raw materials, semi-finished products, etc.
d) unemployment resulting from these.
e) withholding of cargo space.
f) war of nerves.

Nevertheless all this is easier to endure than bombings, land and air raids, perhaps even civil war. The Irish around the world can contribute a lot to save the people of Eire from this terror and to rid the Northern Irish from it again.

8. The Northern Irish Question. Also see IV 5 c.

a) The Irish will never relinquish their claim to unification with their brothers in the North, separated from them by violence and cunning.

b) Only after partition ceases is a trusting relationship between England and Ireland possible.

c) With reference to related statements by de Valera etc.

d) Description of the most recent terror by the English authorities etc. against Northern Irish nationalists.

e) Description of related religious suppression and discrimination. Also see IV 4 b and declarations by Catholic bishops from the recent past.

f) A unified Ireland will be free and then permanently neutral. Compare IV 6 h.

Conclusion

The overthrow of British imperialism is unavoidable since it has afflicted Ireland with so many crimes. It will bring with it Ireland's reunification so that it can sever all remaining connections to the British Empire. Then Ireland will see the fulfilment of its inalienable right to total sovereignty.

Only then will the reconstituted sovereign Irish nation be able to fully contribute, in friendship with all peoples and without link to other powers, to the rebuilding of the true international community of peoples which has been destroyed by England's plutocratic and un-Christian imperialism.

Appendix II
One Woman's Journey from a
Nazi Camp to Holloway Prison

N ot many people could claim to have been shipwrecked twice and thus washed up on the shores of occupied Europe in World War II, but Mrs Susan Hilton was one such person. Born Susan Sweney into a British colonial family in Trichinopoly, India, on 2 February 1915, she was destined — through a bizarre set of circumstances — to become a propaganda broadcaster for German Radio 25 years later. Her father, Cyril Edward Sweney, was born in 1889 and grew up in Wales. From 1908 to 1932 he worked for the British-controlled Indian police force, rising to the rank of superintendent of railway police.

Susan Sweney's brother Edward was born in Madras in 1912, and later moved to Ireland where he became a poultry farmer. When asked to comment on his sister's wartime role in broadcasting and her anti-Allied stance, he said that having been born in India, his sister had seen the British treatment of Mahatma Gandhi and his followers. Later on she had received 'rough treatment' at school in England and had reacted against the class divisions of British society.

In 1936, at the age of 21, Susan Sweney married George Martin Hilton, a Scottish mining engineer from Dumfries. In the same year she became a member of the British Union of Fascists (BUF) — the group founded four years earlier by Sir Oswald Mosley, and of which William Joyce was also a member — 'in the mistaken belief that they were solely interested in keeping the British Empire together'. Two years later she left the BUF 'because of the public attacks by the Union against the Jews', and moved to Dublin where the police Special Branch noted she was living at 8 Upper Mount Street. Back in London in January 1940, she rejoined the BUF and edited its newspaper *Voice of the People* until May that year. Her work for Mosley's fascist paper attracted the attention of the police who raided her flat and seized belongings. By that time Mrs Hilton's health had been affected by the death of her young son and she decided to leave England to join her husband who was working at the Mawchi tin mine in Simla, Burma. But her ship, the *Kemmendine*, which sailed from Glasgow on 28 May 1940 (bound for Rangoon via Gibraltar and Cape Town), was fated never to reach its destination, being sunk by the German raider *Atlantis* on 13 July in the Indian Ocean, 700 miles south of Ceylon.

Mrs Hilton, along with the other passengers and some crew from the *Kemmendine* were put aboard a captured Norwegian vessel turned prison ship, *Tirranna*. But Hilton made it clear from the start what she thought of her new captors who dubbed her the 'devil's roast'. When the story of the *Atlantis* was published ten years after the war, it was revealed that when Hilton was taken prisoner 'she had labelled the men of *Atlantis* with every expletive that the vocabulary of a lady would allow. "Brutes, murderers, people who spent their time shooting at innocent children" were but the mildest terms of her abuse, and beneath her invectives even the toughened marine guards winced and wilted'. Ulrich Mohr, first officer of the Atlantis took it all in good heart, however, writing in his memoirs that Hilton

> was quite a character, we thought, and her grouses eventually more amused us than otherwise. Obviously a well indulged type. Her special complaint was that the bar tender on *Kemmendine* had left his post after the first salvo. 'Would you believe it?', she said, 'Leaving the bar at a time like that! Worse still, the fool locked it!' Certainly the lady was somewhat partial to her 'drop', and our looted scotch provided a frequent panacea to her wounded susceptibilities.

On 4 August the *Tirranna* headed for German-occupied France with 293 prisoners on board. But on 22 September 1940 she was torpedoed off the French port of Royan by the British submarine *Tuna*. The *Tirranna* took only two minutes to sink with the loss of 87 lives. The survivors, including Hilton and a 'frequently intoxicated' Irish doctor, 54 year old Thomas Cormac McGowan from Sligo — who had been the *Kemmendine's* medical officer — were taken ashore and detained at the German naval quarters in Royan until December 1940 when Hilton made her way to Paris.

In the occupied French capital she earned 500 Reichsmarks for giving what she described as an 'innocuous broadcast' about her maritime adventures. Mrs Hilton's potential as a propagandist must have been spotted by the Germans who persuaded her to develop the radio broadcast into a longer memoir eventually published in Hamburg in 1942 under the title 'An Irish woman's experience of England and the war at sea'. Hilton was allowed to work in Paris as a journalist — based at the Hotel d'Amerique in the rue Rochechouart — while the *Tirranna's* other passengers spent the remainder of the war in German prison camps. MI5 files indicate that Dr McGowan did not survive the war. According to Eileen Walsh, the secretary of the Irish Legation in Berlin, Hilton established very close contacts with high ranking German army officers in Paris. But according to Mrs Hilton's own account, given to MI5 in mid-1945, she helped British merchant seamen to escape from occupied Paris with the assistance of an Irish priest, Father Kenneth Monaghan of St Joseph's Catholic church on avenue Hoche, and an Irish lady called Miss Fitzpatrick.

According to Miss Agnes Hannigan, an Irish woman resident in wartime Paris, Fr Monaghan was a British army chaplain who, during the Dunkirk evacuation of 1940, was ordered back to Paris by Military Intelligence in order to establish links with the French resistance. St. Joseph's church in the heart of Paris, near the Arc de Triomphe, was an ideal cover for the priest's underground work. But Fr Monaghan did not escape suspicion and was, in fact, imprisoned and interrogated by the Gestapo in mid-1940. He was later released. According to Miss Hannigan, Fr Monaghan's resistance work was a closely guarded secret known only to a few people in the French underground. This would lend credence to what Hilton told MI5 at the end of the war.

In June 1941 three members of the Deutsche Fichtebund (FB), the German overseas propaganda organisation, visited Hilton in her Paris hotel to sound her out about the possibility of undertaking an overseas spying mission for them. Hilton later travelled via Brussels to Berlin with the head of the Fichtebund, Theodore Kessemeir, and Oscar Pfaus (the spy chosen by German Intelligence to make contact with the IRA in Dublin at the beginning of 1939), former head of the FB in America and then FB leader in Hamburg. The Germans asked Hilton if her nerves were strong enough to undertake work for them in Ireland, the United States or Portuguese East Africa (Mozambique). But she refused on the grounds that she 'didn't want to do anything dirty'.

After moving to Berlin, Hilton undertook a series of jobs, starting with telephone intercept work, and was later taken to see top secret U-boat centres and other military installations so she could produce a propaganda book on Germany's military strength and capabilities. But radio broadcasting was destined to be her principal occupation for the next year in wartime Berlin. Explaining her decision to MI5 at the end of the war, Hilton said: 'I was then drinking an awful lot and I needed the money to pay for it'. She added that she went to Berlin on the promise of getting a safe passage home but once there she was forced to sign a statement 'that the work on which I was to be engaged was secret and that I would be severely punished if I said anything about it'. According to a friend, Margaret Schaffhauser, Hilton 'told them [the Germans] she would only broadcast to keep Ireland out of the war'.

Hilton began her radio work by scripting religious sermons for a black Büro Concordia station called the Christian Peace Movement, followed by personal talks for another Concordia station, Radio Caledonia, beamed to Scotland. For broadcasting these talks from September 1941, under the name of Ann Tower, she received 300 marks a month. In choosing the name Tower for the Scottish broadcasts, Hilton was not strictly using a cover name (although the first name, Ann, was made up) but part of the maiden name of her mother, Dorothy Tower-Barter. Although never broadcasting under her married name, Mrs Hilton did not attempt to hide her identity, using her maiden name of Susan Sweney for all the broadcasts to Ireland following her recruitment by the Irland-Redaktion, where she gave her first talk on 2 January 1942.

A radio colleague, Francis Stuart, said of Hilton:

> She was a nice sort. A great disadvantage for her was that she was evidently a heavy drinker, normally. In those days drink was less available. She didn't seem to have access to the black market. She was always seeing where she could get the next drink, poor woman. She was a nice woman, mind you. I never saw her outside [the radio centre] but I heard from others who knew her more socially that it was always [a matter of] where would she get the next drink.

Susan Hilton's dependence on alcohol meant she was all the more easily controlled by her Nazi bosses. Her predicament was reflected in the depressed tone of letters she wrote in 1942 to family and friends in Ireland (see chapter 13). As the autumn of 1942 approached, Hilton was to commit a professional error that cost her her job at the radio centre in Berlin. The precise details of what happened emerged over a year later, in December 1943, when another broadcaster, John O'Reilly, was interrogated by G2 officers in Dublin following his parachute drop into County Clare. In the course of a debriefing, O'Reilly told G2's Colonel Dan Bryan that Susan Hilton had proved unreliable on the radio and was fond of drink. In addition, another broadcaster, James Blair, was proving unsatisfactory and was believed by the radio chiefs to be getting stale. O'Reilly then told Bryan that 'following a scene in which Susan Hilton used endearing terms to Blair while he was in the announcing box, and still on the air, their services were dispensed with'. Following her dismissal from Hartmann's team Mrs Hilton disappeared — O'Reilly thought she may have gone to Spain — but in January 1943 she reappeared working for the Nazis' Inter Radio service where James Blair also found employment. Given the shortage of trained English language announcers, one part of the German broadcasting service appeared quite prepared to turn a blind eye to what the other half was doing.

In the summer of 1943 Susan Hilton was preparing to embark on a grand tour of some of the Third Reich's main cities with a view to preparing propaganda material for Dr Joseph Goebbels' Propaganda Ministry. But as she undertook her tour of Germany the Gestapo was voicing concern about Hilton's true loyalties. In June 1943 the Gestapo's Göttingen office detailed her itinerary around the country but, more importantly, it clearly labelled her as a suspected Allied spy. The Gestapo document, dated 30 June 1943, was addressed to the district administration of the National Socialist Party and referred to 'the Irish journalist Hilton, who is a spy suspect'. Her address was given as the Kant Hotel in Berlin's Kant Strasse.

The same document detailed a wide ranging trip around the Reich that had been arranged by the Propaganda Ministry, taking in Bayreuth, Passau, Vienna, Salzburg, Munich, Innsbruck, Augsburg, Biberach, Heidelberg, Koblenz, Cologne and Göttingen. The purpose of the tour was to allow Hilton to gather material on the life of the Roman Catholic Church in the Third Reich and, by producing a propaganda brochure, counter Allied propaganda that the Catholic Church was being crushed in Germany. Hilton was also under instructions to take pictures of churches ruined in British and American air raids and to write about them in her article destined for foreign consumption. The document ended with the Gestapo's Göttingen bureau chief instructing the local Nazi Party administrator that 'when Hilton turns up in Göttingen I want to be informed immediately so we can supervise her'.

It is not clear exactly what prompted the Gestapo to label Hilton as a spy suspect. Elements in the Gestapo may have thought her on-air blunder was a deliberate attempt to sabotage part of the radio propaganda effort. There was also the question of her letters home, which the Gestapo may have thought contained coded messages. In addition, she had refused two years earlier to undertake a spying mission for the Fichtebund, and her role in helping British sailors to flee occupied Paris may have been discovered through the arrest of Fr Monaghan in mid-1940. Hilton did not arrive in Paris until six months later but by that time it can be assumed the Irish priest and his circle of contacts were being closely watched by the German occupying forces.

A second letter from the Gestapo in Göttingen, dated 15 July 1943, informed the local Nazi Party HQ that Susan Hilton would 'according to the Propaganda Ministry office in Hanover, not be passing through the South Hanover-Braunschweig region on her trip through Germany'. But why were the authorities so anxious to keep her out of that area at that time? It could have been to hide the extent of Allied bombing in the region near the Volkswagen plant at nearby

Wolfsburg, or to keep secret the movement of troops or prisoners. In addition, important military and civilian radio transmitters were located at Öbisfelde and Helmstedt, both near Braunschweig (Brunswick). But uppermost in the minds of Nazi Party officials in Göttingen must have been the necessity to prevent Hilton discovering anything about the huge Buchenwald concentration camp just 100 km south east of the city.

Later in the war, Susan Hilton was allowed to move from Berlin to Vienna where she broadcast what she termed 'little talks' for German Radio's *Voice of the People* programme. She was paid 50 marks for each broadcast. In Vienna she accepted an invitation to join an SS undercover unit, thinking this would give her 'the opportunity of getting out into Yugoslavia'. She was supposed to spy for the SS on resident Americans as well as Germans suspected of helping the Allies, but after the war she claimed she 'endeavoured to warn them all' instead of informing the SS.

In 1944 Hilton visited the Turkish Consulate in Vienna, attempting to get a visa to leave the Third Reich. When the Gestapo discovered what she was doing, they imprisoned her. Hilton's friend, Margaret Schaffhauser, recalled: 'She was in the condemned cell in Vienna but was reprieved. She said a great calmness came over her there. She was no longer on the run'. Hilton's arrest in Vienna came at a time of heightened tension in the Third Reich, just days after the 20 July plot by army officers to assassinate Hitler.

On 26 August 1944 she was transferred to Liebenau internment camp, north of Lake Constance near the town of Meckenbeuren. According to Schaffhauser, Liebenau was a former asylum for the insane, which 'had been taken over for the camp and the original inmates "disposed" of'. Hilton was still being held at Liebenau when it was liberated by the Allies at the end of the war, by which time she was suffering from severe malnutrition. While other prisoners of the Nazis were released, Susan Hilton remained in the camp in Allied custody for another eight months until December 1945. She gave a series of sworn statements — on 30 May, 30 June, 1 July and 3 July 1945 — to MI5 interrogator Captain Reg Spooner who was later involved in the capture of Lord Haw Haw's colleague, Norman Baillie-Stewart. (After the war Spooner had a distinguished career with Scotland Yard, rising to the rank of Deputy Commander of the Flying Squad.) At Liebenau camp Hilton admitted broadcasting for the Germans and joining an SS unit.

In December 1945 she was taken back to England to face treason charges. Accompanied by an MI5 officer, Iris Marsden, she crossed the channel by ferry to Dover on 11 December 1945. Years after the war, Mrs Iris Cawley (née Marsden) remembered the trip in detail:

> We collected Mrs Hilton from the French and she had her arm in plaster. We were told she had been involved in a road accident and I have no reason to think otherwise but we did get the impression that the French army had used her rather roughly... I escorted her home from Germany to London to stand her trial. I found her a weak sort of character but with some literary ability. She was well aware that she had done what was unacceptable and was terrified at what would happen to her. I told her, from experience, that she would very likely get 18 months in prison... that guess turned out to be exactly right... As to why she was in a concentration camp, I have a vague recollection of her saying it was the safest place to be in the circumstances. I think she was quite devious enough to work that one out. However, I believe that Jim Skardon [MI5's top post-war interrogator who trapped the Soviet spies Klaus Fuchs and Gordon Lonsdale] and I found receipts signed by her from the German radio which were pretty damning. Her attitude to what she had done was much like Tallyrand's secretary when he had been caught out in corruption and said 'One must live!'.

After arriving on English soil, Hilton was formally arrested and charged. *The Times* carried the story on page two in its *News in Brief* section as follows:

> Scotland Yard announces that Mrs Dorothea May Therese Susan Hilton was detained on her arrival at Victoria Station from the Continent yesterday and charged with an offence under the Defence (General) Regulations 1939, and will appear at Bow Street Court.

When she appeared before Sir Bertrand Watson at Bow Street Magistrates' Court, Hilton was charged with assisting the enemy by taking employment in the German Radio propaganda service. Her solicitor told the court that everything she had done for the Germans was done with a view to getting out of Germany. She was committed for trial at the Old Bailey on 5 February 1946. After a postponement the trial eventually took place on 18 February 1946 when Hilton faced a total of ten counts of assisting the enemy. The prosecution evidence was compiled by Special Branch Detective Sergeant Albert Gibson who was based at the London Metropolitan Police Commissioner's office and was also a witness at the trial.

Mrs Hilton was described as a British subject on the charge sheets, although for the Gestapo she had been an 'Irish journalist'. The status of her nationality was shrouded in mystery. She had been given a temporary Irish passport by Count O'Kelly de Gallagh at the Irish Legation in Paris early in 1941. However, the document was not renewed on application to the Berlin Legation the following year. Nonetheless, Hilton had kept her passport locked up in a safe at the Concordia studios in the Reichsportsfeld in Berlin. To add to the confusion, Hilton also carried a German passport. A fellow broadcaster, Hilde Spickernagel (née Poepping), recalls:

> Not only were interim passports handed out by the Irish Legation to people who claimed to be of Irish origin, but also fully valid German passports — with pictures and all the necessary stamps — were made out by the German authorities. Thus, the lady generally known as Susan Hilton once showed me a German passport she also held in the name of Ann Tower.

At the Old Bailey, Mrs Hilton faced the following counts, namely that she:

1. Made a record for broadcasting propaganda on behalf of the enemy, between 1 December 1940 and 1 June 1941;

2. Conspired with other British subjects — Donald Palmer, John O'Reilly, John Brown, Gilbert, Dorothy Eckersley, James Clark [Eckersley's son], Liam Mullally and other persons unknown — to broadcast propaganda on behalf of the enemy;

3. In September 1941, entered the service of the Bureau Concordia, a section of the German Broadcasting System, broadcasting secret propaganda;

4. In December 1941, prepared propaganda on behalf of the enemy, for broadcasting;

5. In January 1942, entered the service of the Irish Redaktion, a section of the German Broadcasting System, broadcasting secret propaganda;

6. In January 1942, prepared, from material provided by the German Foreign Office and by the German Propaganda Ministry, propaganda for broadcasting by the enemy;

7. In September 1942, broadcast propaganda on behalf of the enemy;

8. In January 1943, entered the service of Inter Radio, a station of the German Broadcasting System, broadcasting secret propaganda;

9. In January 1943, prepared propaganda for broadcasting by the enemy;

10. In October 1943, entered the service of the Schutz-Staffel (SS), a German paramilitary organisation engaged in internal security operations.

Hilton pleaded guilty to count 1, as well as counts 3 to 9, inclusive. She pleaded not guilty to counts 2 and 10. The second charge, of conspiracy, was not proceeded with. The tenth and final charge of SS membership was also dropped, despite her earlier admission to MI5 at Liebenau camp that in 1943 in Vienna she had been recruited by a local SS unit. The prosecution's decision to accept only Hilton's guilty pleas — and not to proceed with the conspiracy and SS charges — meant that only the minimum evidence was publicly revealed. Hilton put herself at the mercy of the court and was sentenced to 18 months in prison.

Edward Sweney describes his sister's imprisonment as 'an injustice' and believes 'her name should be cleared because what she did was inoffensive and caused no one any trouble... She was the victim of very cruel circumstances. I do not like to see anyone being exploited and cruelly treated. Susan was, in point of fact, incarcerated by the Germans and this fact should have been emphasised at her trial instead of which, apparently, it was ignored at great prejudice to a fair trial'. Mr Sweney describes his sister as 'someone left helplessly at the mercy of people still suffering from war hysteria'.

Susan Hilton's case is almost certainly unique among wartime propaganda broadcasters in that she managed to be imprisoned by the Nazis and MI5 — both sides considering her to be an enemy collaborator. The facts that she had worked with the French underground, was twice a prisoner of the Nazis, had refused to undertake spying work for them, had tried to flee the Third Reich and had been found half-starved in a Nazi camp were never raised at her 1946 Old Bailey trial which was disposed of in less than a day. In addition, charges against her of conspiracy and SS membership were dropped without explanation by the prosecution team creating the impression that the case dealt purely with someone accused of broadcasting enemy propaganda.

Susan Hilton's own theory about her treatment by the Gestapo and MI5 was that she was the victim of mistaken identity. According to Margaret Schaffhauser:

> From putting two and two together afterwards, Susan was sure that a woman who left the ship [*Kemmendine*] there [in Gibraltar] was an agent and was given Susan's name by MI5 by an extraordinary coincidence. Of course, it would not have been the name that she [the agent] would have had on the ship. She [the agent] must have disappeared or not been found by the Nazis, so when Susan arrived on the scene they thought she was the other one. It is the only explanation she could think of to explain later events — not only by the Nazis but also by the facts not being brought out at her trial and by the special treatment she received at Holloway with her own room and another prisoner assigned to act as maid for her.

The *Kemmendine's* passenger list provides no clue as to the identity of the mystery woman agent whom Hilton believed left the ship when it docked at Gibraltar. The records show that all passengers who boarded the ship in Glasgow stayed aboard until the fateful encounter with the German raider. Extra passengers were taken on board at Gibraltar but none left, although an agent could have been travelling secretly, perhaps with only the knowledge of the captain. Hilton's theory — that she was a pawn in a bigger game of espionage and that she was, in effect, sacrificed to protect the identity of a genuine British agent — appears at first sight to be far fetched. But according to published accounts of the period, an MI5 agent was sent to Gibraltar in June 1940 (Hinsley and Simkins, *British Intelligence in the Second World War*, vol. 4, p. 149) and an MI6 agent was also sent there around the same time (Kim Philby, *My Silent War*, pp. 82-3). This would not, however, explain MI5's insistence on Hilton facing trial at the end of the war, unless MI5 and MI6 had got their lines of communication mixed up; or the intelligence services wished their agent to remain on in post-war Europe as a spy.

When Hilton was released from Holloway in 1947 the prison governor, according to Schaffhauser, 'shook hands with her when she left'. At the gate of the prison she was met by two MI5 agents who

> bent over backwards to help her, telling her she was to contact them immediately if anyone said or wrote anything defamatory about her. They did stop the publication of a book. She always referred to them as 'my friends'. The two who looked after her even sent her Christmas cards every year until first one and then the other retired in the 1970s.

But who were the two MI5 agents who 'looked after' Hilton after the war? Not Iris Marsden, certainly — who had 'no further contact with Mrs Hilton' after delivering her to the authorities in December 1945 — but perhaps Spooner and Skardon? All three agents had worked for a special unit set up to catch British collaborators, which was under the command of Major John Stephenson. In 1962 the MI5 major was knighted and, as Sir John Stephenson, served as a Lord Justice of the Appeal Court from 1971 to 1985. When asked about the Hilton case in April 1994, Stephenson claimed to have 'no recollection' of it. In an appreciation of Jim Skardon, penned for the London *Times* of 23 March 1987, Stephenson wrote:

> Our task was to find some 100 British collaborators and obtain evidence on which they could be prosecuted... The few broadcasters, stool-pigeons, and those who were recruited into the pathetic little body which the Germans called first the Legion of Saint George and, later, the British Free Corps, fell far short of three figures.

Susan Hilton eventually settled down to run a farm and pet shop business in England after working as an international courier. In the 1960s she returned to Germany to meet a hotel owner who had worked as a guard at Liebenau, and to thank local farmers for providing food in those hard times. Hilton died on 30 October 1983 but her name has never been cleared. Despite all her wartime suffering she is still classified as a traitor by the British authorities who have yet to release her wartime file to the Public Record Office. Susan Hilton is the only member of Hans Hartmann's Irland-Redaktion team ever to have stood trial after the war.

Appendix III
John O'Reilly — the Wild Boy from County Clare

J ohn Francis O'Reilly was an improbable broadcaster for the
Nazi radio service. He was an inherent adventurer, almost in
the mercenary mould. The story of how he came to broadcast
from wartime Berlin to Ireland says as much about the haphazard
recruitment methods of German Radio as it does about this vaguely
enigmatic Clare man. He was the only member of German Radio's
wartime Irland-Redaktion who is known to have returned to Ireland
on a spying mission, although Susan Hilton turned down a similar
mission before joining the radio team.

John O'Reilly was born in Kilkee, County Clare on 7 August 1916.
His father Bernard was the local Royal Irish Constabulary sergeant
who had taken part in the arrest of Roger Casement just three and a
half months before John Francis was born. Casement was landed on
the Kerry coast by a German U-boat on Good Friday, 21 April 1916
— three days before the Easter Rising. The RIC man was known
thereafter as 'Casement' O'Reilly. Given that his father had gained
notoriety through the arrest of Casement, there was more than a little
irony in the fact that 27 years later the RIC sergeant's son would be
dropped by parachute from a Luftwaffe plane to spy for the Germans.
According to O'Reilly's own memoirs he duped the Germans into
taking him on as an agent simply to get back home.

In 1943 a secret Garda assessment on the young O'Reilly's
background noted he had 'always been regarded as the wild boy of
the family'. O'Reilly's taste for adventure, his apparent inability to

stick to one job for any length of time and his propensity for globe-trotting, proved early on that 'wild boy' was an apt sobriquet for the young Kilkee man. His early career was varied, to put it mildly. After being educated by the Christian Brothers in Kilrush he got a job as a customs officer at Rosslare Harbour in 1936, but left — reportedly after failing an Irish language exam — to study for the priesthood at Buckfast Abbey in England. But the priestly life was not for O'Reilly who left Buckfast after only two weeks to work as a reception clerk in a London hotel.

O'Reilly was in London when war broke out and in May 1940 he used his savings to travel to Jersey in the Channel Islands for a holiday. When that money was spent, O'Reilly took a job on Jersey's Beaumont Farm helping out with the potato harvest. He chose to stay on there, even when other Irish labourers returned to Britain along with the Dunkirk evacuees and was still doing casual work when the German Army occupied the Islands on 2 July 1940. A chance meeting with a German sentry landed the Clare man a barracks job at St Peter's airfield, then controlled by the Luftwaffe. Later on he distributed rations from the kitchen of an anti-aircraft battery on Jersey.

O'Reilly's aptitude for learning German made up for his earlier failure to master Irish and by March 1941 he was acting as an interpreter and go-between for Irish labourers and the German commander on Jersey. The Germans regarded him as something of a leader. Having manoeuvred himself into a position of trust and limited authority, O'Reilly approached the military commander of Jersey, Prince Van Baldeck, seeking travel papers to get to Germany. O'Reilly later told Irish Army Intelligence officers that his idea was to make contact with the Irish Chargé d'Affaires in Berlin, William Warnock, and get back home to neutral territory. But the Germans had other ideas. Van Baldeck did a deal with O'Reilly, telling him he would get his travel papers for Germany on condition he brought as many Irishmen with him as he could persuade to work in German factories to assist the war effort. The German commander also insisted that O'Reilly make sure there were no British agents or Irishmen with pro-British views among the recruits.

With promises of good pay, generous holidays and their return passage to Ireland to be paid for once the war was over, O'Reilly managed to recruit no less than 72 Irishmen. They set off for Germany on 5 July 1941. But one thing the Germans had not bargained for was the ability of Irish labourers to celebrate the end of seasonal work on Jersey coupled with the promise of lucrative work in the Fatherland. The train journey from the north coast of France to Germany degenerated into bedlam with O'Reilly's 'fusiliers' spending their savings on a massive drinking spree which caused havoc. Reconstructing the events two and a half years later, Irish Army Intelligence officers noted that

> on the journey from Jersey through occupied France, the party was anything but well-behaved. They had a fair amount of money saved and proceeded at once to get completely drunk and out of hand... the train was divided into various compartments according to nationality. O'Reilly's party invaded all compartments of the train and on several occasions pulled the communication cords causing an amount of confusion. As accepted leader of the party, he [O'Reilly] had to bear the brunt of the criticism.

On arrival in Germany the Irish were put to work in the Hermann Goring steel works at Watenstedt. O'Reilly wrote to his parents in Kilkee on 27 July 1941 saying he had a job as an interpreter to the German forces at Watenstedt. But despite Prince Van Baldeck's optimism, O'Reilly's men never quite measured up to the German role model of industrial workers. The Irish, who were kept apart from other nationalities, disregarded the rules: coming back drunk at night, singing and shouting, and — most dangerously from the German point of view — switching on factory lights during the blackout. Tiring of the continuous complaints from the German authorities about his men's drunken behaviour O'Reilly decided it was time to leave. In September 1941, just two months after arriving in the Third Reich and two years into the war, he applied for a job in Berlin writing articles for the new nightly Irish service, known in German as the Irland-Redaktion. At the radio centre in Berlin the Kilkee man was given a microphone test and hired. The fact that he got the job was not altogether surprising as he was then the only Irish national in the Irland-Redaktion. O'Reilly did not get on with some of his 'Irish' colleagues who were in fact German, French, English and Russian. He bluntly told two Frenchmen that they should go and work for the radio's French service.

O'Reilly did not begin broadcasting to Ireland immediately and was given the job of scripting short articles of Irish interest for others to broadcast on air. After doing talks for a while under the fictitious name of Pat O'Brien, O'Reilly began using his real name on air in October 1941. Irish Army monitors heard O'Reilly broadcasting on 28 October 1941 and reported that his 'talk dealt with religion. Ireland in the Penal Laws was compared with Russia under communist rule'.

After his colleagues James Blair and Susan Hilton were sacked in 1942, John O'Reilly was promoted and took on extra duties. As well as his own talks, the 'Flashback' historical series, and Pat O'Brien talks, he also put out three general news bulletins a night. Although O'Reilly had his own ideas about what should and should not be broadcast to Ireland, he was never given a totally free hand to do as he liked. His boss, Hans Hartmann, considered him a relatively low-key member of staff compared, for example, to Francis Stuart, whom the German found 'highly intelligent'. Both Hartmann and Stuart were lecturers at Berlin University. Consequently, Stuart got a freer hand in choosing the subject matter for his broadcasts, although even in his case the texts had to be submitted in advance, first to Hartmann and then the English section. O'Reilly, who was not an academic, did channel his own ideas to Stuart for use in the latter's weekly talks entitled 'Through Irish Eyes'.

From time to time O'Reilly, Stuart and Frank Ryan met to discuss the contents of Stuart's broadcasts, but after the war Stuart said neither man was 'of the slightest help' to him. Stuart saw O'Reilly as a 'pretty nasty character. He was a sort of mercenary, not that he ever did any fighting'. Stuart notes that O'Reilly 'lived in great style' and adds: 'I was very suspicious of him because he could easily have been a double agent'.

O'Reilly's earlier career pattern did not augur well for his tenure at the radio centre and a difficult working relationship with Dr Hartmann caused unease. A row broke out between them when the German academic insisted that O'Reilly read lengthy extracts from Wolfe Tone's diaries on air. Hartmann — who had purchased an Irish translation of the diaries while working as a folklore student in Dublin four years earlier — felt they contained a pertinent message for Irish listeners and had incorporated them as a regular feature of his Irish language talks since taking over the service in December 1941. But, angry at being asked to read what he considered to be 'uninteresting' material, O'Reilly handed the Wolfe Tone scripts back and told Hartmann what he thought of them. The Clare man lost this encounter, however, being rapped over the knuckles and told to carry on.

O'Reilly was also upset that musical items played on the Irland-Redaktion programmes had no 'actual Irish basis'. Eventually, he decided to look for another job. In June 1942, just nine months after joining the radio service, O'Reilly made contact with an American working for an SS unit. The American got him an interview with an SS official who sounded O'Reilly out about working in Spain as an agent gathering military intelligence from refugees, shipwrecked Allied sailors and others. O'Reilly, who by this time wanted to get home to Ireland, told the SS contact that he would prefer to be sent on a mission to Northern Ireland. The German official said he would need at least six months' intensive training for such a task. Three days later O'Reilly was summoned back to the same SS bureau and told his application to work as a German intelligence agent had been approved. But it was to be another three months before he found out what the Germans had in mind for him.

From June to September 1942 O'Reilly continued working for Hartmann's small radio team. Then suddenly he was summoned back to the SS office and informed that the previous three months had been spent checking out his credentials and reliability. He was told to leave the radio and prepare for specialised training as a spy. Back at the studios O'Reilly told Hartmann of his decision to leave. After the war he wrote: 'I knew I could trust Dr Hartmann. He appeared to have considerable influence in the Foreign Office. He was a member of the National Socialist party and he was obviously attached to Ireland'.

Alarmed at losing a genuine Irish member of his team of announcers, Hartmann contacted Helmut Clissmann who, in 1942, was attached to the German Army's Brandenburg Regiment. Clissmann was not able to intervene and persuade O'Reilly to stay.

Hartmann eventually agreed to O'Reilly's departure, however, on condition that the Clare man found another Irish person to take his place at the Rundfunkhaus. The substitute was O'Reilly's friend Liam Mullally, an English language teacher at the Berlitz school in Berlin. As Mullally began work at the radio centre, O'Reilly made his way to Bremen on 17 September 1942 to begin training in espionage techniques.

So it was that by the age of 26, John Francis O'Reilly had made the transition from customs official to seminarian, from hotel receptionist to potato picker, from interpreter to steel worker and on to broadcaster and spy. The Kilkee man was now about to embark on what he called 'my great adventure into the intelligence branch of the German Navy in Bremen'. He still had over a year to wait before making his fateful journey home to Kilkee. Ahead of him lay a tough training programme in wireless telegraphy as well as the construction and repair of radio sets. He also received instruction in the use of invisible inks and how to condense intelligence reports to a minimum. As 1942 drew to a close, plans were afoot to send O'Reilly home aboard a U-boat bound for the west coast of Ireland. But when he returned from three weeks leave in January 1943 he was told the U-boat plan had been dropped. The same month, he was transferred from Bremen to Hamburg for further training.

The various branches of the Nazi intelligence service could not apparently agree on what to do with their new recruit. Francis Stuart felt the Clare man wanted to return home to Ireland for purely personal reasons, while some Germans involved felt O'Reilly would be unreliable as a spy. O'Reilly then became the subject of top level discussions within the Nazi espionage hierarchy. Edmund Veesenmayer, the Nazis' so-called coup d'état specialist, had been picked by Ribbentrop to stir up rebellion in Ireland. His master plan to return IRA leaders Seán Russell and Frank Ryan to Ireland fell through when Russell died aboard a U-boat on 14 August 1940, just 100 miles west of Galway. Despite the setback, Veesenmayer still harboured a desire to get Frank Ryan back home to take over the secret task originally assigned to Russell. He felt the moves to get O'Reilly to Ireland were interfering with the more important Ryan plan, and asked Admiral Wilhelm Canaris, the head of the Abwehr (German counter-intelligence) to cancel the O'Reilly plan.

Veesenmayer directed his right-hand man Kurt Haller to draw up unflattering assessments of both O'Reilly and Liam Mullally. The latter, it had been planned, might be sent back on the spying mission with O'Reilly. Haller pulled no punches in his report for the Foreign Ministry, describing O'Reilly as a 'pig-headed opportunist' and Mullally as 'an irresponsible, albeit affable, chatterbox'. Thus, Veesenmayer's efforts caused O'Reilly's departure by U-boat to be cancelled in December 1942. In his memoirs O'Reilly recalled being summoned to a naval espionage bureau in Bremen where he was told by an 'admiralty espionage chief' that the spy mission was being cancelled because

> Germany wishes Ireland to remain neutral in this war. We have no desire to see England or the United States using Irish ports as a base for operating against our U-boat packs in the Atlantic. The German Foreign Office, which has the last word in such matters, has deemed it advisable, therefore, to veto all operations that might jeopardise Ireland's neutrality.

But O'Reilly was an SS recruit and the SS-run Sicherheitdienst or security service wanted to press ahead with their plan to return him — and another Irishman called John Kenny — to Ireland. Consequently, unknown to either the Foreign Office or the Abwehr, O'Reilly was dropped over his home area of County Clare from a German aircraft at 2 a.m. on 16 December 1943. The parachute landing was made four miles from Kilkee, just across the Shannon estuary from the transatlantic flying-boat harbour of Foynes, where the noise of the Luftwaffe plane's engines would attract less attention. O'Reilly was carrying a wireless in a brown suitcase along with £300 in cash. But the Telefunken transmitter never sent any messages back to Berlin and ended its days gathering dust at the military archives in Dublin.

Within hours of landing O'Reilly was arrested and taken to Arbour Hill prison in Dublin. John Kenny — who had worked for the German Army's transport corps — was also captured shortly after parachuting into County Clare just three days later. O'Reilly and Kenny's swift discovery was due to the fact that British Intelligence had tipped off

G2 that the Luftwaffe planes were on their way to deliver a 'human cargo'. Liaison between Irish and British Intelligence was well developed by that stage of the war and, besides, Admiral Canaris was secretly tipping off Allied intelligence, for which actions he was executed by the Germans towards the end of the war.

The two parachute incidents put a strain on Éamon de Valera's policy of neutrality. The arrival of O'Reilly and Kenny coincided with increasing pressure on de Valera's government by the American Minister to Ireland, David Gray, who wanted Axis diplomats expelled from Dublin. The Dublin government tried to keep the arrest of both men secret but, despite strict press censorship at the time, a newspaper did report that an injured man had been found in a field in Clare. It would have been difficult for G2 to prevent rumours of the parachute drops from spreading in any case since Kenny had been treated at hospitals in Kilrush, Ennis and Dublin for injuries he sustained on landing.

On 20 January 1944 a report of the parachute drops also featured in a secret weekly dispatch drawn up for the American Office of War Information in Washington by Dan Terrell, who was a press attaché with the U.S. Legation in Dublin. Terrell wrote:

> One month after it happened, the Irish public was informed this week about two parachutists who were dropped from German planes. Both Irish, of course. Our favourite angle; John F. O'Reilly, 28 year old Irish Haw Haw, left Berlin with papers permitting him both to leave Germany and land in Éire — even down to an exit permit issued by the Irish Chargé d'Affaires in Berlin! (Such detail, of course, was censored by our old friend, censor Thomas Coyne).

Fearing the parachute incidents would reflect badly on Ireland's delicate neutrality policy, de Valera instructed Joe Walshe, Secretary of the Department of External Affairs, to cable Ireland's representative in Washington, Robert Brennan, with instructions to lobby the State Department there. Walshe cabled Brennan on 27 January 1944, saying:

> Impossible for two raw, ignorant youths to have received such a mission. Incapable of exercising influence on anybody. Obvious purpose was to get home by fooling Germans that they could get information and send it on their portable [radio] sets. Both arrested

within few hours of landing. Both American and British governments know that Ireland is not a centre for any kind of German activities. You should talk to State Department to prevent new campaign for which this may be signal.

The Kilkee parachute landings were first aired publicly in the Dáil on 17 February 1944 when the opposition TD, James Dillon (who had been thrown out of Fine Gael earlier in the war for suggesting that Éire should help the Allies) questioned the Taoiseach, Éamon de Valera about them. De Valera confirmed that his officials were trying to determine why the men (neither of whom was named in the Dáil) had been sent. He did reveal though that both men had been working together on Jersey when German forces occupied the island.

On 21 February 1944 David Gray mentioned the arrival of O'Reilly and Kenny in a diplomatic note to de Valera requesting that Axis diplomats to be expelled from Dublin. De Valera rejected Gray's demand. The parachute landings were raised again by Dillon in the Dáil on 23 February, but the diplomatic row sparked by Gray's note remained secret until leaked to the American press in mid March 1944 when banner headlines were published, such as 'How Ireland harbours Nazi spies'.

On 28 March 1944 Joe Walshe asked the German ambassador Eduard Hempel 'to warn his government once more of the fatal consequences of sending any further agents to this country'. Dr Hempel told Walshe he intended sending 'a further warning' to Berlin in any case. According to Walshe, Hempel 'was completely frank in expressing his own opinion of his government's folly in this matter of sending agents to Ireland. He felt it was due to the absence from the Foreign Office of officials who understood the Irish situation'.

The Germans' plan to use O'Reilly as a spy backfired badly because while the Clare man was under lock and key in Dublin's Arbour Hill prison, Irish Army Intelligence (G2) experts tricked him into disclosing a secret code he had been trained to use for relaying radio messages back to Germany. The plan to trick O'Reilly was devised by G2's Colonel Dan Bryan and his assistant Dr Richard Hayes, a renowned code-breaker who in civilian life was director of the National Library. The plan was described by Hayes' post-war colleague Alf Mac Lochlainn:

Hayes and Dan Bryan fooled this young Clare man into revealing the ciphering system he had been taught. O'Reilly had claimed it was unbreakable and rashly accepted a challenge to test his captors. But they 'cheated' by going to his cell when he was on exercise and taking the ashes from the fireplace where he had burned the papers on which he had done his homework. The ashes were brought to the Garda technical office in Kilmainham where they were laboriously mounted on glass and photographed so that the steps between clear and cipher could be followed.

Within two weeks of O'Reilly's arrest G2 was passing on details of his interrogation to MI5. This was before Dr Hayes had broken the code. On 3 January 1944, MI5's Guy Liddell wrote to Dan Bryan saying he would be 'delighted [to] come over when you think suitable stage of interrogation reached... Information about ciphers and device of great interest. Your preliminary report on radio indicates it may be of type not hitherto known here'. By 21 January, Col. Bryan was able to cable MI5 that O'Reilly's code had been broken: 'Doctor's notes provided solution. Details follow by letter'.

Almost six months later on the night of 5/6 July 1944, O'Reilly sparked a nationwide security alert by escaping from Arbour Hill prison. Wanted posters with O'Reilly's photograph were widely distributed by the police but the fugitive did not remain at large for long. He was rearrested just three days later, on 9 July, at his father's house at Brendan Villas in Kilkee. Bernard O'Reilly, the retired RIC sergeant, turned his son over to the police and pocketed the £500 reward which he invested for 'Jack'. O'Reilly was finally released from prison on 24 May 1945 and used the reward money — plus £300 the Nazis had given him for his spying mission — to open his own pub in Dublin's Parkgate Street, ironically not far from Col. Bryan's office. Some years later on, O'Reilly bought the Esplanade Hotel in Dublin.

The 'wild boy' from Kilkee apparently never found out that he had been tricked into revealing the Germans' secret code by Bryan and Dr Hayes. As late as 1952, under the heading 'How the secret of the codes was kept', he was writing in his memoirs that

> One microfilmed code-card had been discovered with the transmitters, but without the information supplied with the key, the five figure symbols would have no significance... The [family]

house had been practically turned upside down by the police in their search for equipment, and my parents had been cross-examined by military interrogators. They examined everything but the front door mat. The cardboard folder, complete with code and cipher keys, rested undisturbed beneath it, where my father had hidden them. Later he had burned them.

As well as running a pub and hotel, O'Reilly travelled widely — including a period in Nigeria — after the war. He sold his memoirs to the Sunday Dispatch which serialised them every week for six months. At the age of 54, John O'Reilly was seriously injured in a road accident in England. He spent the final months of his life in the Middlesex Hospital near London where he died on 4 May 1971. Nine days later, as Ireland's political leaders gathered at Dean's Grange cemetery to bury the former Taoiseach, Seán Lemass, Jack O'Reilly was quietly laid to rest at Glasnevin cemetery.

Appendix IV

Technical data concerning broadcasts to Ireland by German Radio's Irish service from December 1939 to May 1945.

PERIOD Month/Yr	WAVELENGTH Metres (kc)	IRISH TIME all p.m.	STATION NAME/NO.	STUDIO LOCATION	SOURCE
end-1939	332	8.25 to 8.40	Hamburg	Berlin	AA
	395.9	Sundays	Bremen	Berlin	AA
	31.22	only	DXB Zeesen	Berlin	AA
early 1940	332	as above	Hamburg	Berlin	BBC
	395.9		Bremen	Berlin	BBC
	31.38		DJA Langenberg	Berlin	BBC
mid 1940	19.74	9.30 to 9.45	DJB Zeesen	Berlin	DNA
	1875	Sun/Wed	Kootwyk	Berlin	DNA
Sept. to	28.45	8.00	Zeesen	Berlin	BBC
Nov. 1941	30/31-m band	7.00	Zeesen	Berlin	BBC
Dec. 1941	1154	8-10 various	Oslo	Berlin	BBC
1942	1154	7-11 various	Oslo	Berlin	BBC
to	431.7		Rennes	Berlin	BBC
July 1943	28.43		DZD Zeesen	Berlin	IAMS
Sept. 1943	1293	as above	Luxembourg	Lux.	BBC
Oct. 1943	514.6	7.15	Calais	Lux.	BBC
February to	1293	various	Luxembourg	Lux.	BBC
March 1944	301.5/415.5		Hilversum	Lux.	BBC
August to	41.44	5.15/6.15/7.45	DXJ	Lux.	IAMS
September	514 (582)	as above	Calais I	Lux.	DNA
1944	301 (995)		Calais II	Lux.	DNA
	296 (758)		Bremen	Lux.	DNA
	1875 (160)		Friesland	Lux.	DNA
	41.4	6.15	DXJ	Lux.	DNA
	48.23	7.45	DXR-7	Lux.	DNA
October	396	6.45/8.00	Bremen	Apen	IAMS
1944	301.6	as above	Hilversum	Apen	IAMS
March 1945	301.6	8.45	Hilversum	Apen	IAMS
early April 1945	n.a.	5.45/8.45 & 10.45	Hilversum	Apen	IAMS
mid April 45	n.a.	8.45/9.45	Hilversum	Apen	IAMS
end April 45	n.a.	as above	Bremen	Apen	IAMS
1 May 1945	n.a.	8.45/9.45	n.a.	Apen	IAMS
2 May 1945*	n.a.	8.45 to 8.55	n.a.	Apen	IAMS

(*final transmission of the war by Irland-Redaktion)

See next page for abbreviations used in above table.

Abbreviations used in main table:

AA = Auswärtiges Amt (German Foreign Office) political archive, Bonn
BBC = BBC monitoring service
DNA = Deutsches Nachrichtenbüro (German News Agency), Berlin
IAMS = Irish Army monitoring service
kc = kilocycles (given in brackets)
Lux. = Luxembourg
m = metres
n.a. = data not available.

Transmitter details:

Short wave transmitters: DXJ, DXR-7, DXB, DJA, DJB and DZD
(all located at Zeesen near Berlin, except DJA at Langenberg).
Medium wave transmitters: Calais I, Calais II (both lost to Allied
troops in October 1944), Bremen, Hamburg, Rennes and Hilversum.
Long wave transmitters: Friesland, Luxembourg, Kootwyk and Oslo.

Appendix V
Nazi Party Members in Ireland

NAME	DATE OF BIRTH	DATE JOINED NAZI PARTY	JOB	ADDRESS IN IRELAND
Boden, Hans	24.06.1910	1.6.37	Consul	58, Northumberland Rd., Dublin
Born, Franz	22.02.1896	1.6.37	Professor of Music	Belgriffin House, Carlow
Brase, Fritz	04.05.1875	1.4.32	Colonel	Royal Hospital, Kilmainham, Dublin
Clissmann, Helmut	11.05.1911	1.5.34	Student	2, Trinity College, Dublin
Greiner, Heinrich	04.02.1908	1.2.36	Foreman	c/o Solus, Corke Abbey, Bray
Hartmann, Hans	18.11.1909	1.3.33	Student	Dublin
Hempel, Eduard	06.06.1887	1.7.38	Envoy	Gortleitragh, Dún Laoghaire
Herkner, Friedrich	25.10.1902	1.9.39	Professor	16, Eglinton Terrace, Donnybrook
Kämpf, Reinhold	10.10.1907	1.5.38	Turner	Dublin
Krause, Ernst	16.07.1895	1.4.35		Dublin
Krause, Carl	28.12.1898	1.1.34	Merchant	7, Ardeevin Road, Dalkey
Künstler, Karl	06.03.1897	1.10.33	Engineer	22 Leeson Pk & 7 Fitzwilliam Sq., Dublin
Lohmeyer, Adolf	25.12.1909	1.5.36	Painter	28 Adelaide Road, Dublin
Mahr, Adolf	07.05.1887	1.4.33	Director	37, Waterloo Place, Dublin
Mecking, Heinz	22.09.1902	1.6.31	Manager	Dublin *52 Casimir Road*
Meissner, Hans	09.08.1904	1.9.38	Clerk	Bray, Co Wicklow
Meixner, Karl	03.09.1897	19.12.38	Worker	17, Herbert Place, Dublin
Mühlhausen, L.	16.12.1888	1.5.32	Professor	(see note below)
Müller-Dubrow, O.	14.02.1879	1.10.33	Director	Cross Avenue, Blackrock, Co Dublin
Poepping, Hilde	06.04.1916	20.9.37	Student	University College, Galway
Püster, Walter	03.04.1897	1.6.34		74, Clonliffe Road, Dublin
Pleines, Walter	14.09.1906	1.5.35	Merchant	34, Northumberland Road, Dublin
Reinhard, Otto	14.01.1898	1.9.39	Manager	Rossmore, Silchester Road, Dublin
Ritter, Hermann	15.11.1892	1.10.33	Engineer	2, Henrietta Place, Dalkey
Schmeisser, Karl	15.05.1897	1.12.37	Worker	26, Wellpark Avenue, Dublin
Schubert, Paul	18.07.1893	1.10.34	Manager	Corke Abbey, Bray
Stumpf, Robert	27.07.1888	1.1.34	Radiologist	47, Raglan Road, Dublin
Tanne, Wilhelm	30.08.1873	1.10.34	Pastor (rtd.)	4, St. James, Malahide, Dublin
Thomsen, Henning	11.07.1905	1.8.37	Attaché	German Legation, Dublin
Weckler, Friedrich	16.02.1892	1.6.34	Merchant	3, Sorrento Terrace, Dalkey
Wenzel, Robert	03.05.1885	1.3.35		Dublin
Winkelmann, Franz	03.08.1892	1.6.34	Director	6, Merlyn Park, Dublin.

219

Sources: Berlin Document Center (BDC) and Bundesarchiv, Berlin. The author wishes to thank Dr David Marwell, director of the BDC, and Frau Stach of the Bundesarchiv, Berlin, for supplying the files on which the above table is based. It does not purport to be a complete list of Nazi Party members in Ireland in the 1930s.

Some of the above named Nazi Party members were State employees: Colonel Fritz Brase was director of the Irish Army's School of Music from 1923 until his death in December 1940; Friedrich Herkner was professor of sculpture at the National College of Art; Dr Adolf Mahr worked at the National Museum from 1927 (he was appointed director in 1934 by de Valera's cabinet); Heinz Mecking was appointed as an expert advisor to the Turf Development Board in 1936 (Dr C.S. 'Todd'Andrews was managing director of the TDB at the time); Otto Reinhard was director of forestry in the Department of Lands (Reinhard beat 65 other candidates to get the job); and, after leaving Siemens, Friedrich Weckler was chief accountant of the ESB from 1930 until his early death in 1943.

Note: Professor Ludwig Mühlhausen, who claimed to be a personal friend of President Douglas Hyde, visited Ireland six times from 1925 to 1937. He visited the Blasket Islands a number of times in the 1920s and lectured at UCC in 1928. He studied Connemara Irish in Cornamóna in 1932, and spent two months in Teelin, Co Donegal in 1937.

Oswald Müller-Dubrow was a director of the Siemens company which won the contract to build the Shannon Hydroelectric scheme in the late 1920s. He was Mahr's deputy head of the Nazi Auslandsorganisation which kept an eye on Germans living in Ireland and ensured that party discipline was enforced. As a resident of Cross Avenue in Blackrock, County Dublin, Müller-Dubrow was a neighbour of Éamon de Valera's.

Heinz Mecking was deputy head of the local Nazi Ortsgruppe in Dublin, taking Mahr's place when the museum director left Dublin for Berlin in July 1939.

Sources

Archival sources by country

Ireland

Military Archives, Dublin

File G2/X/0127 Foreign Wireless broadcasts, in six parts covering broadcasts from Germany and elsewhere to Ireland from 1939 to 1945 as follows: Part 1: 1939 to 13 June 1942; Part 2: 13 June 1942 to 27 October 1942; Part 3: 27 October 1942 to 31 March 1943; Part 4: 1 April 1943 to 31 October 1943; Part 5: 1 November 1943 to 30 July 1944; Part 6: 1 August 1944 to 1945.

The Military Archive also holds files on individuals involved, directly or indirectly, with German radio broadcasts to Ireland in World War II, as follows: G2/2473 Ludwig Mühlhausen. G2/0130 Adolf Mahr, personal file, and G2/130 Adolf Mahr, intercepted letters file. G2/0071 Hans Hartmann, and G2/007 Hans Hartmann. G2/4102 Susan Hilton. G2/5129 James Blair. G2/0054 Franz Fromme. G2/0245 Otto Reinhard.

Other files from the Military Archive, Dublin, quoted in this work: G2/X/0099 Translations and Translators, contains details of G2 personnel doing translation work, including translations of foreign broadcasts. G2/X/0676 Irish-German-American Notes, containing details of courier system used by Francis Stuart to communicate between Berlin and Ireland via the United States during 1940 and 1941.

Department of Foreign Affairs, Dublin

DFA A72 Francis Stuart restricted file DFA 205/108 German Broadcasts to Ireland (contains records of diplomatic protests over one Stuart broadcast in December 1942, and others in April and May 1943).

Department of Finance, Dublin

E53/3/33 National Museum: appointment of Dr Mahr as director (containing details of Mahr's appointment by de Valera's Cabinet to head the National Museum in 1934).

Franciscan Library, Killiney, Co Dublin

De Valera Papers, file 953, 'Anglo-Irish Relations. J.P. Walshe: Memoranda, 1932-39'.

National Archives, Dublin

DFA A52 I 'Landing of parachutists John F. O'Reilly and John Kenny.' File contains details on O'Reilly and Kenny, including G2/3824 memo dated 31 December 1943 and entitled 'Notes on John Fras. O'Reilly's activities in the Channel Islands and Germany'. 1/5 Minutes of the 7th Cabinet, S6631 p. 341 (contains minute of Mahr's promotion signed by Éamon de Valera). DFA restricted file 201/36/12 Irish citizenship application at Vichy 1941, Susan Hilton. DFA, A60 Secretary's Office files (re Department of Foreign Affairs, Dublin, and 1943-44 correspondence between Col. Dan Bryan of G2 and Guy Liddell of MI5). D/JUS C766 containing examples of the *Weekly Review* of the German News Agency.

National Library, Dublin

The *Irish Bulletin* (file ref. Ir 94109 i15), an underground pamphlet circulated by the Provisional Government during the Irish War of Independence, 1919-21. Its contents formed the basis of the U.S. Senate document, *The Struggle of the Irish People*, which was quoted by German

Radio's Irish service in the 1941-44 period in the Flashback series.

National Museum, Dublin

Director's file no. 490 (containing correspondence concerning Adolf Mahr, 1946-51). Dr Adolf Mahr's work diaries in three volumes covering the period 1927-35 (the diaries for August 1935 to July 1939 are missing) as follows, Volume 1: 16 September 1927 to 14 February 1931; Volume 2: 15 February 1931 to 31 December 1933; and Volume 3: 1 January 1934 to 31 July 1935.

Oireachtas Library, Dublin

Official Reports, Parliamentary Debates, Dáil Eireann, as follows: Broadcast from Hamburg Radio Station, 27 September 1939, Vol. 77, Col. 195; Alleged Radio References, 30 April 1940, Vol. 79, Col. 1945; Parachute Landing, 17 February 1944, Vol. 92, Cols. 1237-1240; Parachute Landing, 23 February 1944, Vol. 92, Cols. 1509-1510; National Museum Director, 6 December 1945, Vol. 98, Cols. 1549-1551; Committee on Finance - Supplementary Estimate, 13 November 1946, Vol. 103, Cols. 792-797.

University College Dublin, Main Library

U.S. Senate document *The Struggle of the Irish People* is held in the library's United States collection (No. 8 SD 67-1 vol. 9-4).

Public Record Office of Northern Ireland, Belfast

CAB 9CD/207 BBC MR, contains BBC summaries of German and other broadcasts referring to Ireland in the 1941-44 period. The files were originally passed from London to the Northern Ireland Cabinet.

Germany

Berlin Document Center, U.S. Legation, Berlin

Bundesarchiv, Berlin

Up to 1994, the Berlin Document Center held files on all Nazi Party members both inside and outside the Third Reich. On 1 July 1994 the BDC's files were transferred to the Bundesarchiv's Berlin office where they are still publicly available. Nazi Party files from both the BDC and Bundesarchiv have been used to compile the list of party members resident in Ireland in the 1930s which appears as Appendix V in this book.

Auswärtiges Amt, Politisches Archiv, Bonn (Political archive of German Foreign Office)

R 27188 Fremdsprachiger Nachrichtendienst des Deutschen Rundfunks (Foreign language news service of German Radio), 1 December 1939; R 67477 Adolf Mahr, containing details of Mahr's career at wartime Foreign Office from 1940 to 1944; R 67483 Rundfunkpropaganda nach Irland (Radio propaganda to Ireland) report by Adolf Mahr for Foreign Office dated 18 March 1941; R 67482 Sitzung beim Herrn RAM über die Propaganda nach den unter dem Joche Grossbritanniens stehenden Landern (Meeting convened by Foreign Minister concerning propaganda to countries standing under the yoke of Great Britain), 22 May 1941, Berlin.

Bundesarchiv, Potsdam (former East German/DDR national archive)

VA 62407, document no. 168, Englischsprachige Sendungen nach Irland (English-language programmes to Ireland), memo by Adolf Mahr for German Foreign Office, dated 9 September 1941.

Belgium

Institut Geographique National, Brussels

91 (417)-3 document 25 P9/3 Militargeographische Angaben über Irland (Military Geographical Data on Ireland): 5-volume document prepared and printed in occupied Brussels 1940-41, published in Berlin 15 October 1941 by German Army's department of war maps and surveys.

Britain

Lord Chancellor's Department, London

CRIM 1/1745 Rex v Hilton. This file contains details of the treason case brought against Dorothea Susan Hilton (née Sweney) for 'assisting the enemy' by making propaganda broadcasts. It also contains details of statements taken from Hilton by MI5 at Liebenau Camp in Germany on 30 May, 30 June, 1 July and 3 July 1945. CRIM 1/1783 Rex v James Gilbert. This file contains an unsigned and undated statement by Gilbert to British military authorities c.1945, detailing his Gestapo interrogation and subsequent imprisonment in Grossbeeren labour camp for refusing to work for the radio propaganda service. It also details a meeting in Berlin with Adolf Mahr after Gilbert's release.

Imperial War Museum, Duxford, Oxfordshire

E88 BBC original monitoring reports 'Germany in Irish Gaelic', 22 September 1940 to 6 July 1943. C88, C89 and C90 Éire in English 1939-1959.

Public Record Office, Kew

HO 45/25839 William Joseph Murphy in 'Renegade' files. FO 371 46702 Political Intelligence Department [British Military Intelligence/MI5] report on 'Control of propaganda in Germany', 19 December 1945. BT 27/1553-21361, passenger list of SS Kemmendine, 27/28 May 1940 (including Mrs S. Hilton).

Public Record Office, Chancery Lane, London (Criminal Records Division)

CRIM 4/1730 indictment papers concerning trial of Dorothea Hilton at Old Bailey, 18 February 1946.

National Sound Archive, London

4151 2152/1-15 DS 396 Catalogue of German Radio recordings, 1929-1936 (including details of programme changes following Nazi take-over on 30 January 1933). BBC Sound Archive Catalogue, January 1943 to December 1945.

BBC Written Archives Centre, Reading, Berkshire

Left staff records for Angus Matheson 1940-42, and Maurice Irvine 1943-44.
Department of Transport's General Register and Record Office of Shipping and Seamen, Cardiff

File 147892, lists of crew and passengers of vessels Kemmendine and Tirranna (including Mrs Susan Hilton).

United States

National Archives and Records Administration, Washington D.C.

Register no. CL-1566-BG: secret dispatches from U.S. Embassy, Dublin, to Office of War Information, Washington, 1943-1945. Foreign broadcast Intelligence Service logs (contain 35,000 international shortwave broadcasts to North America which were monitored from 1941-45). The FBIS also holds a collection of captured German sound recordings.

Princeton University Archives, New Jersey

The university's Seeley G. Mudd Manuscript Library contains details on the Princeton Listening Center which pioneered American monitoring of foreign broadcasts from 1939 to 1941. The monitoring work was taken over by the Federal Communications Commission in October 1941.

Interviews conducted by the author with:

Mr Charles Acton, Dublin, 2 July 1992.
Miss Mona Brase, Dublin, 8 October 1991, 4 March 1995.
Mr Ned Butler, Dublin, 23 August 1990.
Professor F.J. Byrne, University College, Dublin, 30 December 1991.
Mr Hugh Byrne, Teelin, Co. Donegal, 15 January 1992.
Miss Mary Charleton, Belfast, 1 February 1993.
Mr and Mrs Helmut Clissmann, Dublin, 11 September 1990.
Mrs Elizabeth Clissmann, Dublin, 19 October 1990.
Professor Tomás de Bháldraithe, Dublin, 15 November 1990 and 1 April 1993.
Mr M. Dewinter, Brussels, 22 November 1991.
Mr Noel Dorr, Secretary, Department of Foreign Affairs, Dublin, 13 June 1991.
Lt. Col. John P. Duggan (retd.), Dublin, 8 June 1991.
Miss Ina Foley, Dublin, 19 June 1992.
Mrs Margaret Greiner, Dublin, 25 May 1993 and 26 June 1993.
Miss Agnes Hannigan, Dublin, 29 April 1993.
Dr Hans Hartmann, Cologne, 9 July 1990, 21 October 1990, 28 December 1990 and
        12 May 1991.
Mr Michael Healy, Dublin, 15 October 1991.
Mr Maurice Irvine, Brighton, 31 January 1992.
Mr Seán Mac Reamoinn, Dublin, 8 August 1991.
Mrs Joan Medcalf (née Budina), Dublin, 15 December 1992.
Mr Éimear Ó Broin, Dublin, 10 June 1992 and 15 June 1992.
Ms Bláth Ó Brolcháin, Dublin, 10 October 1991.
Mr Tomás Ó Cathásaigh, Department of Early Irish, UCD, 11 December 1991.
Dr Seán Ó Heochaidh, Gortahork, Co. Donegal, 14 January 1992.
Mr Liam Ó Muirthile, Dublin, 9 October 1991.
Mr Seán Ó Súilleabháin, Dublin, 24 April 1991.
Dr Joseph Raftery, Dublin, 20 May 1991.
Mrs Ingrid Reusswig (née Mahr), Dublin, 28 July 1994.
Mr William Ryan, Dublin, 26 February 1991.
Miss Margaret Schaffhauser, Liphook, Hampshire, 9 November 1992.
Mr Günther Schutz, Shankill, Co. Dublin, 6 September 1990.
Mrs Jean Sheridan-Healy, Cork, 4 January 1992 and 2 March 1992.
Mrs Eileen Slowey, Dublin, 15 November 1990.
Mr Enno Stephan, Cologne, 28 December 1990.
Mr Francis Stuart, Dublin, 17 November 1989, 24 February 1990, 10 February 1992
        and 19 June 1992.
Mr Edward Sweney, Oldcastle, Co. Meath, 9 June 1991, 14 September 1992, 18
        November 1992 and 28 August 1993.
Dr Pat Wallace, Dublin, 5 December 1990.
Miss Eileen Walsh, Dublin, 10 July 1992.
Mr Bob Wylie, Strasbourg, 10 September 1991.
Commandant Peter Young, Dublin, 29 January 1991 and 9 December 1991.

Letters received by the author from:

Mr Charles Acton, Dublin, 27 August 1992.

Professor Bo Almqvist, UCD, Dublin, 24 May 1991.

Professor James J. Barnes, Wabash College, Indiana, 5 August 1991.

Dr Rolf Baumgarten, Department of Celtic Studies, Dublin Institute for Advanced Studies, 8 July 1991.

Dr Wolf Bierbach, Studienkreis Rundfunk und Geschichte, Cologne, 22 October 1990.

Mrs Carolle J. Carter, Menlo College, California, 13 January 1991.

Mr John Cassidy, Public Record Office, Chancery Lane, London, 13 January 1994.

Mrs Iris Cawley (née Marsden), Hindhead, Surrey, 12 November 1994 and 22 November 1994.

Miss Mary Charleton, Belfast, 27 July 1991.

Mr Terence C. Charman, Imperial War Museum, London, 13 September 1990, 19 October 1990, 3 December 1990, 8 August 1991, 4 October 1991 and 5 May 1992.

Miss J. Coburn, Greater London Record Office and History Library, 27 June 1991 and 24 July 1991.

Mr Tom Collins, Athlone, 30 July 1990.

Mr Seán Cronin, Washington D.C., 26 November 1990.

Mrs Siobhán de hOir, Royal Society of Antiquaries of Ireland, Dublin, 10 September 1991.

Dr Ansgar Diller, German Broadcasting Archive (DRA), Frankfurt-am-Main, 23 August 1990 and 16 May 1993.

Lord James Douglas-Hamilton M.P., House of Commons, London, 30 December 1994.

Colonel J.M. Doyle (retd.), Dublin, 14 July 1994.

Lt. Col. John P. Duggan (retd.), Dublin, 17 August 1992.

Mr Friedrich Engel, BASF, Mannheim, 8 February 1991.

Mr Martin Esslin, London, 15 December 1993.

Mr Tony Fahy, RTE, 12 March 1992.

Mr George Fleischmann, Ontario, Canada, 6 May 1991.

Mr M. Flynn, City Librarian, Limerick, 12 June 1991.

Dr Ann Gallagher, TCD, Dublin, 26 April 1994.

Ms Tracy Gallagher, British Embassy, Dublin, 12 August 1991.

The Duke of Hamilton, East Lothian, Scotland, 24 December 1994 and 28 January 1995.

Miss Agnes Hannigan, Paris, 8 March 1993.

Mr J. Harrison, Public Record Office, Chancery Lane, London, 14 August 1991.

Dr Hans Hartmann, Cologne, 28 June 1992, 12 July 1993 and 16 August 1993.

Mr Billy Hawkes, Dept. of Foreign Affairs, Dublin, 18 June 1991 and 18 October 1993.

Dr Louis D. Healy, Mandurah, Australia, 14 January 1992.

Dom Placid Hooper OSB, Buckfast Abbey, England, 16 March 1993.

Fr Ignatius C.P., Broadway, Worcestershire, 28 January 1993 and 18 April 1993.

Mr Maurice Irvine, Brighton, 29 April 1991, 31 July 1991, 10 January 1992, 3 November 1992 and 28 December 1993.

Ms Kate Johnson, Imperial War Museum, London, 18 November 1992.

Frau Jung, Deutsche Dienstelle, Berlin, 29 April 1993.

Mrs Jacqueline Kavanagh, BBC Written Archives Centre, Reading, Berkshire, 20 June 1990, 13 July 1990, 24 August 1990, 26 July 1991, 4 September 1991 and 24 December 1991.

Dr Maria Keipert, German Foreign Office, Bonn, 9 July 1990 and 2 May 1991.

Mr Douglas King, Berlin, 1 March 1991.

Mr Heike Klauss, Foreign Office, Bonn, 7 August 1991 and 17 June 1993.

Mr Pierre Kowanko, Paris, 8 May 1994.

Dr David Lammey, Public Record Office, Belfast, 14 February 1990.

Ms Anke Leenings, DRA, Frankfurt-am-Main, 4 March 1991.

Professor Gearóid MacEoin, Department of Old and Middle Irish, UCG, 5 March 1991.
Mr Tony McKenna, Bord na Móna, Newbridge, Co. Kildare, 5 June 1991.
Dr Alf Mac Lochlainn, Galway, 11 June 1991.
Dr Séamus MacMathúna, UCG, Galway, 23 September 1991.
Mr John Magennis, Northern Ireland Department of Education, Bangor, 22 October 1991.
Mr Gustav Mahr, Berlin, 28 November 1990.
Mr Gerard Mansell, former Deputy Director General, BBC, London, 13 November 1989.
Dr David G. Marwell, Berlin Document Center, 17 September 1991, 24 May 1993 and 30 July 1993.
Dr Ian Maxwell, Public Record Office, Belfast, 24 June 1994.
Mr Hans Heinz Mecking, Friesoythe, Germany, 22 July 1991.   *Son*
Ms Joan Newman, Fort William, Scotland, 2 July 1992.
Miss Isold Ní Dheirg, Dublin, 10 February 1994.
Ms Róisín Ní Mheara, Berenau, Germany, 2 February 1993.
Dr Burkhard Nowotny, Deutsche Welle, Cologne, 28 August 1990.
Mr Éimear Ó Broin, Dublin, 2 July 1992.
Professor Conn R. Ó Cléirigh, Department of Linguistics, UCD, 4 May 1993.
Mr John O'Connell, Department of Finance, Dublin, 18 November 1994.
Ms Deborah O'Donoghue, British Library, London, 8 August 1991.
Dr Seán Ó Heochaidh, Gortahork, Co. Donegal, 20 June 1991.
Dr Oldenhage, Bunesarchiv, Potsdam (former DDR National Archive, 26 April 1991.
Mr Art O'Leary, Oireachtas Journal Office, Dublin, 4 February 1991.
Mr Seán Ó Lúing, Dublin, 9 March 1993 and 16 March 1993.
Mr L. Ó Ronain, Donegal County Library, Letterkenny, 8 May 1991.
Dr Ken Ó Siochfhradha, Dublin, 8 May 1993.
Mr Gerry Power, Queen's University, Belfast, 23 January 1993.
Mr Ben Primer, Princeton University, New Jersey, 4 September 1991.
Mrs Ingrid Reusswig (née Mahr), Gelnhausen, Germany, 9 May 1994 and 10 July 1994.
Dr Heide Riedel, Deutschesrundfunk Museum, Berlin, 5 June 1991.
Dr Ritter, Bundesarchiv, Koblenz, 14 March 1991.
Mr Don Roe, National Archives, Washington D.C., 2 November 1990.
Mr Walter Roller, DRA, Frankfurt-am-Main, 8 March 1991 and 10 May 1991.
Mr S. Roser, German Embassy, Dublin, 25 July 1991.
Mr Vladimir Rubinstein, Reading, 24 July 1990, 2 October 1990, 22 January 1992, 19 January 1993, 17 March 1993 and 18 November 1993.
Dr Michael Ryan, Director, Chester Beatty Library and Gallery of Oriental Art, Dublin, 4 November 1994.
Miss Margaret Schaffhauser, Liphook, Hampshire, 26 November 1992 and 29 January 1993.
Mr Werner Schwipps, Berlin, 17 February 1991, 29 March 1991 and 21 April 1991.
Mrs E. Smith, Lord Chancellor's Department, London, 27 August 1991.
Dr Hilde Spickernagel, Hanover, 11 November 1991, 9 February 1992, 10 August 1992, 31 January 1993 and 31 December 1993.
Mr Enno Stephan, Wachtberg-Villip, Germany, 16 September 1990.
Mr Francis Stuart, Dublin, 9 November 1989, 15 January 1992, 7 July 1994 and 14 July 1994.
Mr Edward Sweney, Oldcastle, Co. Meath, 28 August 1993.
Miss Lorna Swire, Reading, 17 October 1990, 19 November 1990, 20 January 1991, 3 May 1991, 15 July 1991, 8 January 1992, 5 February 1993, 4 November 1993, 25 November 1993.
Mrs V.A. Swyers, Lord Chancellor's Department, London, 24 September 1991, 25 October 1991 and 1 December 1991.

Professor Derick Thomson, University of Glasgow, 27 November 1990 and 16 June 1991.
Ms Ríonach uí Ogáin, Department of Irish Folklore, UCD, 26 November 1992.
Ms Lucia van der Linde, Foreign Office, Bonn, 27 January 1992 and 27 February 1992.
Dr Pat Wallace, Dublin, 30 May 1990.
Mr John Walsh, Dublin, 25 January 1992.
Mr A. Wehmeyer, Staatsbibliothek, Berlin, 10 December 1992.
Ms Elizabeth Wells, National Sound Archive, London, 26 September 1990.
Mr Hans Wirth, Berlin, 18 October 1990 and 17 December 1990.

Books

Andrews, C.S. Tod. *Man of No Property*, Dublin 1979.

Baillie-Stewart, Norman. *The Officer in the Tower*, London, 1967.

Bair, Deirdre. *Samuel Beckett*, London, 1978.

Baird, Jay W. *The Mythical World of Nazi War Propaganda, 1939-1945*, Minneapolis, 1974.

Balfour, Michael. *Propaganda in War, 1939-1945*, London, 1979.

Barnouw, Erik. *The Golden Web: A History of Broadcasting in the United States. Volume II, 1933-1953*, New York, 1968.

Barton, Brian. *The Blitz: Belfast in the War Years*, Belfast, 1989.

Bennett, Jeremy. *British Broadcasting and the Danish Resistance Movement, 1940-1945*, Cambridge, 1966.

Bewley, Charles. *Memoirs of a Wild Goose*, Dublin, 1989.

Boelcke, Willi A. *Die Macht des Radio: Weltpolitik und Auslandsrundfunk 1924-76*, Frankfurt-am-Main, 1977.

Bowman, John. *De Valera and the Ulster Question, 1917-1973*, Oxford, 1982.

Boyle, Andrew. *Poor, Dear Brendan: The Quest for Brendan Bracken*, London, 1974.

Briggs, Asa. *The War of Words*, London, 1970.

Briggs, Asa. *The BBC: the First Fifty Years*, Oxford, 1985.

Brown, James. *Techniques of Persuasion: from propaganda to brainwashing*, London, 1963.

Brown, Terence. *Ireland: A Social and Cultural History 1922-1976*, Glasgow, 1981.

Burden, Hamilton T. *The Nuremberg Party Rallies: 1923-39*, London, 1967.

Campbell, Christy. *The World War Two Fact Book, 1939-45*, London, 1985.

Carney, James and Greene, David. *Essays in Memory of Angus Matheson*, London, 1968.

Carroll, Joseph T. *Ireland in the War Years, 1939-1945*, Newton Abbot, 1975.

Carter, Carolle J. *The Shamrock and the Swastika: German Espionage in Ireland in World War II*, Palo Alto, California, 1977.

Carty, James. *Bibliography of Irish History 1912-1921*, Dublin, 1936.

Cathcart, Rex. *The Most Contrary Region: The BBC in Northern Ireland 1924-1984*, Belfast, 1984.

Clarke, Paddy. *Dublin Calling*, Dublin, 1986.

Cole, J.A. *Lord Haw-Haw: The Full Story of William Joyce*, London, 1964.

Coogan, Tim Pat. *The IRA*, London, 1970.

Coogan, Tim Pat. *De Valera: Long Fellow, Long Shadow*, London, 1993.

Cooper, Matthew. *The German Army 1933-1945: Its Political and Military Failure*, London, 1978.

Cronin, Seán. *Frank Ryan: The Search for the Republic*, Dublin, 1980

Cronin, Seán. *Washington's Irish Policy, 1916-1986*, Dublin, 1987.

Cruickshank, Charles. *The Fourth Arm: Psychological Warfare 1938-45*, London, 1977.

Debray, Régis. *Revolution in the Revolution?*, New York, 1967.

Delmer, Sefton. *Black Boomerang*, New York, 1962.

Dickel, Horst. *Die deutsche Aussenpolitik und die irische Frage von 1932 bis 1944,* Wiesbaden, 1983.

Diller, Ansgar. *Rundfunkpolitik im Dritten Reich,* Munich, 1980.

Duggan, John P. *Neutral Ireland and the Third Reich,* Dublin, 1975.

Duggan, John P. *A History of the Irish Army,* Dublin, 1991.

Dwyer, T. Ryle. *Irish Neutrality and the USA, 1939-47,* Dublin, 1977.

Edwards, Donald. *The Two Worlds of Donald Edwards,* London, 1970.

Elborn, Geoffrey. *Francis Stuart: A Life,* Dublin, 1990.

Ellul, Jacques. *Propaganda: the formation of men's attitudes,* New York, 1965.

Fanning, Ronan. *The Irish Department of Finance, 1922-58,* Dublin, 1978.

Fisk, Robert. *In Time of War: Ireland, Ulster and the Price of Neutrality, 1939-45,* London, 1983.

Flannery, Harry W. *Assignment to Berlin,* London, 1942.

Flynn, William J. *Irish Parliamentary Handbook: 1945,* Dublin, 1945.

Foster, R.F. *Modern Ireland: 1600-1972,* London, 1988.

Fraser, Lindley M. *Propaganda,* London, 1957.

Fromme, Franz. *Irlands Kampf um Die Freiheit,* Berlin, 1933.

Gerstenberg, Joachim. *Éire, ein Irlandbuch,* Hamburg, 1940.

Glees, Anthony. *The Secrets of the Service: British Intelligence and Communist subversion, 1939-1951,* London, 1987.

Gorham, Maurice. *Forty Years of Irish Broadcasting,* Dublin, 1967.

Grandin, Thomas. *The Political use of the Radio,* Geneva, 1939.

Gray, Tony. *Mr Smyllie, Sir,* Dublin, 1991.

Greene, Hugh Carleton. *The Third Floor Front,* London, 1969.

Hale, Julian. *Radio Power: propaganda and international broadcasting,* London, 1975.

Hartmann, Hans. *Über Krankheit, Tod und Jenseitsvorstellungen in Irland,* Halle, 1942.

Herridge, Charles. *Pictorial History of World War II,* London, 1975.

Herzstein, Robert Edwin. *The War That Hitler Won: Goebbels and the Nazi Media Campaign,* New York, 1978.

Hildebrand, Klaus. *Foreign Policy of the Third Reich,* London, 1973.

Hildebrand, Klaus. *The Third Reich,* London, 1984.

Hinsley, F.H. *British Intelligence in the Second World War, Vol. 2: Its Influence on Strategy and Operations,* London, 1978. *Vol. 4: Security and Counter Intelligence* (with C.A G. Simkins), London, 1990.

Hitler, Adolf. *Mein Kampf,* London, 1974 (2nd English translation).

Hoehne, Heinz. *Canaris,* London, 1979.

Howe, Ellic. *The Black Game: British Subversive Operations against the Germans during the Second World War,* London, 1982.

Jones, R.V. *Most Secret War,* London, 1978.

Jowett, Gareth S. and O'Donnell, Victoria. *Propaganda and Persuasion* (2nd edition), Newbury Park, California, 1992.

Kahn, David. *Hitler's Spies: German Military Intelligence in World War II,* London, 1978.

Keogh, Dermot. *Ireland and Europe 1919-1948,* Dublin, 1988.

Kris, Ernst and Speier, Hans. *German Radio Propaganda: report on home broadcasts during the war,* New York, 1944.

Laird, Dorothy. *Paddy Henderson: The Story of P. Henderson & Company,* Glasgow, 1961.

Lasswell, Harold D. *Propaganda Technique in World War I,* New York, 1971.

Ledbetter, Gordon T. *The Great Irish Tenor,* New York, 1977.

Lee, J.J. *Ireland 1912-1985: Politics and Society,* Cambridge, 1989.

Leiser, Erwin. *Deutschland, erwache!: Propaganda im Film des Dritten Reiches,* Berlin, 1968.

Lockwood, W.B. *A Panorama of Indo-European Languages,* London, 1972.

Lyons, F.S.L. *Ireland Since the Famine,* London, 1971.

MacAonghusa, Proinsias. *Quotations from Éamon de Valera,* Dublin, 1983.

McCormack, Lily. *I Hear You Calling Me,* Milwaukee, 1949.

MacKenzie, John M. *Propaganda and Empire: The Manipulation of British Public Opinion, 1880-1960,* Manchester, 1984.

MacLysaght, Edward. *Changing Times: Ireland since 1898,* London. 1978.

Mansell, Gerard. *Let Truth Be Told: 50 Years of BBC External Broadcasting,* London, 1982.

Mohr, Ulrich. *Atlantis: the story of a German surface raider,* London, 1955.

Mühlhausen, Ludwig. *Die Vier Zweige Des Mabinogi,* Halle, 1925.

Ní Mheara-Vinard, Róisín. *Cé Hí Seo Amuigh?,* Dublin, 1992.

Nolan, Kevin B. and Williams, T. Desmond. *Ireland in the War Years and After, 1939-51,* Dublin, 1969.

Ó Broin, León. *Just Like Yesterday,* Dublin, 1985.

O'Callaghan, Seán. *The Jackboot in Ireland,* London, 1958.

Ó Siochfhradha, Padraig. *Beatha Theobald Wolfe Tone,* Dublin, 1932.

Overy, R.J. *Goering: The 'Iron Man',* London, 1984.

Parrot, Jacques. *La Guerre des Ondes,* Paris, 1987.

Peukert, Detlev J.K. *Inside Nazi Germany,* London, 1987.

Philby, Kim. *My Silent War,* London, 1968.

Pohle, Heinz. *Der Rundfunk als Instrument der Politik: Zur Geschichte des deutschen Rundfunks von 1923-1938,* Hamburg, 1955.

Renier, Olive and Rubinstein, Vladimir. *Assigned To Listen: The Evesham Experience, 1939-43,* London, 1986.

Roberts, C.E.B. *The Trial of William Joyce,* London, 1946.

Roller, Walter. *Tondokumente zur Zeitgeschichte 1939/1940,* Frankfurt-am-Main, 1987.

Rolo, Charles J. *Radio Goes to War,* London, 1943.

Sanders, Michael and Taylor, Philip M. *British Propaganda during the First World War, 1914-18,* London, 1982.

Scheel, Klaus. *Krieg über Ätherwellen, NS-Rundfunk und Monopole 1933-1945,* Berlin, 1970.

Schlesinger, Philip. *Putting 'Reality' Together: BBC News,* London, 1978.

Schnabel, Reimund. *Missbrauchte Mikrofone: Deutsche Rundfunkpropaganda im Zweiten Weltkrieg,* Vienna, 1967.

Schwipps, Werner. *Wortschlacht im Äther,* Berlin, 1971.

Selwyn, Francis. *Hitler's Englishman: The Crime of 'Lord Haw-Haw',* London, 1987.

Shirer, William L. *The Rise and Fall of the Third Reich,* London, 1960.

Shulman, Holly Cowan. *The Voice of America: propaganda and democracy, 1941-1945,* Wisconsin, 1990.

Silvey, Robert. *Who's Listening?: the story of BBC audience research,* London, 1974.

Smith, Howard K. *Last Train from Berlin,* London, 1942.

Snyder, Louis L. *Encyclopedia of the Third Reich,* New York, 1976.

Soley, Lawrence C. and Nichols, John S. *Clandestine Radio Broadcasting,* New York, 1987.

Soley, Lawrence C. *Radio Warfare: OSS and CIA Subversive Propaganda,* New York, 1989.

Sproat, Ian. *Wodehouse at War,* New York, 1981.

Steele, R.W. *Propaganda in an open society: the Roosevelt administration and the media, 1933-1941,* Westport, CT, 1985.

Stephan, Enno. *Spies in Ireland,* London, 1963.

Stuart, Francis. *Black List, Section H,* London, 1975.

Stuart, Francis. *States of Mind,* Dublin, 1984

Stuart, Madeleine. *Manna in the Morning: A Memoir, 1940-1958,* Dublin, 1984.

Sturm, Hubert. *Hakenkreuz und Kleeblatt: Irland, die Alliierten und das Dritte Reich, 1933-1945,* Frankfurt-am-Main, 1984.
Talbot, Godfrey. *Permission to Speak,* London, 1976.
Taylor, A.J.P. *The Russian War 1941-1945,* London, 1978.
Taylor, Fred. *The Goebbels Diaries, 1939-1941,* London, 1982.
Taylor, Philip M. *The Projection of Britain: British overseas publicity and propaganda, 1919-1939,* Cambridge, 1981.
Thomson, Oliver. *Mass Persuasion in History: an historical analysis of the development of propaganda techniques,* Edinburgh, 1977.
Trevor-Roper, Hugh. *The Goebbels Diaries: The Last Days,* London, 1978.
Welch, David. *Nazi Propaganda: The Power and the Limitations,* London, 1983.
West, Nigel (pseudonym for Rupert Allason). *MI5, British Security Operations 1909-1945,* London, 1981.
West, Rebecca. *The Meaning of Treason,* London, 1949.
West, W.J. *Truth Betrayed,* London, 1987.
West, W.J. *Orwell: The War Commentaries,* New York, 1985.
West, W.J. *Orwell: The War Broadcasts,* London, 1985.
White, Antonia. *BBC at War,* London, 1940.
Winkler, Allan M. *The Politics of Propaganda: the Office of War Information, 1942-1945,* Yale, 1978.
Wulf, Joseph. *Presse und Funk im Dritten Reich,* Gutersloh, 1964.
Zeman, Z.A.B. *Nazi Propaganda,* London, 1964.

Articles, Pamphlets, Reports, Theses, etc.

Battersby, Eileen. 'Ever the outsider, still unrepentant', *Sunday Tribune,* Dublin, 11 February 1990, p. B1.
Boelcke, Willi A. 'Das Seehaus in Berlin-Wannsee', *Jahrbuch für die Geschichte Mittel- und Ostdeutschlands,* Berlin, 1974.
Bunker, John. 'Memories of a Wireless Man: Thomas George Cole', *Journal of the Police History Society,* No.6, 1991.
Bytwerk, Randall L. 'The Rhetoric of Defeat: Nazi Propaganda in 1945', *Central States Speech Journal,* Vol. 29 (1), Spring 1978, pp. 44-52.
Cox, Colm. 'Militär Geographische Angaben über Irland', *An Cosantoir,* March 1975, pp. 83-96.
Cullen, Paul. An Irish World Service - the story of Ireland's shortwave broadcasting station. M.A. thesis, Dublin City University, 1991.
Duggan, John P. Herr Hempel at the German Legation in Dublin 1937-45. D. Litt. thesis, Trinity College, Dublin, 1979
Duggan, John P. 'Kuno Meyer: Time to Make Amends?' *The Irish Times,* 12 April 1990, p. 11.
Engel, F.K. 'Magnetic tape from the early days to the present', *Journal of the Audio Engineering Society,* July/August 1988.
Fiftieth anniversary report, 1940-1990, of the School of Celtic Studies, Dublin Institute for Advanced Studies, Dublin, 1990.
'Fifty Germans leave for Fatherland', *The Irish Times,* 12 September 1939, p. 7.
Fisher, Marc. 'The Nazi Archives: Mining, and Minding, the Past', *International Herald Tribune,* Paris, 10 July 1990, p. 1.
'Former German Colonists Send Greetings', *Irish Press,* 2 January 1942, p. 2.
Gieseke, D.H. 'Broadcasting in Germany', *BBC Yearbook 1932,* London, 1932.
Graas, Gust. 'Petite et Grande Histoire de Radio-Télé-Luxembourg', *Les Cahiers Luxembourgeois,* Luxembourg, 1961.

Hamilton, Alan. 'Public urged King to spare life of Lord Haw-Haw', *The Times* (London), 8 February 1995, p. 9.

Hayes-McCoy, G.A. 'Irish Defence Policy, 1938-51', Kevin B. Nowlan and T. Desmond Williams (eds) *Ireland in the War Years and After, 1939-51*, Dublin, 1969.

Kealy, Alacoque. *Irish Radio Data: 1926-1980* (RTE occasional paper series no.1). Dublin, May 1981.

Keogh, Dermot. 'The day Dev offered condolences to Nazi Germany', *The Irish Times*, 11 January 1990, p. 15.

Kershaw, Ian. 'How Effectlve was Nazi Propaganda?', in David Welch (ed), *Nazi Propaganda*, London 1983, pp. 180-205.

Kilbride-Jones, H.E. 'Adolf Mahr', *Archaeology Ireland*, Vol. 7, no. 3, issue no.25, autumn 1993, pp. 29-30.

Millward, David. 'Duke joined campaign to spare Haw Haw', *The Daily Telegraph*, London, 8 February 1995, p. 11.

'Ministers expected Haw-Haw to go free', *The Independent*, London, 8 February 1995, p. 8.

Moller, Lynn E. 'Music in Germany during the Third Reich: the Use of Music for Propaganda', *Music Educators Journal*, Vol. 67 (3), November 1980, pp. 40-44.

Myers, Kevin. 'An Irishman's Diary', *The Irish Times*, 19 March 1991, p. 9.

O'Connor, Ulick. 'Alienation of a Black Swan', *Sunday Independent*, 13 November 1994, p 11.

O'Halpin, Eunan. 'Intelligence and Security in Ireland 1922-45', *Intelligence and National Security*, London, January 1990.

O'Reilly, John Francis. 'I was a Spy in Ireland', *Sunday Dispatch* (series of weekly articles published from June to December 1952), London, 1952.

'Pillars of Society: Francis Stuart', *The Phoenix*, 5 April 1991, p. 13.

Rockel, Martin. 'The Growth of Celtic Studies in Berlin and Leipzig', *Celtic Cultures Newsletter* No.6, Galway, August 1990.

Smith, Bruce L. 'Propaganda', *Encyclopaedia Brittanica*, 15th edition, Vol. 26, London 1987, pp. 170-74.

Smyth, Captain John. 'German Broadcasts to Ireland', in file MA G2/X/0127 Foreign Wireless Broadcasts, part 3, 1 April 1943.

Statistical Abstract of the United States 1991, U.S. Department of Commerce, Washington D.C., 1991.

The Struggle of the Irish People, United States Senate document no. 8 of 67th Congress, published by U.S. Government Printing Office, Washington D.C., 1921 (having first been adopted by January 1921 session of Dáil Éireann).

Stuart, Francis. 'Berlin in the Rare Oul' Times', *Irish Press*, 1 September 1989, supplement pp. XII-XIII.

'Substantial level of wartime co-operation with British revealed', *The Irish Times*, 2 January 1991, p. 5.

'They fell from the sky on Éire', *The Cork Examiner*, 2 June 1945, p 5.

Thiele, H.H.K. 'Some remarkable firsts in magnetic recording created and used by the German Broadcasting System until 1944' - paper presented to 84th Convention of the Audio Engineering Society, Paris, March 1988.

Zimmer, Stefan. 'Ludwig Mühlhausen, Leben und Werk', Appendix to 1988 edition of Mühlhausen's book *Die Vier Zweige Des Mabinogi*, pp. 145-151. (The book was first published in Halle in 1925), Tübingen, 1988.

Index